AGING WITH ATTITUDE

————————————— • —————————————

Growing Older with Dignity and Vitality

Robert Levine, M.D.

Westport, Connecticut
London

KH

Library of Congress Cataloging-in-Publication Data

Levine, Robert, 1939–
    Aging with attitude : growing older with dignity and vitality / by Robert Levine.
      p. cm.
    Includes bibliographical references and index.
    ISBN 0-275-98173-8 (alk. paper)
      1. Aged—Psychology.   2. Aged—Health and hygiene.   3. Aging—Physiological
aspects.   4. Aged—Conduct of life.   5. Self-realization in old age.   I. Title.
    HQ1061.L472 2004
    305.26—dc22   2004044374

British Library Cataloging in Publication Data is available.

Library of Congress Catalog Card Number: 2004044374
ISBN: 0-275-98173-8

First published in 2004

Praeger Publishers, 88 Post Road West, Westport, CT 06881
An imprint of Greenwood Publishing Group, Inc.
www.praeger.com

Printed in the United States of America

The paper used in this book complies with the
Permanent Paper Standard issued by the National
Information Standards Organization (Z39.48-1984).

10 9 8 7 6 5 4 3

9/19/07

To Anne
   who is always there.

CONTENTS

Acknowledgments

———————————— • ————————————

A number of people helped me prepare and shape this book with timely suggestions and criticisms. Without their astute observations and helpful encouragement, this project might not have reached fruition, or if it had, in a much different form.

I am indebted to Janet Cohn and Mike Slosberg, Dr. Ernest Shaw and Marna Anderson, and Randi Frank for their incisive comments and recommendations, and the time spent reading early versions of the manuscript. Ms. Jill Golrick, the medical librarian at Norwalk Hospital, was of great help with the necessary research.

Doctors Peter Cohn, Amy Knorr, Myron Glucksman, and Ernest Atlas reviewed the manuscript as it neared completion, adding scrutiny in their particular fields of expertise—cardiology, neurology, psychiatry, and internal medicine. Dr. Alan Lieberson provided discerning observations as well. Their assistance and advice was of inestimable value.

My children Marjorie Levine-Clark and Matthew Levine were tremendously helpful with their critical eyes and keen minds as they negotiated the pages of this work in progress, offering ideas on content and structure.

I also thank my editor at Greenwood Press, Debora Carvalko, who initially saw the possibilities in my manuscript and whose suggestions contributed to the finished work.

Finally, there is my wife, Anne, who was in on every stage of production of this book, offering love and encouragement, but also critical comments and perceptive recommendations, as well as aid in physical tasks like typing and collating. It could not have been completed without her.

Robert Levine
Westport, Connecticut
March 3, 2004

FOREWORD

———————————— • ————————————

Aging connotes an entirely different set of values in 2004 compared to 1954, when Dr. Levine and I were in college and wondering about the future. For one thing, the veneration that we held for our "elders"—though not as great in Western society as in Asian culture—was stronger then. The nuclear family was more apt to include grandparents in 1954 than it is today. Even if not living under the same roof, this extended family was also more likely to reside nearby. Older members of the family would interact frequently with younger members of the family, to the enrichment of both groups. Today, families are more likely to be spread out across the country with visits a special event, not an everyday occurrence. In addition to the difference in societal values before 1954 and in 2004, it would also have been impossible to accurately predict the medical, scientific, and technologic advances that make our current generation so fortunate compared to that of our parents and grandparents, extending survival and quality of life.

For many seniors, especially those who are infirm, "home" is often a facility, whether it be assisted living or a nursing home. How is one to optimize quality of life in such circumstances? Unfortunately, the correct answer is: with difficulty. But does it have to be that way? Can the inevitable aging process be modified to enable its participants to enjoy a more meaningful existence? This is the challenge facing our generation.

Dr. Levine explains this challenge remarkably well in his eminently scholarly yet readable book. He has organized his book into ten chapters, each emphasizing a different aspect of his main theme: you *can* grow older with dignity and vitality. An enlightened discussion of the aging process itself in Chapters 2 and 3 is written in words that everyone can understand, and helps prepare the reader for the chapters that follow. Dr. Levine makes several important points in these opening chapters, not the least of which is that a long time spent in old age is not a normal state in nature, since our bodies are programmed to die to make way for the next generations.

How long we can forestall our demise in the larger societal sense is a direct offshoot of the socioeconomic and medical state of that society. This is why the life span today is much greater than it was fifty years ago and much greater than it was one hundred or five hundred years ago. Each organ system ages, and dies, according to its built-in regulatory factors. These factors can be modified to a varying extent by a nurturing socioeconomic environment, although too much "good living" can have the opposite effect, as with fat-laden diets accelerating cardiovascular disease. But to truly modify the built-in regulatory system that controls the life span of cells, and ultimately organs and organ systems, requires the kind of genetic manipulation that we are just now gingerly probing in scientific laboratories around the world. Paradoxically, the only truly immortal cells are the cancer cells that overgrow and eventually suffocate their normal neighbors. It is not that far-out a prediction to wonder if the ultimate secrets to leading a longer life will come from a more complete understanding of the genetics of these dread harbingers of deadly diseases.

Dr. Levine emphasizes that taking advantage of the scientific advances of modern life requires more than just taking a test for this disease, or a pill for that disease. It requires a new attitude, one that emphasizes quality of life. As a cardiologist who has spent the past thirty plus years dealing with the problems of cardiovascular disease in thousands of patients, I know firsthand how much of it probably could have been prevented with attention to exercise, proper diet, and the kind of healthy lifestyle delineated in Dr. Levine's book. But again, growing old with the right attitude is more than a medical challenge, it is a way of life. The medical part will provide society with more and more senior citizens, people who will live longer after retirement from occupations and/or child rearing, people who will have more time on their hands, people who can and should remain engaged in the world about them.

To age properly, Dr. Levine feels passionately that we have to start preparing when we are younger and I wholeheartedly agree. Once we do grow old we can take charge of the process; by accepting its realities. This is where the suggestions made in Chapters 7 and 8 are especially helpful. You cannot be a passive bystander to the aging process; you have to do more than accept its inevitability. You have to take charge of those areas that you have some control over. Nothing exemplifies this concept more than in the contemporary approach to physical fitness. Whereas in 1954 conservation of strength, that is, "resting," was thought to be beneficial for the elderly, we now know that the opposite is preferable. It is never too late to take charge, Dr. Levine argues, and he is right. There are political and social causes that instill passion, there are religious pursuits, hobbies, pets, volunteering, and the like. Independence should coexist with just the right blend of social interaction.

His concluding chapters look at what the future holds for us—including better and "smarter" houses to live in, replacement of more body parts by prostheses, and more political clout for the elderly. A potpourri of exciting challenges. With its upbeat philosophy of aging, Dr. Levine's book is a welcome addition to the bibliography of this subject, offering a different perspective to accompany both useful facts and factoids of knowledge and practical ideas on growing older. It is worthwhile reading for both the people who are "old" now and for those who are hoping to be older at some point in the future (in other words, the rest of the population). Thus, the readership for this book can really be said to extend from current sixty-fivers (like myself) and persons even older, down to those in their forties and fifties and all the way back to current college freshmen, young people with questions about the future, much like those the author and I had fifty years ago.

Peter F. Cohn, M.D.
Professor of Medicine
Vice Chairman for Clinical Affairs
Chief of Cardiology, Emeritus
Department of Medicine,
SUNY Health Sciences Center
Stony Brook, New York

1

INTRODUCTION

Age is a question of mind over matter.
If you don't mind, it doesn't matter.

—SATCHELL PAIGE

The baseball player and armchair philosopher Satchell Paige uttered the above words many years ago when he was pitching in the major leagues in his fifth and possibly sixth decades. He was dismissing those critics who were insisting that he was too old to pitch at such a high level and showing confidence in his own abilities. Indeed, the way we age and much of what happens to our minds and bodies as we grow older depends on our attitudes and feelings about ourselves and our approach to life. Though there are elements beyond our control, such as illnesses or the death of loved ones, to enhance our lives, we must take advantage of the things we can control while dealing with any adversity that might arise. We should not focus on our mortality and how to live longer, since survival alone is meaningless. What is really important is the quality of our lives and whether we can find satisfaction and pleasure in the things we do in the time available to us.

We are not alone as we face the problems that accompany aging and search for solutions. With life expectancy increasing and birth rates declining, the population of the United States and the rest of the industrialized world has aged significantly in the past half century and will continue to do so in the decades ahead. The roles and lifestyles of the middle-aged and elderly have also changed dramatically, the result of both social necessity and individual desire. People who once would have been considered old lead active, exciting lives, as rich and rewarding as the younger members of society. Some keep working past the normal age of retirement, while others follow creative pursuits, engage in competitive or recreational sports, take courses, collect various objects, or travel extensively. Though these scenarios may be more prevalent among the affluent elderly, they are seen at every economic level. The image of an older man and woman sitting on a porch in rocking chairs whiling away their remaining days, she knitting and he perhaps reading the newspaper, in a placid but boring existence, is no longer the general rule. The Rolling Stones (who are now middle-aged) have sung to us for years about "what a drag it is getting old."[1] But it doesn't have to be that way. Older people are demanding more from life and from themselves and are discovering ways to satisfy these demands.

On the other hand, many of the elderly, for reasons other than illness or disability, find themselves unable to enjoy their final decades of life in a vital fashion. Because of their own behavior and the inability to manage their lives, they often lose their pride and self-confidence. This results in diminished respect and admiration from their families and friends, reinforcing their negative perceptions about themselves.

However, even those older people who are fully self-sufficient may find it difficult retain to their dignity as they try to function in a world that is geared to the young. In a society that measures worth mainly by productivity, older people are less valued. Nevertheless, maintaining dignity and self-respect as we age should be universal objectives and should be attainable for most of us. But what do we mean when we speak of dignity?

Dignity is an intangible characteristic, unique to each individual and manifested differently in different people. It includes feelings of pride, self-worth, and self-esteem, much of it internalized and some of it visible to others in a person's bearing and actions. An individual's dignity is his or her shield against the slings and arrows of the outside world. It allows him or her to exist within a predatory universe, inured to the insults and trauma of daily living, safeguarding his or her spirit. With our dignity gone, we face the universe as naked, primitive beings, powerless and fearful before the shifting currents of our environment.

In my practice over the years, I have seen hundreds, if not thousands, of older individuals with various illnesses, or none at all, who have lived with positive feelings about themselves, with pride and belief in their own self-worth while they were aging. These people did not succumb to either illness or aging, but instead preserved their dignity while making the most of their lives. As examples:

S.W., an 85-year-old widow who lives alone in a condominium in a town on the Connecticut shore, originally came to me over five years ago because of problems with balance. I found that she had a neuropathy (damage to the nerves in her legs) with impaired sensation and, in addition, had previously had several small strokes. Two years later, she had another small stroke from which she recovered and returned to her baseline. I have continued to see her three to four times a year, treating her with medication and encouragement. Thin, with angular features, she is always immaculately groomed and fashionably dressed whenever she comes to my office.

Mrs. W. has remained quite active, not allowing her problems to control her life. She still has minor difficulty with balance, but exercises for forty minutes every day, using a treadmill or stationary bike that she has in her apartment. Two daughters and a number of grandchildren live nearby and are very attentive to her, and she socializes with friends. With one or two family members or friends, she travels into New York City regularly to go to the theater and museums. She and a granddaughter flew to London for a week recently and she is helping this granddaughter plan her wedding. Though she is not happy with her limitations, Mrs. W. tries to overcome them, sustaining a positive outlook while always wanting to do more.

L.R. is 92 years old. Six years ago, he had several seizures due to a minor stroke that caused no discernable deficits. The seizures are now controlled with medication that he takes religiously. Short and stocky, he lives with his wife, who is a year younger than he, in a small home they have occupied for over fifty years; they are still fully able to take care of themselves. Her vision is not good and he does all the driving when they go shopping or visit friends. While he is comfortable driving at low speeds locally, he does not venture onto the highway. He and his wife walk outside for exercise whenever the weather permits. They are not affluent and do not travel much, but are bright and articulate and still enjoy life. He has an excellent sense of humor, delighting in verbal repartee and jokes. His standard comment when I ask him how he's doing is "I can't complain. I'm in fine shape for the shape I'm in."

I have been seeing E.T. for fifteen years and she is now 84. Of medium height and slightly overweight, I initially saw her for a stroke that caused left-side numbness and weakness, leaving her with mild loss of sensation on that side. Subsequently, she developed a neuropathy and also has severe arthritis. Because of these problems, she moves slowly and uses a cane outside her home. Given her status, she cannot exercise, but she is bright, cognitively intact, and optimistic, always smiling and looking forward to new adventures. Her husband is five years older than she and in fairly good health, though hard of hearing. They are both passionate about food and love to travel, taking periodic vacations in Italy and cruises to various destinations. Life remains full of pleasure and excitement for her, as she has been able to overcome different obstacles that aging placed in her path.

I lost track of J.G. several years ago after he had been a patient of mine for five years. Tall and lanky, he was 92 when I last saw him, a widower who was living on his own in a condominium. He had come to me because of pain in his neck and shoulder, the result of cervical arthritis and a "pinched nerve." I treated him with medication and physical therapy, which relieved his pain, though it recurred intermittently and required renewal of medication. Despite complaints of minor difficulties with memory, Mr. G. was quite sharp and able to care for himself. Always nattily dressed, he went into his office at a local law firm a few days a week to handle some cases. He also read extensively, mainly biographies, and loved to do crossword puzzles. Physically very active, he walked daily and went swimming four or five times a week. Every winter, he traveled down to Florida and spent three to four months there with a group of friends. Though he joked about not having much time left, he was always positive about the future, making plans to do things months in advance.

Mrs. G.S., who is now 91, has been a patient of mine for six years. Small and almost birdlike, with a quaint German accent, her original complaint was of headaches, for which a complete workup was unrevealing. Living with her husband in a small home in a rural area, she had always been devoted to exercise and walked several miles every day. Though she did not appear depressed to me, she was somewhat anxious. I treated her with a mild antidepressant (which can help tension headaches) and reassurance, to which she responded quite well. Her cognitive abilities remained intact and she was a voracious reader. Three years after her initial visit, she suffered a stroke and had trouble speaking and walking, which slowly improved over a month. For a short period, as she was recovering with new medication and physical therapy, I saw her more often. It was then that she told me she was a Holocaust survivor and had been interned in two concentration camps during the war, with most of her family having been killed. She had come to America afterward where she had met her husband, who was also a refugee. Never having had children, she had a large circle of friends with whom she met and communicated with frequently. In addition, she kept herself occupied with her reading and knitting, ignoring the arthritis in her hands. With little income other than Social Security, the cost of medication for her husband and herself consumed most of their discretionary income, not allowing for frivolous expenditures. Yet despite her situation and all she had been through, Mrs. S. amazed me as she spoke of her hunger for life and a desire to keep living beyond one hundred years of age. When her stroke had resolved, she resumed her daily walks, unwilling to make any concessions to age or illness.

These vignettes of some of my patients describe people who have had various types of neurological problems, yet have managed to maintain an optimistic outlook as they carried on with their lives, preserving their pride and self-esteem. If these people have done well, there is no reason why others with similar illnesses, or no illness at all, cannot also do as well, or even better. The key perhaps is believing in yourself and having the will to move forward. We must remember that as we grow older, aside from any genetic predispositions we may have inherited, and any random illnesses or accidents we may encounter, we can determine our own destiny. We are in control of the way we age and the quality of our own lives.

From the "biblical era" through medieval times, people lived an average of thirty or fewer years, reproducing as teenagers, then dying off when their children were in their midteens. (Generations were delineated as fifteen years apart, as this was the length of time for the cycle of reproduction to start again.) By 1900, life expectancy had climbed to about fifty years of age and continued to increase through the twentieth century. Now, at the beginning of the third millennium, the average life expectancy in most Western countries is in the upper seventies. "Currently, 12.4% of our population is 65 years of age or over, and 5.3% is 75 years of age or over. By 2015, when the first of the postwar baby boom generation reaches age 65, those proportions increase to 14.6% and 6.0% respectively. As the baby boomers enter their seventies and eighties, the population age 65 or over will comprise 20.1% of the total, with those 75 and over accounting for 9.0%."[2] Put another way, in 1900, one in every twenty-five Americans was sixty-five or older.[3] In 1965 (the year Medicare was enacted), it was one in twelve. By the year 2030, one in five will be sixty-five or older. Other Western countries will have even a higher proportion of older people.

"Global aging will transform the world into societies that are much older than any we have ever known or imagined," Peter Peterson notes in his book *Gray Dawn*.[4] He also warns that the aging of America and other industrialized nations will present serious economic problems that are yet to be addressed.

Economics aside, we can see that today growing old is normal and expected, in sharp contrast to the way things were in the past when it was uncommon for people to survive into old age. Now the elderly are a substantial minority whose existence and needs should be acknowledged by the rest of society. For the most part, older people are also much healthier than they used to be. They have their own living complexes, and their own organizations, and their own magazines and newspapers that cater to them. Yet too often they do not have the respect of the community at large and may be broken and degraded by an unfeeling society.

THE INCREASE IN LONGEVITY

Historically, infectious diseases have been responsible for most human deaths; though, periodically, famines and wars exacted a heavy toll. Advances in medicine, hygiene, and sanitation during the late nineteenth century and early twentieth century controlled many of these infectious diseases in Western countries, accounting for much of the rise in life expectancy. (Improved sanitation was particularly important, with the development of sewage systems, clean drinking water, and garbage collection.) Infantile diarrhea, childbed fever, and diseases like typhoid, cholera, smallpox, and plague, which previously ravaged the citizenry in intermittent epidemics, were virtually eliminated. Leprosy, syphilis, and polio, which caused a great amount of disability as well as death, were vanquished almost completely. Tuberculosis and pneumonia, which took innumerable lives in urban centers over the centuries, were also curbed greatly, though pneumonia still represents the final blow for many of the very feeble and immune compromised. Over the past fifty years, life expectancy has further increased because of progress in the prevention, diagnosis, and treatment of coronary artery disease and cancer, currently the two major killers in the developed world.

WHAT IS OLD?

Relative age is a function of a person's location on a bell-shaped curve of the population in the era in which they live. When life expectancy was thirty, those considered old were much younger than when life expectancy reached fifty, or seventy. In addition, with people now living longer and being productive longer than in the past, and engaged in tasks not necessarily related to physical prowess, categorizing them according to age is more complicated. When everyone in society was occupied hunting or gathering, age was regarded differently than with people working as scientists, lawyers, machine operators, or computer technicians. "Also, individuals age at different rates; differential aging can be observed not only in changes in facial appearance, loss of hair, skin changes, but also in motor, sensory and cognitive processes."[5] These differences in biological aging may be due to inherited factors or related to people's working conditions, nutrition, stress, substance abuse, and so forth—a combination of genetic and environmental elements. Even in healthy people with similar diets and behavior, the aging process affects individuals differently, and at eighty, some may be feeble and some may be vigorous—the saying "You're as old as you feel" is true to some degree. Thus, a person's physiologic age may be quite different from his or her chronological age, as evidenced by his or her lifestyles and activities. For example, a seventy-year-old marathon runner may be younger according to certain parameters than a forty-year-old couch potato.

Of course, any designation or grouping to which men and women are assigned is usually inconsistent and based on the biases of the person doing the classifying. Nevertheless, placing people in categories can be helpful in describing certain observations and perceptions common to individuals within these groups. Traditionally, in industrialized societies, life's stages have been defined by a person's assigned role. Youth was supposed to be devoted to education. In young adulthood, one started to work, with middle age the time of major accomplishments. Then, old age was a period of retirement. Today, however, the boundaries are fuzzier. There are individuals whose crowning success, thanks to the Internet, may come when they are in their early twenties, with nothing afterward that is comparable. In fact, some of these people have been able to retire at age twenty-five or thirty. On the other hand, those studying complex subjects such as medicine, science, or the humanities may not be able to even begin their life's work until they are in their late thirties or forties.

I will arbitrarily define adulthood as starting at age twenty-one, with those below this level considered youth or children. Young adults are those from twenty-one to forty-five; those middle-aged are from forty-six to seventy; and those above seventy are old. However, given the growing number of the elderly, old age can be further divided into the young-old, those from seventy-one to cighty-five, and the old-old, those who are above eighty-five. (There have been previous definitions of the young-old as from sixty-five to seventy-four and the old-old as above seventy-five,[6] and other classifications as well.)

As one would expect, people's outlooks and concerns change at different stages of their lives, shaping their actions and behavior, including patterns of spending and saving. In general, the young tend to be preoccupied with career development, having and raising children, and buying and maintaining a home. For most men and women, middle age is more a period of consolidation: children have left the nest and their interest is now centered on achieving economic security. Occupational issues and the desire to be "successful" still persist, but wind down toward the latter part of this stage. In old age, one's career is over and there are fewer responsibilities. The opportunity to acquire significant financial assets is usually gone. The focus now is on how to live with what you have and how to enjoy retirement, perhaps moving to a smaller home or condominium, a special community, or even to a new region of the country. Without the stresses of children and careers, there is potentially more freedom during this time, though not everyone takes advantage of this.

The old and middle-aged are not a homogeneous group. They differ not only in terms of age and physiologic status, but in terms of health and finances, whether single or married, and whether rural, suburban, or urban. People's physical, cognitive, and emotional status and the way these elements interact is particularly important in determining how they carry on their everyday activities. Financial pressures also affect older people to a greater degree than the young, since they usually live on fixed incomes and cannot return to work to earn more money if the need arises. Their family situations and the presence or absence of a spouse and/or children is critical as people grow older, and may be a major factor in how their energy is directed. Because men die earlier, there are a higher percentage of women beyond middle age at every level. For example, in 1996, the average life expectancy for men was seventy-three years versus seventy-nine years for women.[7] After age eighty-five, there are five women for every two men.[8] Among the older population are individuals who were never married, some who were divorced, and some who were widowed. And those who are still married may have relationships that run the gamut from unpalatable to wonderful. A spouse may also be ill and have to be cared for. This task may be borne cheerfully with love, or there may be resentment because of the previous history and ambivalent feelings toward the spouse. Relationships with children may vary as well and influence peoples' emotional states. But notwithstanding the differences that exist among old and middle-aged people, there are certain common patterns and needs that run through their lives, which can be explored to aid us all in the process of growing old.

In the past, both the Judeo-Christian tradition and Eastern religions instructed their adherents to respect the elderly, as did most primitive cultures.

Age was equated with wisdom and sages were depicted as old men in myths, literature, and art. There was a gender bias to this however, with old women less respected than men and often called by derogatory names, for example, crone, hag, or witch. Of course, since men and women died earlier in life, there were not many elderly in the community and they did not constitute a significant burden to society. Those who reached old age were believed to have special qualities that allowed them to survive and perhaps they were venerated because there were so few of them. Families and the community not only revered the elderly, but if necessary, cared for them and met their needs as much as they were able, sometimes at great sacrifice in terms of their own lives.

Starting in the nineteenth century, attitudes toward older people changed, owing to various social currents, both secular and religious, which will be discussed later. This led to a tendency to devalue the elderly in many ways, which has remained a theme through the present. Instead of regarding seniors as wise and acknowledging their experience, they are often thought of as senile, or near senile, with their infirmities exaggerated. Indeed, there is a bias against older people called "ageism" (a term first used by the geriatrician Dr. Robert Butler in 1968), which makes it more difficult for them to work, or realize their potential in other ways; an extra encumbrance they must constantly deal with. Their expertise is usually not utilized by the community, or even their families, and they are frequently relegated to stand on the sidelines when leadership is needed, or decisions are made. Our culture lionizes youth, as shown daily on television, in music, in the movies, and in the print media, all of which cater to the young. Fashion and styles are also created with the young in mind, giving little consideration to the tastes of older people. Youth is good, age is bad. Young is beautiful, old is ugly. But there are other factors as well that make seniors feel out of the loop. Even the language and terminology of the young is different from that of older people, further hindering communication between the generations. And today, the revolution in computers has left many of the elderly population behind, unable to comprehend just what is going on with this new instrument of commerce and creativity. As they search tentatively for a place in today's complex world, older people are often reluctant to speak up and let their views be known.

But whether the opinions of older people are sought by others in society, or are disdained as being "over the hill," they should put in their two cents on the issues of the day and make their feelings evident. They should be secure in their wealth of experience and recognize that they are wiser in many ways than those who are disinclined to listen to them. They understand more about the intricacies of life, its pleasures, and its pains, and what makes the world go round, since they have lived so much longer.

With the degree of mobility in our country, the extended family has also been vanishing over recent decades to the detriment of the elderly. Older parents often do not live near their children and may not have frequent contact with their grandchildren. The familiarity and emotional ties between family members, and the structure of the family unit, which were related to proximity, encouraging love and concern among the generations, is no longer there. Many children feel less responsibility toward their parents and no longer want to take care of them when there are problems. Indeed, physical or emotional abuse of elderly parents by children or grandchildren is not uncommon.[9] So-called granny-bashing cases are seen in hospital emergency rooms regularly and relatives have been known to abandon the demented elderly, at times without identification. Children also take funds or material possessions from older parents and use them for their own ends, sometimes impoverishing their fathers or mothers.

The United States is composed of many individual ethnic cultures, as well as the prevailing culture. Attitudes toward the elderly and how they are treated by their children and other younger people differ greatly from subculture to subculture. However, as the second and third generations are assimilated, their opinions and beliefs tend to track the dominant culture.

Though people are surviving longer, the quality of their lives can diminish as they age, particularly when they attain the status of being old-old (eighty-five and over). Some of them have chronic illnesses, such as arthritis, diabetes, Alzheimer's disease, Parkinson's disease, or residua from strokes, which leaves them infirm to varying degrees. And if their impairments are severe enough, their lives may be bereft of pleasure, instead filled with emotional and/or physical suffering. Before the era of modern medicine, most of these unfortunate individuals would have fallen victim to infections (usually pneumonia) and died prior to reaching this stage. But with ventilators and IVs to sustain them and antibiotics to combat the bacteria, many now manage to escape death, while passing from crisis to crisis. As the famed physician Sir William Osler noted in his 1927 *Principles and Practice of Medicine*, "Pneumonia may well be called the friend of the aged. Taken off it in an acute, short, not often painful illness, the old escape those 'cold gradations of decay' that make the last stage of all so distressing."[10] (By "taken off it," he meant dying.)

However, those with substantial disabilities constitute only a minority of the elderly population and most individuals in this age group have at least the potential of leading rich, rewarding lives. Even those with mild to moderate impairments or various aches and pains can usually function fairly well and be active in numerous ways. Indeed, aches and pains are a normal part of aging and signal that a person is still alive and able to feel things. If they are not significantly ill, the level of activity that people pursue is largely in their own hands, notwithstanding the constraints society may place on them. While some certainly take advantage of the opportunities offered to them in terms of continued growth, too often older people are lacking in goals or objectives over and above their daily existence. Without work to lend structure to their lives, they do not have a routine and do not make long-range plans. They refuse to consider options that are not easily attained, or that may require physical or mental effort. They are unwilling to be challenged or to explore new worlds, instead allowing their lives to become mechanical and automatic, with an absence of passion and little that is exciting or stimulating. In short, they permit themselves to fall into a rut and then find that climbing out may be a formidable task.

Many seniors also become emotionally or physically dependent on a spouse, children, or friends, when they are actually able to fend quite well for themselves. Taking the easy way out, they have others do things for them that they themselves are capable of doing. Sometimes, this happens because of depression or anxiety, but it can be because of simple laziness, or can even be manipulative in nature. For those elderly who feel lonely and irrelevant, this may be a way for them to gain recognition and to control other people, but it diminishes the recipient's self-sufficiency and independence, and cuts into their dignity.

Some older individuals may be excessively fearful—afraid of death or illness or of being alone. They see their peers dying or disabled and wonder when their turn will come. This anxiety may dominate their daily lives and interfere with their ability to function normally and communicate with others, changing the nature of their relationships. Their fear may chain them to their homes and they may be unwilling to take any chances or expose themselves to any threats, further isolating themselves. Life entails taking chances and putting oneself at risk in one way or another, and those unable to do so deprive themselves of pleasure, settling instead to exist with a relative absence of pain.

There are also some of the elderly who are resentful of how their lives have played out and the situations in which they find themselves. It may be their own fault or not, but that does not lessen their feelings of bitterness. (Of course, it is always easier for them to blame someone else than accept responsibility for their own fates, particularly when the results have not been what they had hoped for and they cannot change what has happened.) This was supposed to have been their golden years, but they wonder who named it so when life is difficult and they are unhappy. They say it is golden only for those who are healthy and economically sound, or not burdened with caring for another person. Anger and depression float to the top of their cups, the scent paralyzing their wills. And they are unable to move forward and find joy in the years remaining, instead feeling sorry for themselves and bringing sadness to those dear to them.

In his 1992 book *The Journey of Life*, Thomas R. Cole queries whether old age has lost its meaning in this era when science tries to answer all questions and sees aging as merely a problem to be solved. The spiritual aspects of aging, its mystery, and its special significance as a part of life seem to have been forgotten. He notes

> that no amount of biomedical research and technical intervention can bring aging fully under the control of human will or desire. Growing old and dying, like being born and growing up, will remain part of the cycle of organic life, part of the coming into being and passing away that makes up the history of the universe. Human freedom and vitality lie in choosing to live well within these limits, even as we struggle against them.[11]

There has been a focus in recent years on "dying with dignity," with innumerable books and papers written on the subject. Individuals mindful of this issue have composed advance directives to make their wishes known about how they want to die. The most discussed aspect of dying with dignity entails not allowing technology to keep us alive when the quality of our lives is poor and the possibility of returning to our former selves is nil. Though much attention has been paid to the manner in which we die, there has been less concern voiced about how we can "live with dignity" as we grow older, a process that lasts longer and is more difficult than dying. Indeed, a large and increasing portion of our existence is spent in middle age and old age. Using that time wisely by getting the most out of those years, in terms of personal growth and satisfaction and productivity and enjoyment, may determine whether we view our lives as having been "successful."

A book with the title *Successful Aging* was published in 1998 by Dr. John Rowe and Dr. Robert Kahn addressing these concerns. According to the authors, successful aging connotes an overall happiness with one's life, and the ability to operate at a high level and with a strong self-image as one grows older. Rowe and Kahn believe this necessitates an engagement with life, an avoidance of disease, and maintaining high cognitive and physical function.[12]

What do I mean by the term *living with dignity*? Is there a special lifestyle or way of living required to maintain one's dignity as one grows older? Not at all. Though remaining independent and autonomous is important, many different lifestyles and individual approaches to life can be rewarding and give a person a sense of worth and self-respect. Each of us has to find the path that is right for him or her and follow that path. If it leads to a dead end, we must search for another road and take it as far as we can. And we must resist attempts by others we encounter during our journey to rob us of our dignity. This includes family members with good intentions who do things for us and take away our independence as they try to be helpful.

All human life has an inherent dignity and there are those who feel that no matter how our lives evolve as we grow old, we should accept what we have and not make an effort to modify our circumstances, or the manner in which we live. I disagree. I believe we should all play a role in shaping our lives and should endeavor to change the way we live if we are not generally content. Living with dignity means that we should try to find activities that are satisfying for us and participate in those we enjoy as much as possible. But life is not all pleasure and we should also try to do things we feel are meaningful and rewarding, for ourselves, for others, and for society at large, giving of ourselves to make the world a better place. We should attempt to fulfill our remaining potential to the best of our abilities, whatever our age or status. Living with dignity also means making our presence known and having our voices heard debating the issues of the day, shouting loudly rather than allowing ourselves to drift quietly into irrelevance. As Dylan Thomas wrote:

> "Do not go gentle into that good night,
> Old age should burn and rave at close of day;
> Rage, rage against the dying of the light."[13]

As a practicing neurologist for over thirty years, I have come to know thousands of middle-aged and elderly people, constituting a significant percentage of my patients. I have seen them in various situations over long periods of time, some sick and disabled, some on the verge of death, but many who were well and functioning independently. I have listened to their fears, their hopes, their despair, and their joys, as I learned a great deal about what it means to grow old and gained an understanding of the aging process. I have also watched three grandparents advance in years and eventually die (one had died before I was born), my parents age, and my father die. Now I am witness to my own aging along with that of my wife and our peers, both friends and relatives. Our aging is on our minds every day, with offhand remarks, frequent discussions, and attempts at humor about our growing limitations. With each birthday and new year that marks the passage of time, we tell ourselves that things aren't really so bad. And perhaps that's true. But at sixty-four, I can visualize my parents at that moment of their lives and remember thinking how old they were. Yet I don't feel old at all. Life is very stimulating and for the most part quite pleasant, and I look forward to every day.

SYNOPSIS OF THIS BOOK

In the chapters that follow, I will examine the barriers that are placed in the paths of all of us as we age, making it more difficult for us to enjoy life and live well. I will explore strategies that can be used to overcome these obstacles and empower people to reach the individual objectives they have set for themselves. I will describe various actions that can help us grow old gracefully, even zestfully, as we live life to the fullest while retaining our self-esteem and our dignity. This is not meant to be a "how-to" book that instructs people on the best ways to grow old. It is more a philosophy of aging and observations about people derived from my own experience and personal beliefs. While the book is meant to be helpful for the elderly, it is also written for the young and particularly the middle-aged, who have the ability to prepare themselves for what lies ahead and then confront aging with the advantage of being ready.

2

THE CONSEQUENCES OF TIME

How the Aging Process Affects Us

———————————————— • ————————————————

Everything about him was old except his eyes and they were the
same color as the sea and were cheerful and undefeated.

—ERNEST HEMINGWAY
THE OLD MAN AND THE SEA

The predominant characteristics of old age are reduced
capacity to adapt, reduced speed of performance,
and increased susceptibility to disease.

—LEONARD HAYFLICK
HOW AND WHY WE AGE

In a hostile universe, old age is an unnatural state for most species. Only
human beings, or animals we have domesticated and keep in a protected environment, away from nature's primitive hands, are generally capable of
growing old. And they are able to live even if they are physically or cognitively
impaired and significantly disabled. Out in the forests and the jungles, however, it is the young, strong, and wily who survive. As animals age and become weaker, unable to run as fast or see as well, they are destroyed through
the natural selection process by predators, disease, or by simply not being able
to feed themselves adequately. For survival of the species, nature has programmed animals to live through sexual maturity and reproduce themselves.

Any existence afterward is merely fortuitous. As Ralph Waldo Emerson noted, "Nature abhors the old, and old age seems the only disease."[1]

Civilization allows homo sapiens to enjoy a major portion of their lives after propagation and child rearing, including those individuals who are no longer economically productive. The more complex and compassionate the social structure of a particular nation, the longer its citizens can potentially survive, with arrangements made for the care and support of its elderly. Thus, ideally, in a modern, democratic state, barring illnesses, we can live as long as we are able, without worrying about predators or starving to death

To understand how the aging process affects our dignity and vitality, we have to know what happens to us with normal aging and about the common diseases of the elderly. During the last half century, gerontology, the study of aging, has made great progress in delineating the changes that occur as we grow older. Much of the knowledge that has been obtained in painstaking research projects has been observational in nature, with scientists reporting on the cellular and molecular transformation that organisms undergo over time. Unfortunately, the reasons why this metamorphosis takes place (perhaps the key to unlocking life's secrets) remain unclear. We know a great deal about what happens, but not why. However, theories abound as to why living cells and larger organisms age. In this chapter, I will look at the changes seen on a cellular level, then briefly discuss some of the theories on aging. I will also survey the alterations that take place in human organs and organ systems over the years. This is not meant to be all-inclusive or encyclopedic in its descriptions, but to provide a general idea of what happens to us as we grow older.

CELLULAR AGING

The trillions of cells in our bodies are smaller subunits (building blocks) of our tissues and organs, each one individually unique and with its own mission to perform in support of the entire organism. During our lifetime, most of our cells divide periodically to replace those that are damaged or are no longer functioning properly. However, all of our cells are constantly active from a metabolic standpoint, even when we are sleeping, like miniature factories, producing various substances, destroying others, moving molecules in and out, and utilizing vast amounts of energy. "In life, entropy (the degree of disorder in a substance or system) . . . is in a constant war with biological forces that try to maintain a well controlled 'homeostatic' environment for the cell. Homeostasis is the tendency for a biological system to keep things steady and unchanged."[2] This battle requires the cell to always be at work preserving a steady state among different elements. Proteins in particular are being created and broken down during every moment of a cell's existence as its needs vary in response to internal and external conditions. This unceasing activity results in certain differences in the cells over time, as parts of the biologic machinery are perhaps worn out.

Though we are able to recognize aging when we look at someone, the changes responsible for what we see occur at a microscopic level, involving cells and their components, and fractions even as small as molecules. "Normal cells have only a limited capacity to divide and function."[3] When that point is approached, cells have become old. In other words, a cell's age can be determined by its ability to divide further in the future. "It takes about forty doublings of a fertilized egg to produce a full grown human adult, allowing for all the cells that are shed from our bodies during a lifetime."[4] Fifty cellular divisions are about the maximum that embryonic human cells can manage, far more than is required during a person's life span. This barrier to infinite cell division is known as the "Hayflick limit" after Leonard Hayflick, the scientist who discovered this phenomenon. The genetically predetermined biologic clock that controls the process resides in the DNA (genes) of the nucleus, in a structure called a "telomere." Each species has its own genetic program with longevity dependent on the number of possible cell divisions.

Recent work on cellular aging has focused on the telomere in determining the limits of cellular division, with some exciting discoveries that have implications for the aging process and the cancerous transformation of cells.[5] It has been found for instance "that the life span of human cells is mainly set not by their chronological age, but by how often they divide. At each division the telomeres—strings of special purpose DNA at the ends of the chromosomes—get shorter, until at a particular minimum length a signal is somehow touched off that forces the cells into the phase of aging and decline known as senescence."[6] This usually occurs at about fifty cellular divisions. An enzyme called "telomerase" can prevent the telomere from getting shorter as the cell divides, thus maintaining its youthfulness, with all the characteristics of young, healthy cells. It appears that telomerase may be able to extend the life span of human cells (in culture) indefinitely, but the significance of this is uncertain. (Telomerase is also produced by cancerous cells, allowing them to multiply unrestrained and to overwhelm normal cells.)

Telomeres and telomerase are not the complete answer to the question of why cells age. There are cells in the body that do not divide after birth (muscle and nerve cells), yet still show the changes of aging, which should not be related to a shortened telomere. (New studies have found that nerve cells may be able to divide and reproduce themselves.) So other mechanisms are probably involved. Research into the different genetic components that might affect aging is ongoing.[7]

Just as cells in different individuals age at their own distinct rates, the cells of different tissues in the same organism do not deteriorate uniformly on the road to malfunction and cellular death. Cells that have divided repeatedly and are near their limit (shortened telomeres) undergo changes that influence all of their metabolic and biochemical processes, affecting proteins, carbohydrates, fats, enzyme systems, and DNA. (Generally, cellular metabolism slows in older cells and the production of proteins is reduced.) This causes their performance to falter and makes them and the entire organism more subject to disease. The tissues or organs that age most rapidly usually determine how long the organism itself will live, particularly if they serve a vital purpose.

THEORIES OF AGING

In searching for the causes of aging in large organisms such as human beings, it is important to remember that although the rate of change that takes place may vary among individuals, it is a universal process. One must also differentiate between the normal changes that are seen with aging and those changes caused by diseases that are more common in an older population, but not universal. In addition, it must be appreciated that when changes are found in aging cells or aging organisms, it may be difficult to determine whether they are simply byproducts of aging, or whether they are actually responsible in some way.

Though the role of the telomere in the aging process is intriguing, a number of different theories have been propounded as to why aging occurs. These remain speculative, with hypotheses falling in and out of favor among investigators in the field, and with no proven cause to date. It may ultimately be found that several mechanisms are involved and that their interaction produces aging, rather than one specific factor. "According to the two main lines of thought, the aging process either results from genetically programmed changes or it occurs because of an accumulation of genetic errors due to environmental damage."[8] Thus, either a biologic clock within our bodies prearranges the aging process, or aging occurs because of a series of random events that act on our bodies. A variety of theories may fall under the umbrella of these two broad categories, though there are others that stand alone.

Free Radical Theory

Free radical compounds may be implicated in age-related changes as well as being linked to a number of disease states. It is known that as a consequence of cell metabolism, various molecules combine with oxygen to form free radicals—unstable molecular fragments that react with other cellular substances to cause significant damage and interfere with normal cell activity. Free radicals have been demonstrated to injure genetic material (DNA) and are involved in the production of the characteristic plaques of Alzheimer's disease and in the generation of age pigment. It has also been established that older animals produce more free radicals with resultant damage to DNA and that resistance to oxidative stress is linked to longevity in some species.[9] Antioxidants, like vitamin E and vitamin C, are compounds that interfere with the formation of free radicals and have been shown in experimental circumstances to retard the changes that occur with aging and to also increase longevity. However, it is uncertain whether antioxidants actually affect aging per se, or may instead reduce the diseases associated with aging, such as cancer, Alzheimer's disease, Parkinson's disease, and cardiovascular disease, extending life in this fashion.

Changes in the Immune System

Some biologists have theorized that alteration of the immune system induces aging, perhaps programmed in by atrophy of the thymus gland in the chest as we grow older. The immune system protects us against alien invaders like viruses and bacteria, and also combats dangerous internal threats by destroying cells that have undergone cancerous changes. Specialized cells of the immune system (white blood cells) and certain proteins generated by the immune cells (antibodies, compliment, and the like) are the bulwarks that safeguard our bodies. If the immune system goes awry, it can sometimes attack healthy tissues because it fails to distinguish between what is foreign and what is self. In these instances, it produces what are known as "autoimmune diseases" like rheumatoid arthritis, multiple sclerosis, myesthenia gravis, certain types of diabetes, and a host of other ailments that can cause serious disabilities or even kill affected individuals. If the immune system is dysfunctional, an individual may be more susceptible to infections and less able to suppress neoplastic (cancerous) changes when they occur. Though the immune system is generally less effective as we grow older, there is no evidence that this transformation is a significant factor in aging.

Errors in the Cellular Reparative Processes

Another hypothesis proposes that errors in the cellular reparative processes cause aging. As would be expected in a living, vital organism, there are constant breakdowns in various components of human tissues with subsequent repair. This cycle is ongoing. The mechanism for restoration of damage lies in the genetic DNA in the cell nucleus that replicates itself and is necessary for the production of proteins within our cells. Over time, after going through multiple cycles of repair, imperfections known as "mutations" are seen in the very complex structure of the DNA. These may lead to errors in cellular proteins whose generation is controlled by the DNA. The flaws produced may be even further exaggerated over additional cycles in the unending sequence that is life. The proponents of this construct believe it is possible these cumulative mistakes are related to the aging process and when severe enough result in certain diseases, even leading to death. Exposure to various environmental factors over the years, such as sunlight, radiation, various chemical substances, and so on, may initiate the mutations in the DNA.

Other Theories

An additional theory suggests that a diminution in the effective handling of waste materials by the cells may be the key element in aging—like factories no longer able to dispose of their byproducts. These substances then accumulate within the cells and may be toxic, producing cellular dysfunction. While it is true that lipofuscin (age pigment) is found increasingly in neurones (nerve cells) and cardiac cells in elderly people, this may just be an epiphenomenon (something associated with a process) rather than the actual cause of cellular aging.

Cross-linking is seen in complex proteins like collagen in older cells. This may also occur in the genetic material (DNA) in the cells. But is it cause or effect? These occurrences could impair cellular replication or metabolism in older people and cause the changes that are inherent in aging.

Other hypotheses have implied that aging may be initiated and sustained by hormonal signals originating in the brain that act on tissues and cells all over the body.[10] The hormones direct the cells to burn glucose, producing free radicals that result in cellular damage and aging. Another proposal is that wear and tear to cells and tissues due to the cumulative effects of repeated small injuries, even at a molecular level, are responsible for aging. Of interest is the observation that in lower organisms like rats, restricted caloric intake and lower body weight has been shown to prolong life span by about 40 percent.[11] There is a suggestion that this is also true in higher primates like rhesus monkeys, though these studies are ongoing. Why this occurs is uncertain, but may be related to the specific gene SIR 2 (silent information regulator) and a protein it produces that silences gene activity. The bottom line is that no research has yet come up with a definitive answer as to why we age.

However, one would not know by the proliferation of special remedies available to halt or reverse aging that an explanation for the aging process has not been found. Various products with secret formulas, unique prescriptions, and exclusive methods promise to keep us from growing older, or at least delay the consequences of time. But there is nothing on the market today of proven value as an antidote to aging. If one were to do anything, it might be reasonable to take vitamin E or vitamin C in appropriate doses. These may have some minor effects on cellular aging because of their antioxidant qualities, are not prohibitively expensive and are not harmful. For some people, this may provide some psychological benefit. On the other hand, the use of unregulated patent medicines has the potential to be detrimental to one's health and pocketbook.

Recently, investigators have discovered certain substances that appear to have the potential of prolonging life, though availability for humans is years away.[12] One of these chemicals is resveratrol, which is found is some red wines. A number of other compounds are also being studied. These substances act in a manner similar to a very low calorie diet and it is possible that if humans behave the same way that rats do, life expectancy could be increased by 30 percent. Scientists are very excited by these compounds since caloric restriction has already been shown to extend life in lower animals. It would have been impossible to place people on this type of diet, but taking a pill that produced this effect would be a wonderful solution.

Also of interest in terms of theories of aging are those rare genetic diseases that cause accelerated aging. The most striking of these is progeria, caused by a mutation in the LMNA gene, which results in a defective type of protein named "lamin A."[13] This takes place in about one in eight million newborns. In this condition, aging occurs at about seven times the normal rate, with a ten-year-old child having the cardiovascular, pulmonary, and musculoskeletal system of a seventy-year-old. These children appear elderly—with baldness, wrinkled skin, pinched nose, small face and jaw, dwarfism, and arthritic joints, as well as generalized atherosclerotic vascular disease. Death usually ensues in the teenage years. Unfortunately, though this syndrome mimics premature aging, it has not provided any answers to investigators as to what causes aging.

NORMAL CHANGES IN VARIOUS ORGANS AND ORGAN SYSTEMS

General Changes Seen with Aging

Loss of height occurs universally as we grow older starting at about thirty, with most of us reluctantly surrendering several inches by the time we enter our eighties. Much of this is due to shrinkage of the intervertebral cartilagenous discs up and down the length of the spine, with alterations in posture and bowing of the hips and knees also playing a role. Total body fat also increases, with a difference in distribution noted as well, particularly in greater abdominal girth. Lean muscle mass is reduced and the body's metabolism falls, as does oxygen consumption. A lessening of abdominal muscle tone adds to the bulging seen in older people.

The Brain and the Nervous System

As a concomitant of aging, everyone's brain weight diminishes. Atrophy is easily recognizable at autopsy in pathological specimens of the elderly who have died, and in CAT scans (computerized axial tomography) and MRI scans (magnetic resonance imaging) of the living. The gyri (the convoluted tissue that makes up the surface of the brain) shrink, the sulci (the fissures between the gyri) widen, and the ventricles (the cavities in the brain) dilate. There is a decrease in the number of neurones (brain cells) in the gray matter seen microscopically, particularly in the frontal regions, but not as severe nor as widespread as previously believed. Subcortical neurones (deep in the brain) are lost in greater proportions and the white matter appears to shrink. The production of certain proteins is reduced, among them enzymes that are important neurotransmitters (chemicals that transmit impulses between nerve cells), such as acetylcholine and dopamine, in systems that control memory and motor activity (movement, balance, coordination, and so forth). In the past, it was believed that neurones were immutable and incapable of adaptability or regeneration when damaged. In the last few years, studies have shown this to be untrue, raising the possibility that with the proper stimulus, injured nerve cells in the brain and spinal cord may be able to be induced to regenerate. "Perhaps the most exciting recent data suggests that the adult CNS (central nervous system) may be capable of impressive self repair, encouraged through activity or rehabilitation."[14]

From a physiologic standpoint, the outstanding effect of aging on the brain is the increased time that is necessary to perform various tasks. As we grow older, "there is continual loss in speed of learning, speed of processing new information, and speed of reaction to simple or complex stimuli. There is loss of sensory functions, . . . in muscle strength and motor efficiency."[15] Though central processing within the brain is slowed, most tasks can be accomplished and new information learned. It just takes longer. As Leonard Hayflick commented, "Loss of mental capacity with age is not inevitable. The old idea that senility is a normal accompaniment of age is simply wrong."[16]

Memory is also affected to some degree in virtually every person, starting in the fifties and becoming more pronounced with each succeeding decade. Explicit memory (where there is intention to recall) is particularly involved, with long-term and working memory remaining remarkably intact in numerous older people. Many individuals are quite concerned over their problems with memory, believing it heralds the onset of Alzheimer's disease. But it is a normal occurrence and is not commonly disabling.

Balance also deteriorates with age, though the level of dysfunction is variable. Those who are physically active tend to have fewer difficulties. Hand coordination and fine movements are frequently impaired as well, usually owing to a combination of both brain and musculoskeletal factors, with arthritis often playing a role. In addition to the changes that occur in the brain, there is a delay in the conduction of impulses in the sensory and motor fibers of the peripheral nerves. This may also contribute to some of the decline in motor abilities (strength and balance) and sensory perception (touch, pain, cold, heat). But usage and activity can help maintain function.

Sleep patterns that are controlled by the brain normally change as we grow older. Hormonal alterations may be partially responsible for these differences. The total time we sleep each night is less, with a decrease in the percentage of deep sleep. There are repeated interruptions during the night, originating in the brain and because of the need to urinate. The elderly generally arise earlier in the morning, even if they go to sleep late at night, though most do retire earlier. Napping during the day is common and quite refreshing for many individuals.

The Heart and the Cardiovascular System

The incidence of cardiovascular disease in the general population is also directly related to age. The older you are, the more likely you are to have problems. In the absence of heart disease however, the ability to pump blood does not change to any major degree as we grow older and our hearts are able to work surprisingly well. But heart muscle has been found to lose some of its elasticity and becomes somewhat stiffer and thicker. The maximal heart rate also declines, though cardiac output can go up when demands are made on it. This happens by raising the quantity of blood pumped out with each contraction. The heart may also not respond as quickly to various stimuli in the elderly. All of these factors make vigorous exertion more difficult. Some of this is often due to deconditioning from lack of exercise and those who are physically active may be able to retard many of the alterations seen with aging.

Most of the changes that occur in the blood vessels of the elderly are caused by atherosclerosis (commonly known as hardening of the arteries, but due mainly to the deposition of fatty materials on and within the wall of the arteries), which in the past was felt to be an expected part of aging. In reality, however, it is a diseased state and these findings are minimal in healthy individuals. The changes that occur are related to cholesterol and lipid metabolism, with genetic predisposition and diet playing roles. But there is normally some thickening of the lining of the arteries (intima) in older people and some rigidity of the blood vessel wall. Systolic blood pressure (the higher of the two numbers) may also be somewhat elevated. The normal changes in the blood vessels of older people probably makes them more susceptible to the development of atherosclerosis.

The Respiratory System

The lungs become less elastic as we age, because of a transformation in the connective tissues (collagen, elastin). This leads to increased pulmonary volume and expansion of the thoracic cavity, the latter easily recognized in many elderly people as a barrel-like chest. Vital capacity of the lungs also diminishes. Calcification occurs between the ends of the ribs and the sternum (breastbone), resulting in reduced flexibility of the chest wall. Because of this, less air moves with each breath, necessitating more work in breathing, particularly the deep excursions that accompany strenuous activity. Many of the small terminal sacs (alveoli) that are deep within the lung tissue are damaged or collapse with age, compromising the surface area where air and blood interface. Thus, the transfer of oxygen from the air through the membranes of the lungs into the blood is less efficient in the elderly and oxygen levels in the blood are reduced. Again, exercise can prevent and even reverse some of these changes.

The Gastrointestinal System

> A man hath no better thing under the sun than to eat,
> and to drink, and to be merry.
>
> —ECCLESIASTES 8:15

Without the gastrointestinal system, it would not be possible to eat, or drink, or be merry. Our nutritional status depends on this allied group of organs that is involved in the intake and digestion of food and the elimination of waste. It consists of the mouth and oral cavity, salivary glands, esophagus, stomach, small and large intestines, liver, gall bladder, and pancreas.

In the elderly, the swallowing mechanism may be impaired to a minor degree and the act may take longer. Emptying time of the stomach may also be increased and less acid may be produced. Atrophy of the lining of the large and small intestines can be seen along with small sacs in the wall of the large intestine (diverticula) that can become inflamed if food lodges in them. Because the muscles and contractile function of the walls of the intestine weaken with age, the passage of food takes longer and there is a higher incidence of constipation. Gas and eructation (belching) are also more common in the elderly. All the glands in the gastrointestinal system (salivary, stomach, intestines) are reduced in number and secrete decreased amounts of enzymes, which may cause some problems with digestion and food absorption. The liver shrinks in size and there is less blood flow to this organ and less enzymatic activity. Since the liver is responsible for the metabolism of many chemical compounds in the body, older people are often more sensitive to medications and may require lower doses and careful adjustments of any drugs that are prescribed. The pancreas may also atrophy and the production of its enzymes may be reduced, particularly lactase, which digests the sugar in dairy products.

The Genitourinary System

In the urinary tract, liquid waste is excreted actively and by passive filtration as urine by the kidneys. It then passes through the ureters into the bladder where it is stored until it is released through the urethra. The genital system in the male consists of the testes with its various tubules, the prostate and the penis. The female genital system is made up of the ovaries, fallopian tubes, uterus, cervix, vagina, and clitoris.

As we age, our kidneys shrink and there is decreased blood flow and renal function. This may cause problems in eliminating some medications. Concentration of urine is also more difficult to achieve and we may have trouble regulating salt. Because the kidneys do not work as well in the elderly, older people are more prone to dehydration. They may also find it more difficult to urinate and empty the bladder because of weakness in the muscles of the bladder wall. Changes in urinary sphincter tone may cause problems in controlling urination and lead to incontinence. The enlargement of the prostate gland around the urethra in elderly men can cause urinary frequency, nocturia (a need to urinate during the night), hesitant urinary flow, and even urinary retention.

As men grow older, there is a decline in the frequency of sexual activity along with a reduction in sexual hormone levels (testosterone). However, sperm counts in ejaculates are unchanged. Some scar tissue develops in the prostate and the penis, and there is diminished blood flow to the latter as well. There may also be less sensitivity of the penis to tactile stimuli, and less sexual daydreaming and fantasies, which appears to correlate with sexual desire. General erectile ability may be impaired and the refractory period after orgasm increases considerably in older men (the time before an erection and subsequent orgasm can be achieved). "There is some belief that intercourse maintains the prostate in good condition. This prompted one urologist to suggest that his patients remember the three stages of sexual activity: "tri-weekly, try weekly, and try weakly—but do try."[17]

Women go through menopause in midlife (generally late thirties to mid-fifties) with a reduction in estrogen levels and a halt in ovulation. The ovaries tend to become atrophic and the drop in estrogen can lead to hot flashes. The lack of female hormones also results in shrinkage of the uterus and vagina, with thinning of the walls of these organs and diminished vaginal secretions. This may lead to discomfort during intercourse (dysparunia) unless corrective measures are taken. (One of my professors used to joke that "Dysparunia is better than no parunia at all." But this pain is no joke to the women who have it, leading to avoidance of sexual intercourse and possible strains on relationships.) Breast tissue shrinks as well after menopause, with the breasts becoming smaller and flabbier. In some women, libido is decreased, resulting in a decline in sexual activity.

The Endocrine System

The production of hormones in the body is felt to be regulated by the "master gland," the pituitary, which in turn may be controlled by a part of the brain called the "hypothalmus." In addition to the pituitary and the reproductive glands (the testes and the ovaries), the endocrine system includes the thyroid, adrenal, and the insulin-producing cells of the pancreas. There is a feedback loop between these glands and the pituitary–hypothalmus that determines how much of the various hormones are manufactured and released. As we grow older, almost all of our glands produce diminished amounts of hormones. In the past, this was felt by some to be responsible for the aging process and hormones, particularly growth hormone—testosterone and estrogen—were given in an attempt to reverse the changes of aging and prolong life. But these have not been shown to be of significant benefit in terms of increased longevity.

Recently, however, there have been a number of clinics and physicians who have been giving hormone injections in an attempt to retard aging.[18] In fact, there is an American Academy of Anti-Aging Medicine that now exists and claims to have eight thousand physicians as members. The injections given are usually a combination of growth hormone (which is produced by the pituitary gland) and the sex hormones—testosterone for men and estrogen and progesterone for women—along with melatonin, vitamins, and antioxidants. There is no question that increased muscle mass, loss of fat, and heightened vigor and sex drive can result initially from these treatments. But the long-term results are less certain and they do not appear to make people stronger, do not improve cognitive ability, and do not increase life expectancy.[19] (In fact, in animal studies, those with increased growth hormone died earlier.) And there are significant side effects from growth hormone including severe joint pain, swelling of the legs and feet, elevated blood sugar or diabetes, and high blood pressure. It is possible that further studies in the future may come up with a formula that can be given with the proper proportion of hormones helpful in slowing the aging process and with minimal side effects, but for the time being the evidence does not favor their use.[20]

The Musculoskeletal System

This is comprised of the bones, cartilage, joints, muscles, ligaments, and tendons. As we age, we lose bone tissue, usually starting in the fifties, though the degree of this loss varies from individual to individual. Normally, there is a balance between the production of new bone and reabsorption of old bone. With aging, this equilibrium is altered, with bone growth slowing and bones thinning, resulting in osteoporosis. Women are affected much more than men, particularly after menopause.

Alterations in the joints occur frequently in the elderly, and manifest as osteoarthritis. The cartilage undergoes chemical changes and some of this tissue is lost. Though much osteoarthritis can be attributed to excessive wear, it is not seen universally.

Muscle as a percentage of total body weight diminishes as we grow older, along with strength and stamina, as evidenced in the performance of different tasks requiring these elements. Though some of this is an integral part of the aging process, considerable enhancement of performance can be fostered with proper exercise and dietary intake.

The Skin

Our skin protects and insulates our bodies and is visible to the outside world as an easily distinguishable indicator of age. However, the changes seen are not uniform throughout the population and certain factors cause alterations disproportionate to a person's chronologic age. The most important of these is exposure to ultraviolet rays that are part of sunlight. Thus, people who are outdoors a lot without adequate protection are more likely to have damaged skin that appears old. Wrinkles are for many the first sign of aging. This is caused by the loss of a protein called "collagen" and an increase in another called "elastin." There is also a loss of some subcutaneous fat and thinning of the skin, which becomes less flexible over time and sags. Age spots (senile keratoses) are also seen more frequently, particularly in the old-old. Though aging skin may not be as esthetically appealing as young skin, it functions quite effectively in the job for which it was designed.

Fingernail growth slows significantly in most people in their later years. Color may change as well to a yellow or gray and the nails may look duller than previously. There are also differences in hair color and in patterns of hair growth. (Male pattern baldness occurs in younger men who have a genetic predisposition and high levels of testosterone.) Hair becomes thinner on the scalp and generally over the body, though it may increase in the nostrils, ears and eyebrows. Women may grow more facial hair after menopause. Of course graying of the hair is another marker of age, but is quite variable in terms of time of onset, degree of involvement and rapidity of development. Graying is due to a decline of cells in the hair bulb that produce melanin, the pigment responsible for coloration of skin and hair.

NORMAL CHANGES IN THE SENSORY SYSTEMS

With aging, acuteness of sensation is blunted to differing degrees in all of us as our vision diminishes and our hearing fades, usually a slow decline that allows us to remain functional into our later years.

Vision

A change in the lens of the eye is noted at midlife for most people, becoming thicker and less flexible. This results in difficulty focusing on near objects (presbyopia) and is usually easily correctable with eyeglasses. Problems seeing in dim light or in the presence of glare are also more common as we age, as is dark adaptation.

Hearing

Structural changes also develop in our ears as we get older. The eardrum becomes thicker, the canal atrophies, and degenerative changes may take place in the small bones of the middle ear. Higher frequencies of sound are not heard as well (presbycusis) because of these differences. Pitch discrimination is also impaired, which may make it more difficult to locate sounds and understand speech, particularly when background noises in the environment are masking it, such as in a crowded room.

Smell and Taste

The ability to perceive different odors as well as taste declines markedly later in life.[21] The diminished sense of smell may be due to changes in the areas of the brain responsible for interpreting smell, or to the loss of cells that detect various odors. This impairment of smell is potentially hazardous in the elderly, if they are unable to recognize toxic elements, gas, burning, and the like.

The tongue atrophies somewhat as we age, though this does not appear to affect our taste buds. But because the sensation of taste is partially dependent on smell, it also becomes muted. This can lead to less enjoyment of food and in some instances, poor eating habits and impaired nutrition.

Touch

The appreciation of light touch and pain sensation also lessens with age. Whether this is on a peripheral basis (delayed nerve conduction) or of central origin (loss of neurones in the brain or spinal cord) is uncertain.

DENTAL PROBLEMS

The loss of teeth with aging is unfortunately widespread, with the elderly often depicted as edentulous (toothless). However, this does not occur universally and with proper dental care can be avoided. For many people, the loss of teeth is undesirable for cosmetic reasons and in terms of self-image. Tooth decay and cavities usually result from poor oral hygiene and when severe may require teeth to be extracted. Periodontal disease (problems with the gums and supporting structures) can also cause tooth loss. Regular dental examinations and care, proper oral hygiene, and fluoride additives for children may all be helpful in maintaining our teeth in our later years.

CONCLUSION

Having reviewed the normal changes that occur with aging, one might believe that the prognosis for all of us is poor as we grow older. But that is not the case. The fate of most of us remains in our own hands to a large degree until the last stages of our lives. However, we must remain physically active, mentally stimulated, and socially engaged if we are to have a positive influence on the course of our aging.

3

UNDERSTANDING THE ENEMY

The Diseases and Disorders Associated with Aging

•

Growing old ain't for sissies.

—ATTRIBUTED TO THE ACTRESS BETTE DAVIS

Growing old is certainly not easy for many of us. Normal aging takes its toll and then we have to deal with various diseases and disorders that may attack us when we are vulnerable. It takes courage and spirit to face down the enemy, battling him to a standstill whenever that is possible and overcoming him when the opportunity is there. But to fight back, we have to understand our adversary in order to devise a strategy and marshal our forces, to emerge victorious whenever we can.

People do not die of old age. Death is caused by various diseases that affect people when they are old (see Table 1). These are abnormal conditions and the older we get, the more likely we are to be stricken by one or more of these disorders, since the aging process itself makes us more susceptible to illnesses and injuries that can kill or disable us.

Not all illnesses result in death. Less serious problems that interfere with quality of life are also common in many seniors. In assessing disabilities among the elderly who live outside of nursing homes, one study found that 38 percent had arthritis, 29 percent had hearing impairment, 20 percent had vision impairment, and 29 percent had heart conditions.[1] Yet, in a survey several years ago, it was found that overall quality of life and health in

Table 1
The Leading Causes of Death, 2000

	Number	Death Rate*	Percentage of Total Deaths
All Causes	2,403,351	873.1	100.0
1. Heart Disease	710,760	258.2	29.6
2. Cancer	553,091	200.9	23.0
3. Stroke	167,661	60.9	7.0
4. Chronic respiratory diseases	122,009	44.3	5.1
5. Accidents	97,900	35.6	4.1
6. Diabetes Mellitus	69,301	25.2	2.9
7. Influenza&Pneumonia	65,313	23.7	2.7
8. Alzheimer's Disease	49,558	18.0	2.1
9. Kidney Disease	37,251	13.5	1.5
10. Blood Poisoning	31,224	11.3	1.3

*Per 100,000 population.

Source: National Center for Health Statistics, U.S. Department of Health and Human Services in The World Almanac—2003, 76.

those people who were living longer did seem to be getting better.[2] We should keep that in mind as we explore the diseases and disorders of older age. People are generally living longer and their quality of life is better than at any time in the past.

DISEASES OF THE BRAIN AND THE NERVOUS SYSTEM

Alzheimer's Disease and Dementia

Dementia is a general impairment of cognitive function with a number of different causes. About three-quarters of those afflicted by dementia have Alzheimer's disease alone or in combination with cerebrovascular disease.[3] Its ravages do not spare the wealthy, nor the famous, with Ronald Reagan, Rita Hayworth, and Charlton Heston among those who have been victims of Alzheimer's. However, those with higher levels of education may have some degree of protection from the disease (or perhaps a greater reserve before dementia is evident).[4] Other important causes of dementia are Pick's disease (frontotemporal dementia), Lewy body disease, and vascular dementia (cerebrovascular disease without the changes of Alzheimer's).

We now know that dementia is not a normal accompaniment of aging, instead being the result of specific illnesses whose incidence increases with age.[5] There is an estimate that 4–5 percent of the population of the United States over age sixty-five has severe dementia, with an additional 10 percent having mild to moderate impairment.[6] The highest rate of involvement is in the old-old over the age of eighty-five, with 25–50 percent said to be affected. There is a hereditary predisposition to Alzheimer's, particularly when it develops at a younger age, that is, seventy or below. A clear association has also been shown to exist between the APOE E4 genotype and Alzheimer's disease, with much greater risk in those people who are homozygous for APOE E4 (that is, have two copies of the gene).[7]

Alzheimer's disease and other forms of dementia cause a decline in all parameters of intellectual performance, with memory and ability to reason most severely compromised. In Alzheimer's it is felt that deposits of a substance called "amyloid" in the brain destroy cells and interfere with the transmission of signals between neurons. Microscopically, one sees amyloid plaques and neurofibrillary tangles scattered throughout the brain, concentrated in those areas that control memory and thinking, increasing as the disease progresses. Cell death increases as well and, over time, the brain atrophies. The initial symptoms may be partially due to diminished acetylcholine, a chemical that transmits signals between brain cells.

At the onset, those who are ill may seem mildly forgetful, though otherwise normal. But in time, they become unable to drive, manage simple finances, dress, prepare food, or take care of themselves. When not being watched, they may wander out of the house and get lost. Comportment may also be transformed. They may become paranoid, claiming that others are stealing from them, and on occasion may be agitated or combative. Eventually, they become incontinent and incapable of simple hygiene. Language function is lost and they are unable to communicate their needs or understand what they are being told. Balance and motor ability is usually involved rather late, following which they may become bedridden. Death usually intervenes mercifully through pneumonia or other intercurrent infections.

At this point, there is no cure for Alzheimer's disease or dementia and it usually runs its course over a number of years. In the early phases, there are drugs called "cholinesterase inhibitors" that improve memory somewhat and slow the disease's progression, but their effects generally last for only a year or two.[8] Antidepressants are also helpful at times. As Alzheimer's advances, other medications may be useful in controlling agitation, paranoia, or behavioral changes, aiding the caregiver with management. New experimental treatments are on the horizon, but their usefulness is yet to be determined.

Of particular interest are chemicals that block the enzymes that break down amyloid precursor protein into amyloid, the substance that is toxic to the nerve cells.

Strokes

Strokes are caused by cerebrovascular disease—atherosclerotic changes within the blood vessels that supply the brain. They are also known as "CVAs" (cerebrovascular accidents). The risk factors are the same as those for atherosclerosis in general (this will be discussed under the section "Coronary Artery Disease"). Stroke is the third leading cause of mortality in the United States and the primary cause of disability. "Stroke incidence rates rise exponentially with increasing age, with a hundred-fold increase in rates from about 3 per 10,000 population in the third and fourth decades, to almost 300 in the eighth and ninth decades."[9] About one in four men and one in five women can expect to have a stroke if they live to age eighty-five. A lack of blood flow to an area of the brain due to blockage of an artery, or bleeding into the brain from the rupture of a blood vessel cause strokes. Emboli, or clots that originate elsewhere (the heart) and travel to the brain arteries and obstruct them, are also responsible for some strokes. The problems that result depend on the severity of the insult and the region of the brain involved.

Strokes can vary from temporary loss of function with no residual difficulty, in which case it is called a "TIA" (transient ischemic attack), to massive permanent deficits, or death. Paralysis of an arm, a leg, or one side of the body; sensory loss, the inability to speak or swallow; problems with balance; or visual dysfunction can all be seen. Improvement may occur over time with rehabilitation, or there may be little return to normalcy. Partial or total disability may result with a need for full- or part-time care. In the worst instances, a nursing home or round-the-clock assistance at home may be required.

Over the last decade, there has been evidence that if a stroke is treated within three hours with drugs that dissolve the clot blocking the artery, it may result in long-term improvement in outcome. This treatment, however, does have associated risks and only a small percentage of stroke patients are candidates for these compounds. Several types of blood thinners may also be utilized as therapy. But once a major deficit is present, the chances for functional recovery are not good. Because of this, prevention of strokes in susceptible individuals is exceedingly important. Reduction of high blood pressure, lowering of blood cholesterol, proper diet, adequate exercise, and cessation of smoking can all contribute to stroke prophylaxis. Aspirin on a regular basis has also been shown to lower the incidence of strokes. In some people who have significant narrowing of the carotid arteries (the major arteries in the neck that go to the brain), surgery to open up the blood vessels may be beneficial.

It should be emphasized again that all strokes do not result in permanent disability, even those that initially seem severe. I recently saw an eighty-two-year-old man in my practice with an acute stroke that had caused significant left-side weakness, difficulty speaking, and an inability to see things on the left side. Over a period of days, his symptoms improved dramatically, to the point where he had only a mild limp while walking and minimal thickness of his speech. After a short course of rehabilitation, he was able to return to his apartment and continue living independently.

Another patient of mine, a woman of eighty-five, had residual mild problems with balance after a stroke, requiring the use of a quad cane to make her feel more secure. She was also able to live completely independently afterward and care for herself. In addition, she travels alone to various cities around the country to visit her children and grandchildren, and even went with her family on a vacation to Ireland.

A further example of triumph over stroke is the actor Kirk Douglas. He has returned to making movies, even though his speech is somewhat slurred because of the CVA that affected the motor area of his brain that controls speech.

Small vessel ischemic changes (from reduced oxygen supply) scattered throughout the white matter of the brain are ubiquitous among the elderly population seen on brain imaging (CAT scans and MRI scans). These are due to diminished blood flow in the smallest arteries and may be responsible for some of the cognitive difficulties and problems with balance seen so often in this age group.

Parkinson's Disease

Parkinson's disease is also known as "shaking palsy." There are more than 250,000 patients with Parkinson's in the United States (based on a population of 250 million) with approximately 50,000 new cases arising each year.[10] A number of factors probably contribute to the development of this condition. All of them cause a loss of cells in a part of the brain called the "substantia nigra," and a diminished production of a neurotransmitter called "dopamine" that transfers impulses between neurones in the extrapyramidal system (a related group of nerve cells that influence motor activity and balance). Because of this missing chemical, people exhibit problems walking: a stooped posture, small steps, and unsteadiness. Speech volume is low, there are difficulties with fine movements and coordination, and a tremor is often present. All motor functions are slowed and, in the later stages, intellectual decline may be present as well. Patients may require help with the tasks of daily living and greater degrees of care as the disease progresses. If another unrelated illness does not intervene (heart attacks, cancer, and so forth), death can result from pneumonia or other infections, usually after a prolonged course.

Treatment is directed toward replacement of the chemical that is deficient. In the early phases of the disease, patients may appear quite normal, with or without medication. But eventually it becomes necessary to give a drug called "L-dopa" (usually in combination with other drugs) that is converted by the brain to dopamine, the substance that is lacking. Medications that act similarly to L-dopa (dopa agonists) may also be utilized. As the process advances, higher dosages of L-dopa or dopa agonists become necessary. In time, patients may become more refractory to treatment and greater disability may occur. Even so, with current therapy, life expectancy has improved dramatically and disability usually does not occur for many years.

There are many examples of people in public life who have had Parkinson's disease and continued functioning on a high level. Pope John Paul II has been the leader of the Catholic Church for a number of years now with Parkinson's disease, following a hectic schedule and traveling around the world. Janet Reno served as attorney general of the United States with Parkinson's disease. She was also able to campaign vigorously before Florida's Democratic primary for governor, which she eventually lost. The actor Michael J. Fox, who developed Parkinson's at a much earlier age, has worked to increase funding for research in Parkinson's disease, while continuing his acting career.

Peripheral Neuropathies

Damage to motor and sensory nerves is seen frequently in older people, more often in the legs, resulting in numbness, tingling, and weakness and problems with balance and walking. Diabetes is often responsible, but a host of other metabolic, nutritional, and inflammatory processes can also produce this type of nerve impairment. Control of the underlying condition and physical therapy can sometimes be helpful. Often when the elderly complain of trouble with balance or walking, multiple factors are involved, including peripheral neuropathies, cerebrovascular disease, arthritis, and other degenerative disorders.

CARDIOVASCULAR DISEASES

Cardiovascular diseases together are the leading cause of illness, disability, and death among people sixty-five and older.[11] About half of all deaths in the elderly population result from these conditions: 45 percent of men and 52 percent of women.[12] The definition here of cardiovascular disease encompasses coronary artery disease, high blood pressure, peripheral vascular disease (arterial disease of the lower limbs), abdominal arterial disease, and strokes. Even alone, coronary artery disease is the number one killer in the United States. In 1993, it was reported to be responsible for 743,460 deaths, one-third of all the deaths in the country.[13] Though these numbers seem huge, the death rates from cardiovascular disease have actually declined dramatically over the last half century, a major public health triumph. "In 1950, the death rate from heart disease was 307.4 per 100,000 people. In 1996, it was 134.6. In 1950, the stroke death rate per 100,000 people was 88.8. In 1996, it was 26.6."[14]

The risk factors for coronary artery disease, strokes, peripheral vascular disease, and abdominal arterial disease (variants of the same disorder: atherosclerosis) are naturally quite similar, some of which can be controlled by behavior change and others that cannot be modified. In addition to cholesterol and lipid deposition in atherosclerosis, another substance that appears harmful is an amino acid called "homocysteine," a byproduct of normal metabolism. Homocysteine may damage blood vessels, magnifying other cardiovascular risk factors such as smoking and hypertension, leading to an increase in heart attacks, strokes, and peripheral vascular disease. Even a small rise in the blood level of homocysteine may make a person more susceptible to these various problems. However, it is also possible that homocysteine is a marker of atherosclerotic vascular disease, rather than causing some of the damage. Reducing the ingestion of meat and taking B vitamins, particularly folic acid, B_6 and B_{12}, can lower homocysteine levels and may decrease cardiovascular risk.

In the last decade, inflammation of the arteries has also been discovered to play a role in the production of atherosclerosis.[15] The exact mechanism by which this occurs is speculative, but it appears that certain infections or inflammatory processes may initiate atherosclerotic changes by damaging arterial walls and making them more receptive to the deposition of cholesterol and lipid material. Further accumulation of this material results in narrowing and finally blockage of the blood vessels, depriving the target organs of oxygen. C-reactive protein (CRP) levels can be used as a marker of inflammation.

Coronary Artery Disease

Narrowing (stenosis) or occlusion of a coronary artery by atherosclerosis causes heart attacks—MIs (myocardial infarction or death of cardiac tissue) and angina (myocardial ischemia or lack of oxygen to cardiac tissue), both of which present as chest pain. An MI can kill a person or produce heart damage that results in reduced cardiac function. This can be responsible for congestive heart failure and decreased levels of activity in survivors. Injured heart muscle makes the heart less able to pump blood throughout the body, particularly when the demand rises, such as with exercise. If enough heart damage has occurred, patients may be chronically fatigued and short of breath, with fluid accumulating in the legs (edema) and lungs (pulmonary edema). When congestive failure is severe enough, the patient may become a cardiac cripple, unable to sustain minimal exertion, because of the heart's diminished capacity to pump out blood.

If medical care is given within the first six hours of an acute heart attack, permanent damage to the heart muscle can often be prevented through the use of what are called "antifibrinolytic agents" (clot busters), which can lyse the clot in the coronary artery that is causing the heart attack. This may have to be followed by a surgical procedure called "CABG" (coronary artery bypass graft) where veins from the leg or arteries from the chest wall are used to replace the blocked coronary arteries and reestablish blood flow to the heart. Another option may be angioplasty, where the narrowed segment of the artery is dilated by a balloon catheter to improve blood flow, or stenting, where a small springlike coil is used to keep the artery open. These procedures do not change the basic process of atherosclerosis, but may buy the patient more time to alter his or her behavior and reverse, or at least prevent, progression of the atherosclerotic changes. Chest pain may be noted during a heart attack, or it may be a warning sign beforehand. Various types of stress tests, coronary angiography (a catheterization study of the heart's blood vessels with X rays taken after the injection of dye), and the use of radioactive isotopes may help establish the diagnosis of coronary artery disease and direct proper therapy.

Coronary artery disease may also cause alterations in the rhythm of the heart (arrhythmias) by damaging the intrinsic electrical system that regulates cardiac contractions. This can result in dizzy spells, blackouts, or even sudden death, by reducing blood flow to the brain and the rest of the body. Arrhythmias can be treated with various medications, but if the anatomic cardiac pacemaker is severely disrupted, an implanted permanent pacemaker may be necessary. With this hardware, those afflicted with arrhythmias may lead many more years of productive life.

Examples of people who have suffered severe heart attacks and continued an active or even stressful life for many years afterward are legion. President Dwight Eisenhower had a significant myocardial infarction during his first term in office. In spite of that, he was elected to a second term, which he served to completion without difficulty. Lyndon B. Johnson had a major heart attack in 1955. Following that, he was able to continue functioning as majority leader of the U.S. Senate, then was elected vice president and then president of the United States, easily handling the stress of his jobs. He died in retirement some years later. The current vice president, Dick Cheney, has had several heart attacks and cardiac arrhythmias, and has an implantable defibrillator in place. Yet he is able to meet the demands of his office and manage an extremely hectic schedule.

Other Vascular Syndromes

As part of the condition of generalized atherosclerosis, patients develop narrowing of the arteries leading to the brain, causing strokes. Peripheral vascular disease involving the arteries of the legs is also common, resulting in pain with walking that disappears with rest (intermittent claudication). Changes in the aorta (the main arterial trunk that leads out of the heart) can produce aortic aneurysms (weakening and dilatation of the arterial wall). Peripheral vascular disease and aortic aneurysms often require surgical repair to allow life to continue in a normal fashion. Severe atherosclerosis of the intestinal arteries may also require surgical intervention.

Hypertension

Hypertension or high blood pressure is a condition associated with aging that is a major risk factor for the development of atherosclerosis, strokes, and heart and kidney damage. It is estimated that about 50 million Americans have high blood pressure (one in four adults). Hereditary factors play a role in its development and it occurs more commonly in African Americans. Elevated blood pressure can also be related to a sedentary lifestyle and lack of exercise, obesity, stress, high salt intake, and heavy alcohol use, as well as decreased ingestion of potassium and calcium. Because those with hypertension often do not have symptoms early on, it is known as a silent killer.

Two parameters are measured to obtain blood pressures: the systolic being the higher number (when the heart muscle contracts) and the diastolic the lower one (when the heart muscle relaxes). Measurements above 140/90 are indicative of hypertension, with the higher the levels, the more dangerous it is to the individual, increasing the chances of stroke, myocardial infarction, and/or heart or kidney failure. Recent articles have suggested that blood pressures of 120/80 to 139/89 be considered prehypertensive and be treated aggressively, though there is some controversy about this.[16] But most would agree that "the relationship between blood pressure and risk of cardiovascular disease is continuous, consistent, and independent of other risk factors."[17]

Treatment of elevated blood pressure should include lifestyle changes such as dietary modification, weight loss, increased exercise, and constraints on alcohol use. Restrictions on the use of salt is quite important for someone who is hypertensive. Medications should be utilized whenever necessary, as there is no question of the risks of hypertension. It is also well-known that the condition is undertreated by many physicians and disregarded by many patients who do not develop symptoms until it is too late.

DISEASES OF THE RESPIRATORY SYSTEM

Chronic Obstructive Pulmonary Disease

Chronic obstructive pulmonary disease (COPD) is a significant cause of disability among the elderly, provoking wheezing, shortness of breath (dyspnea), and coughing. Emphysema and chronic bronchitis are the usual perpetrators, though asthma can produce similar symptoms, more commonly in a younger population. COPD is invariably the result of smoking for many years, with environmental factors and exposure to certain toxins occasionally contributing. In emphysema, the alveoli (terminal sacs) in the lungs are severely damaged or destroyed, making the exchange of oxygen between air and blood more difficult. In chronic bronchitis, the tubes that carry air in the lungs are inflamed and produce copious amounts of mucous (phlegm) that clog the tubes and prevent oxygen from reaching the bloodstream. The patient coughs intermittently and brings up this material, which may be infected as well. Shortness of breath hinders exertion and can be frightening at times, making patients feel as if they are suffocating. Those who have dyspnea on a chronic basis may become pulmonary cripples and have difficulty performing the simplest tasks. Usually, people do not have emphysema or chronic bronchitis in isolation, but instead are afflicted with a combination of the two conditions.

Cessation of smoking is an important element of treatment of COPD, but the underlying destructive process may already be advanced by the time that decision is made. (If every smoker could be forced to walk through a ward of patients with COPD and see them wheezing and gasping for breath, perhaps they could be induced to abandon tobacco earlier.) A number of different medications may be used to relieve some of the shortness of breath and diminish the production of mucous. Oxygen can also be helpful and it may be necessary for patients to carry an oxygen supply with them wherever they go. Because of their lung damage and inability to clear secretions, they are very prone to pulmonary infections and these should be treated early and aggressively with antibiotics.

Pneumonia

Pneumonia remains to this day a major killer of the elderly, particularly among the old-old and residents of nursing homes. The reasons for its prevalence include the diminished effectiveness of the immune system as we age, compromised pulmonary function, and COPD in many older people. There is also a tendency toward aspiration, or inhalation of fluids or foreign substances into the lungs, seen in people with impaired swallowing mechanisms, such as might occur following a stroke. When foreign substances enter the lungs, they produce a chemical irritation, increased secretions, and a fertile medium for infection. People who are feeble, chronically ill from any process, or bedridden may have a suppressed cough reflex and an inability to clear secretions, making them prime candidates for pneumonia. Treatment with antibiotics and improved pulmonary toilet (clearing secretions in the lungs) can often salvage patients with pneumonia, if their underlying problem is not too severe.

DISEASES OF THE GASTROINTESTINAL SYSTEM

While complaints relating to the gastrointestinal (GI) system are common among seniors, they are usually not indicative of serious conditions. Among the more frequent GI complaints are constipation, heartburn, gas, decreased appetite, abdominal pain, problems swallowing, diarrhea, and fecal incontinence. Older people often focus on their bowels, wanting "youthful regularity," and are overly concerned when they are constipated. Lack of exercise, poor abdominal muscle tone, diminished intake of fluids and bulky foods may all play a role, with regular straining at stool producing hemorrhoids. Gall bladder disease, hiatus hernias, and GERD (gastroesophogeal reflux disease), diverticulitis, and cancers of the GI tract all occur more often in the elderly, and structural abnormalities such as these must be sought if there are persistent symptoms.

DISEASES OF THE GENITOURINARY SYSTEM

Genitourinary problems are also not life threatening for the most part, but raise quality of life issues, particularly urinary incontinence. Urinary symptoms in the elderly, including frequency, urgency and difficulty voiding, may at times respond to medication, but some older men may require surgery to remove part of the prostate gland.

Urinary Incontinence

Urinary incontinence occurs in about one-third of the population over sixty who are living in the community and about 50 percent of those in nursing homes.[18] Patients in nursing homes may develop breakdown sores of their skin if the urine is not cleaned up quickly after they are incontinent. A number of different factors can be responsible for incontinence, including neurologic dysfunction, urinary tract infections, mechanical abnormalities, shrinkage of the bladder, weakness or damage to the pelvic muscles, inability to get to the bathroom in time because of neurologic or orthopedic problems, medications, dementia, and psychiatric disorders. It is important that medical evaluation be undertaken in those who have this condition, as a significant percentage of them can be helped. If no solution is found, the use of diapers or condom catheters may allow activities to continue and make the incontinence more tolerable.

Sexual Function

Sexual dysfunction in the United States appears to be prevalent in all age groups. A recent study showed that 43 percent of women and 31 percent of men had sexual problems, often associated with poor physical or emotional health and impaired quality of life.[19] But this is far from universal and can be amenable to treatment.

Though a decreased libido (sexual drive) in older people is a normal consequence of aging, some degree of intimacy and pleasurable sexual activity can be achieved by most healthy couples. In addition to one's physical situation and desire, there are many elements that play a role in deciding sexual behavior as we grow older. "The most important factor may be the presence of a willing and able partner. Social and cultural circumstances tend to reinforce the decline in sexual activity, especially for older women."[20] Interest in sexuality may be suppressed in the healthy elderly because of societal pressures and false beliefs that this is abnormal, wrong, or even immoral. In general, those who were most active sexually when they were young are most active when they are older, even with the expected reduction in frequency. The presence of physical illness in a person, or his or her spouse, can also severely limit sexual ardor. Cardiac disease, strokes, COPD, cancer, arthritis, osteoporosis, or fractures are some of the many conditions that can interfere with sexuality. And psychological problems, such as anxiety or depression, usually suppresses desire in both men and women.

Notwithstanding the difficulties noted, many healthy postmenopausal women have greater enjoyment of sex than when they were younger, and the desire for sexuality and sexual intercourse still remains in most men well into their eighties. However, impotence (the inability to have and maintain an erection necessary for sexual intercourse) is a common problem for a great number of older men. Again, many factors, both emotional and physical may be involved. From the physical side, atherosclerosis of the arteries that supply the penis can result in impotence, as can diabetes or any process that causes a neuropathy. Impotence, as well as lack of libido, may also occur as a side effect of certain medications. From an emotional standpoint, in addition to generalized depression or anxiety, a fear of failure or "performance anxiety" may underlie impotence, becoming a self-fulfilling prophecy.

ENDOCRINE DISORDERS

Thyroid

Thyroid dysfunction occurs with some frequency in all age ranges, including the elderly population. Hypothyroidism, or decreased thyroid function, is most common, where the output of thyroid hormone by the thyroid gland is reduced. This can cause symptoms of fatigue, weakness, weight gain, lassitude, mental dullness and loss of memory, depression, hair loss, cold intolerance, and decreased libido. It is easily amenable to treatment with thyroid hormone replacement, resulting in marked improvement in symptoms.

Diabetes

Diabetes is caused by diminished insulin production by the islet cells of the pancreas, or a lack of responsiveness by the body's cells to insulin. Older people have predominantly the latter kind of diabetes called "Type 2," or noninsulin-dependent diabetes. With this disease, glucose (sugar) metabolism is not well regulated and the levels of glucose in the blood and in the urine are elevated. Initial symptoms may include increased thirst and fluid intake, increased urine output, undue fatigue and lower levels of energy, generalized weakness, and weight loss.

As the disease progresses, various organ systems are affected to a greater degree. Diabetic retinopathy in the eyes can cause loss of vision. A peripheral neuropathy develops with numbness and tingling in the extremities, particularly the feet, which can be quite painful. Balance and strength can be impaired, and impotence and incontinence may occur. Diabetes also appears to worsen atherosclerosis and circulatory problems, with a rise in the incidence of cardiac disease, peripheral vascular disease, and strokes. Susceptibility to infections and delayed wound healing also is common. Because of the neuropathy and reduced blood flow to the legs, diabetic ulcers and gangrene may develop, necessitating amputation of the toes, feet, or legs.

Treatment consists of controlling the blood sugar through dietary restrictions, oral medications, and exercise if possible. If this is not effective, then insulin may be prescribed. Blood sugar levels are checked on a regular basis to monitor adequacy of treatment. Keeping the blood sugar within the normal range appears to lessen the rate of complications, though it does not eliminate them completely. If blood sugars are extremely high and the diabetes is poorly controlled, diabetic coma may result. It is also critical that blood sugars not drop too low (hypoglycemia), for that can produce hypoglycemic coma and seizures. Good hygiene and diet and avoidance of injury and infections are salient rules for all older people, but are particularly critical for diabetics. Weight loss can reduce the need for medication, and eliminating smoking and controlling cholesterol and blood pressure in diabetics are also extremely important.

Recent studies have shown that regular exercise can significantly reduce the incidence of diabetes. For anyone who is overweight, or with a family history of diabetes, an exercise program as part of his or her daily routine is imperative.

DISORDERS OF THE MUSCULOSKELETAL SYSTEM

These conditions include osteoporosis, hip and other bony fractures, arthritis, and joint problems, all of which are responsible for a reduction in the quality of life for older people. Inflammatory diseases of muscle (polymyalgia rheumatica, polymyositis) occur less frequently.

Osteoporosis

Osteoporosis is usually thought of as "softening of the bones" and is a loss of bone mass and bone density. Though it is a normal accompaniment of aging, when excessive, it greatly increases the chances of compression fractures of the spine and fractures of the hips or long bones. Also with this condition, the spine often bows out causing a hunched-back appearance (kyphosis). Predisposing factors include reduced estrogen levels after menopause in women, a sedentary lifestyle, smoking, alcohol, and certain medications. A deficiency of calcium, possibly due to problems with absorption of this mineral, may be important, as may diminished vitamin D and parathyroid hormone metabolism. People with osteoporosis often develop fractures with minimal trauma.

Prevention appears to be the most efficacious way to deal with osteoporosis. Increased calcium intake can compensate for the reduction in age-related absorption, and regular weight-bearing exercise, such as walking, may help strengthen bone and reduce fractures.[21] In postmenopausal women, hormone replacement therapy may also be beneficial, but may increase susceptibility to breast and ovarian cancers as well as vascular complications. Bone densitometry testing can be used to predict the risk of fractures and the degree of osteoporosis, perhaps leading to more aggressive therapy when bones are thought to be fragile.

Bony Fractures

Though osteoporosis is the primary condition leading to fractures in the elderly, other disorders (osteomalacia, cerebrovascular disease, cardiac arhythmias, and so forth) also contribute to this problem. Compression fractures of the thoracic and lower spinal vertebrae are most common, resulting in back pain that varies in severity, but can be quite excruciating. These may develop with heavy lifting or straining, a jarring step, or a drop from a short height. Pain may necessitate bed rest and relative immobilization for a short period. Back braces to limit movement of the spine may alleviate some of the pain when walking or standing, but time (usually a few months) is necessary for healing.

Hip fractures are a major cause of disability among older people and usually result from falls. In the United States, there are approximately 250,000 hip fractures each year, or 80 per 100,000 persons.[22] This is estimated to double by 2040. The severity of the fall necessary to produce a hip fracture depends on the degree of osteoporosis and the strength of the bone. Fractures may occur in different regions of the hip, may be displaced (out of alignment) or nondisplaced, or impacted (jammed together). Pain in the hip and groin, particularly with movement, is almost invariably present. If the fracture is nondisplaced or impacted, it can be stabilized surgically by the use of pins that allow the patient to be up and around quickly, eliminating the complications that arise with prolonged bed rest.

Displaced hip fractures can also be stabilized in younger people who can participate in an active physical therapy program. In most cases however, hip replacement is recommended to prevent deformity and problems with healing. The use of a prosthesis allows rapid weight bearing, usually with the aid of a walker. Physical therapy is again important to restore a person to some level of independent ambulation. If a patient is bedridden in a nursing home prior to the fracture, the treating physician may elect to merely keep him or her at bed rest rather than pursuing a more aggressive approach that will end in failure.

Wrist fractures are also seen frequently among the elderly owing to falls. For the most part, these are easily treated with casts or splinting and do not result in significant disability.

Arthritis

Arthritis can involve virtually any joint in the body, the result of degenerative changes, or inflammatory disease. Osteoarthritis, a chronic degenerative condition, is the most common form of arthritis, attacking mainly the hips, knees, spine, and hands. It is felt by some to be a consequence of wear and tear of the joint, though the degree of the changes seen on X ray and pathologically do not necessarily correlate with the amount of usage. Loss of cartilage that lines the joint spaces occurs first, followed by overgrowth of the ends of the bones near the joints, forming knobby protuberances called "osteophytes." Stiffness, pain, and swelling are the usual complaints, but at times, progression can lead to total dysfunction of the joint. Aspirin or nonsteroidal anti-inflammatory drugs (NSAIDS) such as Motrin and Naprosyn can often provide relief, particularly in the early stages. Hip or knee replacements by artificial joints may be required in some patients, when pain is unrelenting or walking is significantly impaired.

Involvement of the small joints of the spinal column by osteoarthritis may produce a different picture, which is called "spinal stenosis." Though spinal pain does occur, the more important symptoms are the result of pressure on the nerve roots and occasionally on the spinal cord itself in the cervical region (neck). The overgrowth of bone in the spinal column often in combination with degenerative disc disease causes a narrowing of the bony canals where the nerve roots are located (neuroforamina), or of the spinal canal. In addition to local discomfort, pain may be seen in the distribution of any nerve root that is compressed (radicular pain). Numbness, pins and needles, or tingling may occur when a sensory nerve root is compromised and weakness may occur if there is pressure on a motor nerve root. (Similar symptoms can be seen with herniated discs, which are more common in a younger population.) If the spinal cord is constricted in the neck, it may cause numbness or weakness in the legs along with balance problems and urinary and bowel dysfunction. Various medications can be used to reduce the pain of spinal stenosis along with physical therapy, but in some cases, particularly when the spinal cord is involved, surgical decompression may be necessary.

Rheumatoid arthritis is a generalized chronic inflammatory disease that can strike various organ systems as well as the joints. Though there is a propensity for the small joints of the hands and wrists, the process may also attack the elbows, shoulders, ankles, knees, and hips. An inflammatory reaction in the joint capsule damages all the elements there (cartilage, ligaments, and tendons), eventually causing changes in the bones as well. The mechanism is believed to be autoimmune in origin (the body produces antibodies that damage its own tissues) and affects women more often than men, resulting in swelling of the joints, restriction of range of motion, and pain. Severe joint distortion can occur, considerably limiting activity. Aspirin and NSAIDS may be helpful in relieving some of the discomfort and can increase mobility. Corticosteriods are often quite effective, but high doses may have serious side effects. Other immune suppressive therapies and gold injections are also utilized to control the disease. In recent years, new types of injectable drugs that block the effect of TNF (tumor necrosis factor) have been found to be very useful in the treatment of rheumatoid arthritis and additional treatments are expected in the near future.

SKIN DISORDERS

Most skin disorders in the elderly, aside from cancers, are only significant cosmetically and for the emotional distress they cause. Various techniques, including plastic surgery, can be utilized to destroy or remove offending lesions if patients so desire. There are several conditions that are in a different category however and are worth mentioning.

Shingles

Shingles is caused by a virus, herpes zoster, which is also the agent for chicken pox. It occurs more often in older people, or those whose immune system is compromised. The virus produces a painful rash with blisters or vesicles within the distribution of a nerve root that stands out sharply from the surrounding normal skin. The pain can be quite unpleasant, with repeated sharp jolts or burning, made worse by any minor contact with the affected area. Though the active disease usually runs its course in four to eight weeks, with the rash drying up and fading away, excruciating pain can persist for some time afterward (postherpetic neuralgia). Antiviral agents given early often abort the process and promote healing. A number of other medications, particularly anticonvulsants that are used for epilepsy and antidepressants, are helpful in controlling the pain.

Stasis Dermatitis

Stasis dermatitis results from poor circulation in the lower legs and increased venous pressure, and is manifest by discoloration, mainly darkening of the skin, shininess, and swelling. Itchiness and flaking of the skin also are seen and the involved areas are much more prone to injury, skin ulcers, and infection. The use of support stockings to reduce fluid accumulation and aid in venous return may be beneficial.

Pressure Sores

Pressure sores or decubitus ulcers are areas of skin breakdown resulting from prolonged pressure on the skin from a boney prominence against another surface outside. These commonly occur over the heels, buttocks, elbows, or back in a patient who is bedridden or wheelchair confined and whose position is not changed frequently enough. However, these ulcers can be seen at times even with good nursing care. They are found more often in older people with limited mobility, particularly hospitalized patients and nursing home residents. Other predisposing factors in addition to immobility include malnutrition, stool or urinary incontinence, the inability to feel or react to discomfort (strokes, coma, neuropathy), and diabetes. These lesions can result in severe localized infections, osteomyelitis (bone infections), and septicemia (infections spread throughout the bloodstream), which can cause death. Indeed, the presence of pressure sores in a hospitalized or nursing home patient is a predictor of increased mortality. Treatment consists of removing any source of pressure from the involved area, frequent change of position, cutting away (debridement) of any dead or infected tissue, antibiotics, and improved nutrition. The best treatment however is prevention, by greater attention and protective measures for those patients who are at risk.

VISION

Though circulatory problems involving the eyes and diabetic retinopathy can cause visual difficulty, there are three major processes that affect sight, predominantly in the elderly.

Cataracts

Cataracts are opacifications of the lens of the eye caused by changes in their proteins. Exposure to the ultraviolet rays of sunlight, uncontrolled diabetes, and the use of steroid medication all contribute to this condition. Whether there is interference with vision depends on the location and severity of the opacity. If sight is significantly impaired, the lens can be removed surgically in a simple procedure and an artificial lens implanted at the same time. With this technique, the vast majority of people have satisfactory restoration of vision.

Glaucoma

Glaucoma is an increase in pressure within the eye that can cause injury to the optic nerve and diminished acuity. The elevated pressure is the result of blockage of the pathways within the eye where fluid is resorbed. Various eye drops and oral medications can be used to lower the pressure and reduce the danger of blindness by protecting the optic nerve. If conservative measures do not work, surgery or laser therapy can be utilized to improve the flow of fluid within the eye and reduce the pressure.

Macular Degeneration

In macular degeneration, the central pigmented cells of the retina are damaged, substances are deposited in the retina, and new blood vessels grow into the tissues, bleeding at times. This leads to decreased vision and ultimately to blindness, and is the major cause of visual loss in the elderly. It is believed the process is genetically determined and cannot be prevented or cured. Laser treatment may retard its progression, but not the ultimate outcome, and low vision aids may be helpful for a period of time. In the future, it is possible that gene therapy may be able to arrest the condition, or even provide a cure. And recent reports hold the promise of other fruitful approaches.

CANCER

Cancer is a special category of disease, actually many different diseases, affecting virtually every organ and organ system in the body. About 1,170,000 new cases of cancer were diagnosed in the United States in 1993, exclusive of skin cancers and carcinoma in situ (a very early stage of cancer).[23] Though cancers kill at any age, they are particularly prevalent and deadly among seniors. Cancer is the leading cause of death in women aged 55–74, the second leading cause among men in that age group, and second among both men and women above age seventy-five.[24] "Persons 65 years of age and older bear the greatest burden of cancer; 55 percent of all malignancies occur in this age group,"[25] with two-thirds of all cancer deaths. These statistics are even more impressive given that this segment constituted only 13 percent of the total U.S. population during this survey.

Cancer rates rise steadily as people grow older. From 1983 to 1987, the annual age-specific cancer incidence rate per 100,000 for persons 45–49 years of age was approximately 300.[26] This more than doubled to 750 for those ten years older. From 65–69, the rate was 1,400 per 100,000, rising to 2,200 for those 75–79 years of age, then peaking at 2,500 in those 80–84 years of age.

In the past, a diagnosis of cancer usually indicated a hopeless situation. Now however, with early detection, improvements in surgical techniques and radiotherapy, and new chemotherapeutic agents, a large percentage of patients with cancer can be cured, while others can coexist with their disease and lead productive lives for a number of years. There are many different types of cancer that affect mankind and many different etiologies (causes). These include environmental toxins, genetic factors, viruses, tobacco, diet, radiation, sunlight (ultraviolet rays), and so forth.

Whatever the etiology or etiologies for specific cancers, a change takes place in the mechanism that controls cell growth and division, allowing the neoplastic (cancer) cells to reproduce in an unlimited fashion, with no intrinsic brakes and no external controls. As previously mentioned, the usual check on cell division resides in the end section of the chromosomes called a telomere, which gets shorter each time a cell divides until it is gone and no further divisions can occur. However, cancer cells produce a substance called telomerase, which keeps the telomere at the same length, so that the cell can continue to divide indefinitely. And the immune system that would ordinarily work to destroy abnormal cells does not function adequately in patients with neoplastic disease. Thus, without intervention, the cancer continues to grow until it kills its host, by eroding a blood vessel, compromising a vital organ, or interfering with nutrition, and so on.

The most common cancers affecting older people originate in the lungs, colon, breast, and prostate. Other neoplasms seen frequently include bladder, ovarian, other GI sites (stomach, pancreas, gall bladder), lymphoid tissue and bone marrow (lymphomas, leukemias, myeloma), head and neck cancers, and brain tumors. Though squamous cell carcinoma and basal cell carcinoma of the skin are ubiquitous, they rarely kill people, since they are very slow growing, are usually discovered early and can be treated effectively. Malignant melanoma, however, which also arises in the skin, is quite dangerous and, if not treated aggressively and at an early stage, will metastasize and kill.

The key to cancer control is prevention if possible and early detection. Avoiding agents that are known to be carcinogenic (producing cancer) is important. This includes not smoking cigarettes nor using other tobacco products, limiting exposure to sunlight, a diet that is low in red meats and saturated fats, and staying away from environmental carcinogens and radiation. If cancer does occur, survival may depend on finding it and instituting treatment while it is localized and liable to be more responsive to therapy. However, some scientists feel that whether a cancer is aggressive and liable to spread depends more on its genetic makeup than its size, particularly for breast cancer.

There are various screening tests helpful in discovering cancer at an early stage, the first of which are regular physicals by a physician. Women should do self-examination of the breasts periodically, with physicians' exams every year and mammography every one to two years. The upper age limit for routine mammography, however, is still a matter of debate.

In screening for colon cancer, stool should be examined for blood at least annually. For patients at risk for colon cancer, colonoscopy should be done every one to three years, depending on the degree of risk (strong family history, previous polyps or colon cancer, and so on). As for the general population, there is no consensus, but every five years is probably reasonable. (Colonoscopy is a procedure where a long, flexible tube with a fiberoptic system is passed through the colon after it has been thoroughly cleaned. It is usually performed under heavy sedation or anesthesia.)

Prostate cancer can often be picked up by a blood test—prostate specific antigen (PSA)—followed by a prostate biopsy. How frequently the PSA test should be done, however, remains controversial. Very early, small cancers may be found and then excised surgically, which usually is curative. Radiation therapy, either external beam or seed implantations, is another option. But the expected course of these early cancers is unknown and treatment, particularly surgery, may result in impotence and incontinence. For some men, watchful waiting may really be preferable to aggressive intervention with its potential complications and impact on quality of life. Digital palpation of the prostate gland through the rectum should be done every year to help uncover any larger cancers.

For women, yearly gynecological examinations are also warranted to look for cancers and any other abnormalities. As part of the exam, a pap smear can aid in finding early cervical and uterine malignancies, though its efficacy in older women who have had previously normal studies is questionable.

Genetic screening tests to delineate cancer risk have been available for the past several years for breast, ovarian, and colonic cancers. There has not been complete agreement over proper use of these tests, including the ethical problems they raise and what to do if they are positive. Some women with a strong family history and positive genetic testing have opted to have bilateral mastectomies to eliminate the threat of breast cancer. In general, the tests seem to be more valuable in the younger age group, to give people an idea of what the future holds. Positive testing does allow those at high risk to be watched more carefully.

Cancer treatment must be individualized to take into consideration the tissue of origin, the stage of involvement, and the age and condition of the patient. For most cancers, if a single lesion is found without evidence of spread (metastasis), it is removed surgically. At times, even if a tumor cannot be excised completely, as much of it as possible may be cut out (debulking) to make radiation and chemotherapy more effective. With cancers that are multicentric in origin (starting in many places, such as lymphoma or myeloma) or with generalized spread, radiation and chemotherapy may be the only options. And in some instances, this type of regimen can effect a cure. Hormonal therapy may also be utilized in certain types of responsive cancers (breast, ovary, prostate, and so forth).

Palliative therapy is also important in treating cancer patients. This aims at eliminating pain and suffering, and making the patient as comfortable as possible, rather than working for a cure. It is usually utilized when the cancer is widespread and the likelihood of cure is remote. To reduce anxiety, patients have to know that even if the cancer is going to kill them, there are medications and techniques available to treat their pain, and that their suffering will be minimal.

MALNUTRITION

Malnutrition among the elderly may produce deficiency diseases, weakness, and weight loss. Problems with swallowing owing to mechanical factors or strokes, diminished senses of taste and smell, decreased appetite, and problems with absorption of food can all be responsible. Disinterest in food may be particularly prevalent in patients with cancer or chronic infections. Medications, alcohol abuse, and dental problems may also play a role. People who are demented or depressed (especially those who are living alone) must be watched carefully by family and social agencies, or their nutritional intake may be inadequate. Those who are disabled from various conditions and unable to shop for themselves or prepare food, must also be monitored, particularly since some of them may be too proud to seek assistance.

PSYCHIATRIC DISORDERS

Depression, anxiety, and alcoholism are all common in middle-aged and elderly people. Hallucinations and confusional states, which might suggest psychosis in a younger group, are usually the result of organic processes, such as dementia, cerebrovascular disease, reactions to medications, and metabolic disturbances.

Depression

It has been estimated that of 34 million older American, 6 million suffer from moderate to serious depression.[27] Depressive symptoms and depressed mood may interfere with daily activities and can lead to physical decline.[28] Depression can result from situational factors that induce sadness such as the loss of a loved one (reactive depression), or can arise without a specific precipitant (endogenous depression). As we age, there are many events and losses (illnesses, physical disabilities, death of a spouse, and so forth) that make us unhappy. These losses are usually dealt with through the normal process of grieving, which can last weeks to months. But sometimes, grief can evolve into depression and compromise functioning to varying degrees. Some older people have a previous history of depression and/or periods of inappropriate euphoria or manic behavior, or agitation and irritability, and may have what is known as "bipolar disorder" (manic-depressive illness).

The symptoms seen in a major depression include

- depressed mood,
- loss of interest or pleasure,
- significant weight change or change in appetite,
- sleeping difficulty,
- severe restlessness or agitation, or significant slowing of movement,
- decreased energy, fatigue easily,
- feelings of worthlessness or excessive guilt,
- decreased ability to think or concentrate,
- recurrent thoughts of death or suicide.[29]

It is necessary for five or more of these symptoms, including one of the first two on the list, to be present for a period of at least two weeks, to establish a diagnosis of major depression.

Depressive symptoms may also be a component of organic illnesses, particularly Parkinson's disease, cancer, Alzheimer's disease, and strokes. Indeed, early Parkinson's and Alzheimer's can appear so similar to depression at times that it may be difficult for even an experienced clinician to differentiate between them.

Questions may arise in older people as to where normal sadness ends and depression begins. And how aggressively should sadness or depression be treated when it seems to be a logical response to life's adversities. Should we expect people in their eighties or nineties to be happy if they are alone after the death of a spouse or other loved ones, limited by chronic illnesses, and unable to care for themselves? Should they be given medication or psychotherapy to try to lift them from the depths of despair that might be expected with the cumulative losses they have suffered? There are no easy answers.

Anxiety

Symptoms of anxiety in the elderly and near-elderly can be due to real problems (serious illnesses, financial worries) and may be appropriate, or they may be excessive and inappropriate. Sometimes, there may not be a specific focus for the anxiety and it may be free-floating or generalized. Generalized anxiety disorder may also be induced by multiple stressors in a person's life, some of which he or she may be aware of and others that are hidden. Physical illnesses may often be present. The symptoms of anxiety include jitteriness or nervousness, tremulousness of the extremities, tension in the muscles, rapid breathing, shortness of breath, palpitations, rapid heart beat, dizzy spells, lightheadedness, abdominal cramps, nausea, diarrhea, difficulty sleeping, inability to concentrate, sweatiness and trouble swallowing.

Alcoholism and Drug Abuse

Alcoholism can be seen in older men and women in all social classes, to the degree that it is thought to be a hidden epidemic by some experts, since older people may drink alone and keep their drinking concealed from others.[30] It was once believed that single men were most at risk, but a recent report notes that 1.8 million women sixty and older abuse alcohol and 2.8 million women abuse mood-altering prescription drugs.[31] The pattern may begin early in life and continue into the later years, or it may arise when a person is older, possibly in reaction to the problems that must be faced with aging. Not infrequently, alcoholism is symptomatic of other psychiatric illnesses such as depression or anxiety. Alcohol is less well tolerated in the elderly than in younger people because of changes in their metabolism and alcohol's greater effect on the brain and central nervous system. Malnutrition may also occur with alcoholism, causing permanent brain damage, liver damage, or peripheral neuropathies, producing confusion, impaired balance, numbness, tingling, and weakness of the legs. Alcohol can interact as well with many medications with potentially dangerous outcomes.

Though the use of street drugs is relatively uncommon in the older population, prescription drugs such as sedatives and minor tranquilizers including Valium, barbiturates, sleeping pills, and similar compounds are generally available and can be addicting. Because of their potential for abuse, which can have serious consequences, these drugs must be monitored carefully by the treating physician. In addition to dependency itself, they can be responsible for accidents and injuries that can kill or disable both users and innocent bystanders.

COMPRESSION OF MORBIDITY

Given the fact that older people are prone to develop many different diseases, one would think that as individuals age, they would be less healthy, with a greater amount of disabilities and overwhelming medical bills. In actuality, this is true only for the middle-aged and young-old, but then changes. People who die in their fifties, sixties, and early seventies are more likely to have had multiple chronic illnesses (diabetes, hypertension, coronary artery disease, COPD, strokes, which are preventable to a large degree) with disabilities and high medical bills than those who die in their eighties and nineties. Those in the latter group are generally in much better shape until their final illness supervenes and spend less annually on medical care than those who die when they are younger. In addition, total cumulative medical spending for healthy people at age seventy who have greater longevity is similar to those whose health is poorer and who die earlier.[32] This phenomenon is known as "compression of morbidity with aging." Thus, many people who live to a ripe old age have a good quality of life. "The payments (for medical care) associated with an additional year of life and the average annual payments over an enrollee's life time (from Medicare) both decreased as the age at death increased."[33]

Of further interest, a recent medical report that reviewed a number of other studies showed that a reduction in old age disability has occurred in the last decade. The authors note that "disability and underlying physical, cognitive and sensory limitations are not inevitable consequences of aging."[34] The improvement in disability rates not only suggests that a better quality of life for seniors is emerging, but is also happy news for the Medicare program as it forecasts reduced expenditures. Care for a disabled older person costs three times as much on average as for someone who is not disabled. The reason for the decrease in disability is uncertain, but may be related to less tobacco use, increased educational level among seniors, and perhaps the perception of self-efficacy—that older individuals are able to do something for themselves to improve their own health.[35]

FACTORS THAT ACCELERATE AGING

There are a number of reasons why some people age faster than others. They may be genetically programmed to do so, they may have been ravaged by illnesses, they may have worked in a hostile environment, or other external influences may have acted upon them. Though certain changes in our bodies are inevitable as we grow older, there are other factors we can control that appear to accelerate the aging process, either in a general fashion or by damaging certain critical systems.

Smoking

As is well-known, smoking is a major contributor to human mortality, causing lung cancer, pulmonary diseases, coronary artery disease, peripheral vascular disease, and strokes. There is also a greater incidence of cataracts and facial wrinkles in smokers.

Alcohol Abuse

While moderate amounts of daily alcohol intake (one to two drinks a day) appear to reduce coronary artery disease and other vascular problems, excessive drinking can increase mortality and impair quality of life.

Obesity

"In the United States, approximately one-fourth of white men and one-third of white women between the ages of 65 and 76 are overweight."[36] Excessive weight gain can result from lack of activity, overeating, or metabolic dysfunction. Whatever the reason, obesity causes increased arthritis in weight-bearing joints, disc problems, and lower back pain. It is also a major factor in high blood pressure, diabetes, coronary artery disease, and generalized atherosclerosis.[37] Greater cumulative disability has also been noted in people who are obese when present with other risk factors.[38]

Sedentary Lifestyle

In addition to contributing to vascular disease and atherosclerosis, lack of exercise leads to a loss of muscle mass, weakness, and reduced stamina. It is also of major importance in the development of osteoporosis, and spine, hip, and long bone fractures.

Poor Nutrition

Lack of adequate food intake can cause deficiency syndromes with brain damage, peripheral nerve damage, muscle loss, and osteoporosis.

CONCLUSION

Though the diseases and disorders associated with aging can obviously disrupt our lives in major ways, all is not hopeless. Those individuals who take proper care of their bodies have the potential to avoid debilitating illnesses and enjoy life even as they grow older. Just as aging is accelerated by the factors covered in the last section, it is possible to retard the aging process and the diseases that accompany aging by behaving in certain ways. Not smoking, not using drugs, and not drinking excessively does not delay aging but does allow us to grow old in a normal fashion, as does control of blood pressure in those who are hypertensive. On the other hand, regular and sustained exercise as a substitute for a sedentary existence is an important weapon in defending ourselves against time's assault. In fact, it is probably the most important weapon in our armamentarium. (How much and what type of exercise will be discussed in Chapter 7.) Physical activity is even helpful in those who are overweight, though keeping one's weight down is also important in extending life and improving quality of life. Proper nutrition, including limiting the intake of fats and simple carbohydrates, eating a well-balanced diet with sufficient amounts of vegetables and grains, can also aid us in our battle. In addition, having a positive attitude will assist us immeasurably as we enter into combat with age.

> Mortality, behold and fear,
> What a change of flesh is here!
>
> —Francis Beaumont
> On the Tombs in Westminster Abbey

4

THE LUCK OF THE DRAW

How Age and Disease Can Rob Us of Dignity and Vitality

"We are helpless in this world.
The years and months slip past
Like a swift stream, which grasps and drags us down.
A hundred pains pursue us, one by one."

—YAMANOUE OKURA
THE IMPERMANENCE OF HUMAN LIFE

Growing old is like going for a walk on a cool, cloudy day. Suddenly, it begins misting, but that doesn't bother you. As you continue walking, the mist becomes a steady drizzle. You debate whether to turn around and go home, but it isn't heavy enough to warrant that. You persist and, almost imperceptibly, the rain gets stronger. Again you wonder about seeking shelter, but convince yourself it isn't that bad. Perhaps it'll let up a bit or even stop in a while. So you keep on trudging through the rain until it's pouring and you're wet and cold, and far away from home. There is no turning back as we grow older and are slowly dampened then finally drenched by the ravages of old age. At each stage, we convince ourselves it isn't that bad until we're completely soaked. And there's nowhere for us to go to dry off.

There are three general considerations regarding the loss of dignity and vitality as we age. The first is how the physical, cognitive, and emotional changes that are part of growing older affect the way we live our lives. These will be covered in this chapter. The second are the consequences of the various losses we all face. The third is the way that society's attitudes and actions impact on older people. These other factors will be discussed in the following chapters.

Though there are some changes we undergo with aging that we are unable to influence, we can modify our response to these changes and the way we behave to make aging less onerous. But we must take action, rather than complaining about our circumstances. The way that society treats the elderly can also be modified by the elderly themselves, if they work as a group to bring about a transformation. The political and economic power to do so is in their hands.

It is important to remember that besides racial, ethnic, economic, and regional differences, "older people" are not a homogeneous group in terms of age. A ninety-five-year-old and a fifty-five-year-old will often not react the same way to a particular situation. And loss of dignity may have disparate meanings for the middle-aged and young-old compared to the old-old and true-elderly. The middle-aged and young-old are more likely to be battling the effects of aging, as many have not yet accepted the fact they are growing older. Bodily changes that the true-elderly are nonchalant about may cause great angst and concern for those younger. Even so, middle age is usually a time of contentment for most people as shown in a recent study by the MacArthur Foundation Research Network on Successful Midlife Development (middle age was defined as thirty-five to sixty-five). People in this age range reported "increased feelings of well being and a greater sense of control over many parts of their lives."[1]

PHYSICAL PROBLEMS

As I have described previously, the physical transformation occurring in the elderly makes them look different than the rest of the population and feel differently and act differently as well.

Musculoskeletal System

Deterioration in the musculoskeletal system can be a major limiting factor. Because of the loss of muscle strength and the pain and immobility of arthritis, osteoporosis, and spinal stenosis, older people move more slowly, walk more stiffly, and often have a flexed posture. Their ability to perform physical tasks may be significantly diminished. They may complain of pain with any movement, or even with no movement at all. Depression may amplify their complaints and they may be averse to trying to push themselves to do things. However, the way older people move and get about their business defines their own self-image and how other people see them.

Deconditioning in the normal elderly and those with minor physical problems is an important element that restricts their ability to lead fulfilling lives. Having ignored proper exercise over the years, they may discover that physical exertion is difficult or impossible for them. They may be unable to travel to certain places or take certain types of vacations and are incapable of playing various sports or even just going for a walk in the country. Despite this, it is never too late to make a commitment to recapture the strength and stamina that was allowed to dissipate. Starting a program of stretching and exercise at any age can arrest and even reverse some of the changes that have occurred in the musculoskeletal system.

Cardiopulmonary Compromise

Cardiac and pulmonary disease often robs the elderly of their capacity to operate physically. For some, shortness of breath and chest pain may intervene whenever they are active, their symptoms proportional to the level of heart or pulmonary damage. Many note that they lack energy and feel generally weak, and that this impacts negatively on what they can do. Dizzy spells and blackouts owing to changes in heart rhythm may also occasionally act as a check upon older people. In addition, some individuals with or without pathology, develop cardiac neuroses, fearing that exertion may cause a heart attack and perhaps kill them. In those with minimal or no cardiac abnormalities, fear directs their lives, rather than the disease process itself. And some who have suffered cardiac damage, and may be restricted in certain ways, become depressed or anxious, feeling sorry for themselves and unwilling to work to try to restore their previous physical state. Of course, the key to what people are able to do is the amount of disease that is present, for at times this may preclude any significant effort and require a passive existence. Nevertheless, everyone with any illness should try to maximize whatever function remains.

Alteration of lifestyle is essential in the treatment of coronary artery disease and other forms of atherosclerosis. This includes dietary modification to lower cholesterol and control blood pressure, regular exercise, and cessation of smoking. Though stopping smoking does not drop its risk to zero immediately, there is a gradual decline that makes the elimination of cigarettes at any age worth-while. The use of aspirin prophylactically to prevent clots from forming is also of benefit on a long-term basis for anyone with risk factors for atherosclerosis. In addition, cholesterol-lowering drugs, such as the statin group, have been shown to reduce coronary artery disease, as well as atherosclerosis in general.

Cerebrovascular Disease

People with cerebrovascular disease may have fixed structural deficits be-cause of strokes (paralysis, sensory loss, balance problems, speech difficulty, and so forth) that define how they live and whether they are able to maintain their dignity and vitality. The severity of their problem ascertains their level of independence and usually changes little when six months to a year has passed after the attack. Obviously, a major paralysis means partial to total depen-dency, even for the simple tasks of daily living, such as feeding one's self, dressing, use of a toilet, or basic hygiene. Patients who have speech impair-ment from a stroke, such as aphasia (language difficulty) or dysarthria (me-chanical difficulty speaking), may be unable to communicate well with other people to make their needs known. Inability to swallow adequately may re-quire a feeding tube, pureed food, or other special diets. Those who have loss of bladder control may need diapers, a condom, or an indwelling catheter.

Those patients with cerebrovascular disease who have TIAs instead of com-pleted strokes, nonetheless may be restricted by these transient events. Frequent or even occasional dizzy spells, blackouts, loss of balance, speech problems, blindness, or paralysis, whether temporary or not, can have a chilling effect on one's activities.

But within the bounds of one's limitations caused by strokes or TIAs, the individual should strive for as much control and independence as possible. A reasonable quality of life can be attained by many, even with some disabilities.

Parkinson's Disease

Parkinson's disease also affects a person's dignity and self-image. Many people are embarrassed by the tremor that occurs, especially early in the course of the disease before they are disabled in any way. Drooling is another symptom that may be bothersome. As the condition progresses, mobility di-minishes and there is trouble arising from a chair or turning over in bed, along with difficulties with walking and balance. Eventually, patients may need assistance with most motor tasks. Hallucinations and confusion (from the disease and the medications) and general cognitive decline may also develop, imposing further reductions on that person's autonomy.

Essential Tremor

Older people may have shaking of their head or hands unrelated to Parkinson's disease called "essential tremor." (The actress Katharine Hepburn had this condition.) Though this can occur in any age group, it is more prevalent in the elderly. Stress or anxiety seems to make it briefly worse, such as when a person is being observed. It is usually of familial origin, but can result from a severe head injury, a period of cerebral anoxia (lack of oxygen supply to the brain), residua of encephalitis, and various other types of pathology. Bringing a spoonful of soup to the mouth may be an adventure when the tremor is pronounced, and it can interfere with handwriting and fine movements. Though it does not cause any major disability like Parkinson's does, from an emotional standpoint it can be very distressing, even more so for public figures who may have to speak before large audiences. Medication can often be quite helpful in reducing the tremor. Mild tremulousness and involuntary movements around the mouth are also noted at times in the elderly population.

Neuropathy

Severe neuropathies in the elderly may cause limitations because of problems with balance, weakness, sensory loss, and pain. However, physical therapy and medications can significantly reduce dysfunction and discomfort in many cases.

Cancer

Cancer deprives individuals of vigor and dignity in a number of ways on the road to death. It begins when the diagnosis itself is made and the illness is named. The word *cancer* conjures up visions, not just of dying, but of a horrible death, and immediately unleashes a torrent of fear and anxiety, even though cancer is not the overwhelming killer it once was. An element of anger is present as well at the outset, with the question being asked, Why me? But as treatment is given and time passes, the apprehension and dread diminishes in many patients, particularly if the prognosis appears favorable. (Even if patients are not told the diagnosis or true prognosis, or if they attempt to deny it, on some level they know what is happening.) However, if the person is not improving or is getting worse, the fear and anxiety may increase. The focus then is not only on death, but on the pain and suffering that is anticipated. Constant reassurance to the patient that the pain can and will be controlled may be necessary. Depression also begins to materialize with the realization that death is nearing and there are no options and no way out. There is a sadness over leaving loved ones and leaving life behind, and concern about being a burden to family and friends. As the disease advances further, people realize they have lost control of their bodies, as they see themselves slowly wasting away, lying around waiting to die. Or they may be heavily sedated by medication to reduce pain and distress, moving in and out of consciousness, their thoughts muddled as death approaches. But proper care during the process of dying can make it much more tolerable for both patients and their loved ones.

Sphincteric Control

Loss of sphincteric control with urinary and less often stool incontinence in the elderly may interfere with daily living and is a direct assault on dignity. It can be quite embarrassing and when it is recurrent or severe in people who are otherwise independent, it may limit their social interactions and have a profound effect on their lives. In mild cases, diapers can be used to keep the person clean and dry. But condom catheters and indwelling catheters may need to be utilized if the problem is severe, particularly if the individual is bedridden or in a nursing home. Constipation is not a social problem, but diarrhea may be when combined with a deficient sphincter. Passing flatus (gas) may also occur involuntarily and make people feel mortified. Frequency of urination and nocturia (getting up at night to urinate) owing to an enlarged prostate may be an annoyance for some men, but only causes real problems in those who have impaired mobility and ambulation.

Difficulty with Vision or Hearing

Poor vision or impaired hearing in the elderly often causes a decline in quality of life and obstacles to communication. Both conditions may result in social isolation. Depending on the cause of the visual dysfunction, relief may be possible with surgery or other types of intervention, though some men and women may refuse to wear extra-thick lenses or other low vision aids because they feel ashamed. Similarly, hearing aids may be a cause of embarrassment for some individuals, though for the most part, the new aids are easily concealed. Being hard of hearing or having very poor vision is difficult for many seniors to accept and they try to hide it, for it is perceived as another marker of old age and feebleness.

Sleep Disorders

Excessive daytime sleepiness often combined with insomnia (difficulty falling asleep or staying asleep) are frequent complaints among the elderly and may detract from their quality of life. "Between 12% and 25% of healthy seniors report chronic insomnia, and these estimates are even higher among older adults with coexisting medical or psychiatric illnesses,"[2] particularly depression or anxiety. Sitting at home watching television or reading a book, older people may slump in their chairs and fall off to sleep. Sometimes, embarrassingly, it may also happen during conversation, while at the movies or the theater, or during other periods of inactivity. It becomes dangerous if it occurs while driving or other operations that involve some risk. The reasons for the insomnia and sleepiness during the day should be sought, for they may be amenable to various types of therapy. Occasionally, merely stopping medication may be the answer. However, for most, taking a nap during the day is quite normal and is to be encouraged, as it may relieve feelings of fatigue, increase energy, and enhance activities.

COGNITIVE CHANGES

Cognitive decline with aging has a profound effect on all of us and, when severe, contributes even more than physical damage to loss of dignity. But differentiation must be made between normal cognitive decline and dementia. As mentioned, problems with memory are almost universal among the elderly, although the degree of involvement can vary considerably, with some of the old-old still having minimal difficulty.

In the middle of the spectrum between the normal changes of aging and true dementia is what is called "mild cognitive impairment" (MCI).[3] Those who have this condition have greater problems with memory and thinking than the normal older population, but are still able to function fairly well and be self-sufficient. However, there are reports that these people are at consid-erable risk for developing dementia, with a large percentage succumbing each year after they have been diagnosed.[4] Studies are now in progress to see whether the use of certain drugs may delay or prevent the progression of mild cognitive impairment to full-blown dementia.

With mild cognitive impairment, objects in the house may be misplaced and people may walk into a room for something and forget what they were looking for. While speaking, individuals may search for words that are not forthcoming, then moments later, or even hours later, it may come to them. Similarly, when meeting someone, his or her name may escape them and they fumble to cover up their gaffe, using a general term to address that person, or not introduce a companion, unwilling to admit their forgetfulness. Then, after the person has gone, they suddenly remember his or her name. To some degree, these are all normal signs of aging if they occur occasionally. Who among us has not blocked a word, a name, or a thought, having it return abruptly moments or hours later.

Because of problems with memory, older people may, at times, be late for ap-pointments or not show up at all. Important events (birthdays, anniversaries) may occasionally be missed and not celebrated, to the chagrin of the person who forgot, and disappointment on the part of the one who was forgotten. In addition, bills may not always be paid on time because they were mislaid, or it was forgotten that they were due. Many older people also have difficulty in learning new tasks and procedures, and in retaining new information.

A further manifestation of a decline in judgment and reasoning may be the observation that some older individuals are less fastidious with personal hygiene than they had been. Clothing may be worn when dirty or stained, and stockings and underwear may not be changed. They may also forget whether they have showered, shaved, or brushed their teeth. Of course, there may be other rea-sons for these problems. Washing or cleaning garments may be beyond some senior's physical abilities (mobility, balance, vision), or they simply might not be able to drive to the cleaners or afford the cost. But the more physically or cognitively compromised a person is, the more hygiene and cleanliness suffer.

An additional byproduct of cognitive compromise is the unseemliness and discordance of dress of some of the elderly. The outfit chosen for a particular situation or event may be unsuitable, or components may not match. Women may wear too much jewelry, and excessive amounts of makeup may be ap-plied. Men may not get their hair cut as regularly and may not always shave, or will shave erratically, when they should be well-groomed.

"Disinhibition" is another behavioral change that may occur in some older people related to cognitive dysfunction. What is meant by this is that the normal constraints controlling people's actions and speech are no longer completely operative and things may be done or said that are inappropriate or even hurtful. The thoughtfulness, courtesy, and good manners that guided individuals when they were younger is somehow missing. Examples might be someone pushing to get in line ahead of another person, trying to get food first at dinner, or beginning to eat before everyone else is served. Other examples would be an individual revealing something that he or she was told in confidence, or mentioning a bit of information that is embarrassing to someone in a group. This type of behavior can be disruptive to relationships, even if others are aware of this predilection.

Another characteristic of some seniors is rigidity in their habits and daily routines, and the inability to adapt easily to new situations. They are less flexible and less interactive with the world around them, and more fixed in their ways. Some of this may be because they have lived in a certain manner for so long, making change difficult for them, but some of their inflexibility is due to the trouble they have with learning. Moving to a new home or apartment may be extremely disturbing to them and cause great anxiety or possibly temporary confusion. Being taken out of their environment to go to the hospital may be even worse, with disorientation and agitation occurring.

Some older people are also excessively self-involved, focusing on themselves and their problems, particularly their illnesses. This may be manifest in frequent complaining to others, the result of disinhibition, or perhaps an attention getting mechanism. It may also be used to manipulate family and friends; to make them feel sorry for the person.

There is a Yiddish expression for complaining about physical ailments called "kvetching." The term can be used as either a verb or a noun. Thus, someone who kvetches constantly is also known as a "kvetch," a very disparaging description. Unfortunately, some of the elderly are perceived as kvetches because of their complaining, which makes them less sympathetic figures. In fact, the response to complainers is usually negative and people tend to avoid those who are chronically lamenting their lot in life. On the other hand, people admire those who bear their crosses with good humor and minimal grumbling, and are more likely to seek them out for companionship. That does not mean that one should not express sadness about one's limitations, or not reveal feelings that are present. But complaining should not be a constant refrain, for it will sour relationships, driving away friends and relatives.

Latent personality traits also may come to the fore in those elderly individuals who have cognitive impairment. Obsessive behavior may become more pronounced. Someone with an impulse disorder may become uncontrollable. Or a mild alcoholic may decompensate and drink heavily. There is often a lack of insight into the problems that are present and an unwillingness to listen to peers or even spouses and children. And all of the disturbances that occur with normal aging or mild cognitive impairment are even more prominent with true dementia.

More than any other aspect of aging or of any other disease process, dementia robs the involved person of all vestiges of his or her dignity. In the very early stages, patients may show only minor problems with memory and cognitive ability, and be able to operate at a fairly high level. They may understand that things are not completely right, but full insight is usually lacking. It is commonly the family, rather than the patient, who brings the condition to the attention of a physician. At this point, the affected individuals are generally able to manage their own lives, perhaps with minimal assistance, being able to stay alone in their own homes, keeping lists of things to help them remember. However, as the disease progresses and they become more intellectually compromised, they gradually lose the capacity to function independently and care for themselves in any way, until they require assistance and supervision for their most basic needs around the clock.

Driving may be one of the first skills to go, with difficulty in making decisions and reacting to conditions that may arise in traffic or on the highway. Following directions to reach a specific destination, or even remembering customary routes, becomes impossible. Soon, even local driving with familiar landmarks cannot be negotiated without getting lost. Usually, a family member will then attempt to take away the car keys and there may be verbal battles between the family and the individual with dementia, before he or she is willing to accept the fact that driving is not permitted. Periodically, one sees articles in the newspapers about a person with Alzheimer's disease who went out for a drive and wound up in another state. (I had a patient with Alzheimer's who took the car one day to pick up some medication for his wife at a nearby pharmacy. The couple lived in a town on the Connecticut shore. After an hour, when the patient did not return, the police were called. But the patient was not found until a day and a half later when he was discovered driving around the streets of Brooklyn with no idea how he had gotten there.)

Eventually, a person with dementia may not even be able to leave the house for a walk without getting lost and being unable to find his or her way home. The doors may have to be secured with deadbolts or special locks to keep the person inside and not permit him or her to wander. In time, he or she may even get lost within the house, uncertain which way to go to find particular rooms. With no recall of where possessions might have been put, demented individuals can become paranoid, charging other people with steal-ing things they cannot find. The problems with memory and judgment also cause them to sometimes accuse spouses of infidelity when they are out of the house for a while in the course of normal daily activities. (Another patient of mine with Alzheimer's repeatedly accused his eighty-five-year-old wife, who was crippled by severe arthritis, of having an affair with their eighty-nine-year-old neighbor who was confined to a wheelchair after a stroke.) In some cases, suspicions of infidelity have been present earlier in life and come to the fore with the dementia, even when the situation is ridiculous.

Managing finances is another proficiency that is lost early. Those who have used a computer are unable to do so. Checks are not written properly, de-posits are not made, and bills are not paid. The checkbook is not balanced correctly and becomes chaotic, before being abandoned completely as the bills pile up. There is difficulty using a credit card, or even making the neces-sary calculations to use cash when shopping. Judgment about money matters is very poor and imprudent purchases or investments may be made. On the other hand, some people with dementia become overly concerned about their money, worried that they are going to lose it, or that someone is going to steal it from them and they are going to become impoverished, even if they are very wealthy.

Because of their inability to drive and handle money as the disease pro-gresses, those with dementia cannot shop for food or any of the necessities of life and other people have to do it for them. After a while, they are unable to pick out clothes or dress themselves. They cannot prepare their own food and, ultimately, cannot even feed themselves. Hygiene also becomes a serious problem as they do not know when or how to bathe or wash. They become incontinent of urine and stool, not remembering when or where to go to the bathroom and are indifferent to being soiled. Skin breakdown, bedsores, and infections may develop because of the incontinence. An attendant becomes necessary to provide full-time care for them, either at home, or in a nursing home, feeding and dressing them, washing them and keeping them clean.

As the dementing process worsens, language function deteriorates and finally disappears. Gait and balance are affected and muscle strength is lost. Unable to walk, these individuals remain in bed or in a wheelchair, often with contractures of their extremities. Vision and swallowing may also be involved, and a decision may be necessary about whether to place a feeding tube to maintain nutrition. They may aspirate food or fluids and pneumonia is a common cause of death. But by the time these patients are ready to die, their minds are totally gone, and they have become mere shells of their former selves.

EMOTIONAL ILLNESS

Emotional disorders may also contribute to breeching the wall of dignity in the elderly. As mentioned previously, depression and anxiety are the twin culprits responsible for most of the damage.

Depression

The severity of the depression in older individuals determines how disabling this condition will be, defining how that person lives, his or her social interactions, and what physical symptoms may result. In mild depression, people may appear fairly normal to most observers, but feel sad, with a diminished zest for life and a general absence of enthusiasm. Friends may be abandoned and family obligations met grudgingly, or ignored. There is less initiative and an aura of apathy—a willingness to sit around much of the time doing nothing. Appetite is usually poor and libido is absent or considerably decreased. Often there are complaints of difficulty sleeping at night, though the patient may fall asleep during the day. He or she may grouse about a lack of energy and a feeling of fatigue. Emotional responses generally seem flat.

In those whose depression is more pronounced, the symptoms mentioned above are accentuated. Unable to concentrate on any tasks, individuals become completely unproductive, unwilling to begin any activity or finish any project. Feelings of despair, dejection, and inadequacy are more manifest and people become increasingly withdrawn. They seem to have no interest in things going on around them, even events of personal significance. Indifferent as well to their own condition, they do not take care of themselves, neglecting to eat and bathe properly, and disregarding medications and other health needs. Spouses, family members, or close friends have to manage every aspect of their lives to be certain they do not develop serious physical problems. Sometimes, if the depression is bad enough, there may be paranoid or guilty delusions, or a suicide attempt may occur. Psychiatric hospitalization may be necessary in intractable cases, with outpatient follow-up. Psychotherapy and the use of drugs is almost always required and, if pursued vigorously, may lift the person from the depths of despair.

The most frustrating aspect of major depressions for family and friends is that the affected individuals cannot be motivated to try to pull themselves out of this terrible state. They may resist professional treatment and no matter how much they are cajoled or exhorted, they refuse to get moving and take responsibility for themselves. Perhaps the frustration is also there for the depressed people themselves, but it is impossible to tell because of their apathy and lack of emotional reaction. Given their withdrawn state, repetitive complaints and unwillingness to do anything about their problems, after a while it becomes hard for them to generate sympathy from those who have contact with them on a daily basis, perhaps reinforcing their own feelings of worthlessness.

Anxiety

Older people who are hobbled by anxiety are also unable to carry on their lives and function at a high level. Those with this condition may be fearful of riding in a car, flying in a plane, being in crowded places, or being in open spaces. They may be afraid of picking up germs by touching something, or afraid of just leaving the house. At an extreme, they are phobic rather than merely anxious, though phobias certainly produce anxiety. There may also be concern about physical illnesses that actually exist but are exaggerated, or others that are completely imaginary. (People with depression as well as anxiety may "somatisize"—develop physical symptoms without a physical cause—but it seems to be more pronounced, or at least more verbalized, in those with anxiety.) They may worry about having a massive heart attack, or choking to death from something getting stuck in their throats; of contracting cancer, or of just dying from any cause. All day long they may sit in their rooms, paralyzed into inactivity by their fears. Or they may come out and try to do things by using elaborate rituals they believe will protect them and counteract their fears. Of course, it rarely works completely, and some element of the anxiety always seems to remain.

Depending on how oppressive the anxiety is, it can be as disabling to individuals as depression or a physical illness; a major obstacle that will not allow them to lead a placid existence. This is particularly true of those who have panic attacks, severe symptoms of anxiety that appear suddenly and are incapacitating. The complaints that accompany anxiety include dizzy spells and blackouts, chest pain and palpitations, shortness of breath and difficulty swallowing, and headaches and tremulousness. However, the one aspect of anxiety common to all patients, no matter what the external manifestations may be, is fear, which may be overt or denied by the individual. As with people who have severe depression, those with relentless anxiety, with constant fearfulness and worry about physical symptoms, also have trouble relating to friends and relatives because of their affliction.

SEXUALITY AND COMPANIONSHIP

Sexual dilemmas in older people may, at times, contribute to a loss of self-esteem. While the need for sexual release in the elderly may be reduced, there is still the need for intimacy and companionship, the need to be held and touched and loved by another person. With the death or incapacity of a spouse, the ability to satisfy these desires may be lost and difficult to establish with someone new.

People may respond to the need for intimacy and sexual pleasure in ways that may be seen by some as "undignified." Sometimes these actions may not even occur on a conscious level and an element of disinhibition may also play a role. As an example, an older woman may dress and act in a se-ductive manner, wearing low-cut dresses or short skirts with heavy makeup, and moving in a way that is sexually provocative. (This may also be an at-tempt to appear youthful.) She may also make off-color or suggestive com-ments to men that are inappropriate. Some women who are widowed may use all of what they believe are their wiles in an attempt to "hook a man" and regain the intimacy and, at times, the security that comes with having a male companion. (In retirement communities, these women are thought of as predators who go about stalking available, and sometimes unavailable, men.) It is also true that some women have a poor self-image and feel they are incomplete or powerless without a man.

Because there is an excess of women compared to men as the population ages, older men in general have less trouble finding women for sex or com-panionship. However, the more desirable women (those who are healthy, at-tractive, and affluent) may disparage attempts at courtship and avoid any involvement. A common saying around retirement communities regarding older single men is that they want "a nurse with a purse" to take care of them.[5]

Men may also act in ways that compromise their dignity, looking for women much younger than they are and with whom they have little in common. An ex-ample of this is when wealthy and successful middle-aged or elderly men di-vorce their spouses with whom they have shared their lives for many years in favor of physically attractive younger women who may not be their intellectual equals. These "trophy wives" may be the subject of derision by the man's peers (perhaps admixed with a bit of envy), who may have difficulty communicating with the woman.

On the other hand, there is nothing wrong with an older man or woman finding a younger spouse or companion if the relationship is meaningful on an intellectual and emotional plane as well as physical. It is also understand-able when an older person separates from a long-standing spouse if that marriage is devoid of love, or compassion, or shared interests, or they just grew apart over the years.

In their quest for sexual fulfillment or "relationships," men can also look foolish in ways similar to women. They can dress inappropriately while trying to appear younger or "with it," say things that are totally out of line or indiscreet, or "make moves" that are totally uncalled for. They may proposition women who are horrified by their advances, or physically grope or start the sexual ritual without receiving the proper signals from their partner. Some of it may be male vanity with a belief they are irresistible. Some of it may be naivete, inexperience, and a misreading of the signals that are given. Or they may just lack knowledge of what to do after forty or more years of relating to one woman. And some of the actions may be the result of disinhibition.

For both older men and older women, making the right connections to find intimacy and sexual satisfaction are not easy tasks, and can lead to put-downs and embarrassment on both sides.

THE RELATIVITY OF TIME

As one grows older, time moves faster. This is almost a universal perception as people age, our minds playing tricks on us, though it is unclear why this is. Intuitively, one would expect the opposite to be true, since people are less active and proceed more slowly when older, with fewer tasks to occupy their time. Perhaps it is because the passage of any unit of time is a smaller fraction of our existence and the totality of our experiences as we grow older. For example when a child goes from two to three years of age, the additional year is 50 percent of its life, while a person going from age fifty to fifty-one only adds another 2 percent to his or her experiences. The more reason to use our remaining time well.

And I must continue to emphasize that we do have the ability to affect the evolution of our lives even as we grow older and face the increased possibility of encountering a physical or cognitive disorder. But we must concentrate our efforts in those areas in which we realistically have a chance of being successful, while accepting what we cannot change.

5

AGING AND LOSS

What It Means in Terms of Dignity and Vitality

---•---

We grudge life moving on
But we have no redress.
I would become as those
Firm rocks that see no change.
But I am a man in time
And time must have no stop.

—YAMANOUE OKURA
THE IMPERMANENCE OF HUMAN LIFE

Growing old entails accommodating to a succession of losses starting early in life that accelerate as we age. We lose people who are close to us and whom we love: our parents, peers, siblings, friends, colleagues, and acquaintances. We lose our skills, proficiencies, power, competence, drive, and initiative. We lose our muscle strength, coordination, mobility, balance, bladder control, memory, and abstract reasoning. Also, as we age, many of us lose our autonomy, self-image, and unique identity—what makes us who we are.

Being older and having lost various functions, we may need support from others in order to manage our lives. This may necessitate a minor or major effort from these people (spouses, children, other relatives, friends), depending on what our requirements are. Whether this support is forthcoming and the way in which it is provided may have a lot to do with our ability to preserve our dignity. Mere existence, or survival alone, has nothing whatsoever to do with dignity. Rather, it is the quality of our lives that is of supreme importance in determining that characteristic. And it is up to us to manage as best we can with the hand we have been dealt; to enhance our life situations at each stage and derive the most satisfaction from whatever time we have left.

LOSS OF INDEPENDENCE

For many older people, living alone or with a spouse of the same age presents a series of challenges that must be overcome on a daily basis and repeated over and over again, the result of physical limitations, cognitive compromise, or psychological problems. These can be due to the normal aging process, or to the various disorders that afflict the elderly. While some may be able to carry on their lives without significant hardship as they grow older, others may have difficulties performing even mundane activities and may eventually need assistance of one sort or another.

There are four types of support that older people may require. The first is help with physical tasks. The second is administrative assistance in running their lives. The third is emotional support. And the fourth is financial aid that may be necessary to solve an immediate dilemma, or on an ongoing basis owing to inadequate resources.

Evolution of the Loss of Independence

For most of us, the period when we are completely free and independent is quite brief, from our postadolescent years through early adulthood. Before that, we are under the wings of our parents and after that time we are usually answerable to spouses, children, our co-workers, and our bosses. But even though we have certain obligations that must be met, for the most part we are still in control of our own lives, able to make decisions and execute those decisions, perhaps with input from others at times, but expressing our own free will. As some of us begin to have physical or cognitive difficulties as we get older, the freedom we once had may be threatened and it may no longer be possible to do everything for ourselves. Even for the majority without significant problems, an initial phase of loss of independence usually occurs in middle age and may be so subtle we are not even aware that anything has changed. With a bad back, we may no longer be able to shovel snow or carry something heavy and may request help from our children, friends, or neighbors, or pay someone to assist us. Or we may ask a child or a grandchild to program a new appliance or piece of equipment for us because of difficulty deciphering the instructions. A classic example of this is a teenager teaching his middle-aged parents how to operate the VCR, or set a new digital watch, or use a computer. It is not that we cannot manage these chores ourselves, it is just that it takes us longer to absorb the new information and perhaps we are more easily frustrated by unfamiliar and perplexing directions. And even when we have been shown how to do something or have figured out the intricate steps ourselves, we may have to go over it repeatedly before we are secure in our knowledge and ability.

As time goes on, our reliance on other people to perform simple or complex tasks for us increases. The degree to which this occurs and the ages at which various functions are transferred to others are different for everyone. There are ninety year olds who do just fine on their own, running their lives with minimal or no assistance, and sixty year olds who need constant help with their activities. Indeed, two people with identical physical problems at the same age who are cognitively intact may require totally disparate levels of support. The wild cards here are the emotional states of these individuals, their feelings of pride, how they lived previously, and how important it is to them to remain self-sufficient. There are some people whose self-respect would suffer grievously if they had to call on others for assistance in the tasks of daily living, and some who acquiesce and scarcely blink an eye.

In past generations, extended families normally cared for the elderly when they could no longer survive on their own. Though family members still play a major role in furnishing aid to the elderly, society has become the caregiver of last resort when relatives either cannot or will not assume responsibility for someone. At present, "about 22 million families, nearly 1 in 4, are providing some form of assistance to an older relative or friend, according to the National Alliance for Caregivers."[1]

Dependency on a Spouse

Dependency on a spouse is perhaps easiest for people to accept, as it is what society has built into marriage ("for better, or for worse, in sickness or in health"). However, if love was lacking or flawed within the marriage before the need for help occurred, problems may arise for both the recipient and the caregiver. The recipient may be reluctant, bitter, hostile, or apathetic about taking the assistance offered, or may appear accepting and grateful but use his or her disability in a manipulative fashion to try to control the behavior of the spouse. Similarly, the caregiver may be quite angry at the role he or she was assigned by fate, and provide help with visible resentment, or try in some way to punish his or her mate who needs assistance by not being properly responsive. However, even if the marriage had been strong previously, the feelings generated by dependency may not be predictable. The person being aided might feel guilty about being a burden to a loved spouse, which might engender hostility toward the caregiver, driving him or her away and perhaps increasing the recipient's anger and depression. As evidence that dependency can be destructive to relationships, the government's National Health Interview Survey in 1994 of 50,000 households found that 20.7 percent of disabled adults were divorced or separated versus 13.1 percent of those without disabilities. Another survey showed that over the past two decades, increasing numbers of the disabled were getting divorced: 13 percent of those with disabilities were divorced in 1998, compared to 11 percent in 1994 and 9 percent in 1984.[2] (These surveys did not focus on older people.)

It is obvious that both partners suffer when one has a chronic illness. Recent studies have shown that in addition to psychiatric morbidity, caring for a disabled spouse is a risk for higher mortality.[3] Spouses who were under stress in providing care had "mortality risks that were 63 percent higher than non caregiving controls."[4]

When it is necessary to provide care for a husband or wife who is chronically ill on a long-term basis, healthy spouses react in different ways, affecting their own lives as well as those of their mates. A few examples follow from my practice.

R.B. is a 69-year-old woman whose husband had multiple sclerosis for eighteen years before dying of pneumonia. He had been wheelchair bound for the last ten years of his life and R.B. gave up her job and devoted her life to caring for him, her only other activity being church on Sunday mornings. They survived on Social Security and disability payments in a small home. When I began seeing her husband, R.B. was a petite brunette. Over the years, as he deteriorated and her life was more restricted, she ate incessantly, reaching a point where she was markedly obese. When her husband died, she tried to return to the workplace, but already in her sixties, was unsuccessful. According to an acquaintance of hers, her days are spent watching television, with few friends and few interests.

L.C. is an 82-year-old woman whose husband, a successful attorney, began to have shaking of his hands and problems walking in his late sixties. Within five years, he was demented and hallucinating, with gait instability. The diagnosis was felt to be Lewy body disease, a progressive dementia. Initially, his wife cared for him at home, with some assistance from a daughter and a nurse's aide who came in to help when the task became overwhelming. Eventually, he had to be admitted to a nursing home where he died after two years. Throughout his illness, his wife managed to have a life of her own, albeit limited. She walked at the beach almost daily, went to the movies and dinner occasionally with friends, and was an insatiable reader. After his death, she pursued the same activities, but also became a volunteer at the hospital. Now, ten years later, she appears reasonably content with her life.

T.T. was a working woman in her early sixties who was quite attractive and youthful. She had been married for ten years to a gentleman about five years her senior who was an advertising executive. It was a second marriage for both. They were a handsome couple and had led an active social life until four years earlier when he began to become forgetful. Alzheimer's disease was diagnosed, which progressed unusually rapidly, reaching a point in about two years where he could not care for himself. Whenever they came into the office, she would complain bitterly about the way her life had changed. I learned subsequently that she had taken her husband to visit his daughter in a town near Boston one weekend and had left him there. She had told the daughter that she could no longer look after him and would not permit him to return to their home in Connecticut.

Assistance from Children

Having to receive assistance from one's children may be more injurious to a person's self-esteem than care from a spouse. How both parents and children deal with this issue again is contingent on the relationship that existed before the help was provided. Invariably in a parent who is cognitively intact, there is some element of guilt about having to enlist a child's aid. But if the assistance is given willingly and lovingly, the parent is more apt to receive it in a similar vein. On the other hand, if help is proffered grudgingly and complainingly, the recipient may refuse it and even show hostility to the child who is rendering the aid. Of course, the kind of assistance that is necessary also plays a role in determining the reactions of both parent and child. Whereas minor aid may be accepted as making life easier, major help with the tasks of daily living may be seen as more threatening to the recipient's autonomy, and may produce resentment and obstruction. These feelings may be particularly prevalent when an elderly person is encouraged or forced to give up his or her home, to live with a child, or, even worse, to go into an assisted living residence or nursing home. If several children are involved in caring for a parent and share the commitment graciously, there may be more compliance on the part of the parent as it may eliminate some of the feelings that he or she is being a burden. Complicating the efforts to take care of elderly parents for many children are the day-to-day demands of raising their own children, a particular dilemma for the so-called sandwich generation that finds itself in the middle of these two competing calls.[5]

Sometimes pride gets in the way of older individuals allowing children to manage their affairs as they stubbornly guard their independence. This can have various consequences. A retired pharmacist who was a patient of mine had accumulated a fair amount of wealth through prudent investments after selling his business. In his eighties, he began to suffer from macular degeneration and mild cognitive impairment. His wife had been disabled by a severe stroke some years earlier and required full-time care from a live-in aide. Two children—a son and a daughter—were very attentive, yet the patient refused to turn over management of his finances to them or even explain what he was doing. When he died suddenly of a heart attack, his records were indecipherable, leading to difficulties getting his estate in order. This caused some problems in caring for his wife, as well as considerable tax losses, as his will had not been updated for twenty years.

Assistance from Other Family Members

Other family members (nieces, nephews, cousins, and the like) may also be called on to assume responsibility for an elderly relative when there is no spouse or children. Even friends may play this role if there is no one else who is able to do it. As always, the prior bonds that existed, the attitude of the caregiver, and the level of care necessary determines whether the new arrangements will be successful. But no matter how close the helpmate and recipient were before the need for help arose, it is even more difficult for someone who is not a spouse or a child to furnish support on a continuing basis.

A recent study demonstrated that there was a significant economic cost to caregivers of elderly relatives who were still working.[6] Wages, benefits and promotions all had to be sacrificed in order for them to be able to provide care.

Assistance from the Extended Family

Because fewer children are being born to each couple, and there are higher rates of divorce and a greater degree of mobility than in the past, the extended family has been slowly disappearing. Previously, within the milieu of the extended family, older people (usually women) served valuable functions that enhanced their feelings of self-worth—helping to care for young children, preparing meals, and assisting with the housework. Then, if a time came when the older people themselves required care, the family as a whole contributed to their support in whatever ways were necessary. Indeed, older parents living with married children and grandchildren, with brothers and sisters, or with nieces and nephews nearby was considered a normal scenario. A change in this pattern of behavior came about as the extended family began to disintegrate and children became more resistant to having parents sharing their space—being more protective of their own privacy and freedom. There is also a greater reluctance on the part of parents to being under their children's thumbs. With older people living longer, as well as being more vigorous and independent, they want to maintain their own lifestyle without the constraints imposed by living with children or other relatives.

Though the environment of the extended family no longer exists for most of our population, there are some cultural groups where it is still seen to varying degrees, with strong feelings of respect for the elderly and the desire to assume responsibility for one's parents. It is particularly prevalent among peoples of Mediterranean origin (Spanish, Italian, Greek, and so forth), Asians (Japanese, Chinese, Koreans, and so forth) and African Americans. A report from the AARP (American Association of Retired Persons) in 2001 showed that Asian Americans furnished the most care for elderly family members; white Americans the least.[7] Forty-two percent of Asian Americans provided care or financial support for older family members, white Americans less than 20 percent, African Americans 28 percent, and Hispanic Americans 42 percent. Interestingly, those who were the most caring also felt the most guilt about not doing enough for their parents. A study for the National Institute of Aging noted that "older blacks were twice as likely as whites to receive care from family members when their health declined."[8] Providing this care has long been a tradition in African American families, perhaps born of necessity, since the poverty rate was higher and other resources were not as likely to be available. Recent immigrant groups from all countries also generally care for elderly family members, following the traditions of their homelands.

In the United States today, fewer than 20 percent of adults over the age of sixty-five live with their children, compared to 55 percent in Japan.[9] However,

as evidence of the changes occurring in Japan, as recently as 1970, 80 percent
of older Japanese were part of their children's households.

Help within the Home Setting

Depending on the person's level of functioning, minor aid may be all that
is necessary to keep that individual living at home. This may be provided by
children or a spouse, or by outside agencies. Sometimes, if a person is homebound, the delivery of one or two meals a day may be needed. Social contact
may be maintained if arrangements can be made to transport this individual
to senior day care for a day or a half day several times a week.

The more affluent families are, the less likely they are to provide direct
physical support and care for their spouses, parents, or other elderly relatives.
However, they are more willing (and able) to give financial assistance. Among
the upper-middle and wealthy classes, caregivers are usually hired to dispense
the hands-on help, whether it is paid for by the parents themselves or their
children. Thus, home health aides and nurse's aides may assist with the tasks
of daily living (bathing, dressing, going for walks, dispensing medications,
even feeding) that the elderly person cannot handle adequately alone, instead
of the spouse, child, or others. In some cases, round-the-clock home care
from these aides may be required when severe impairment is present.

For those individuals who have suffered blackouts, dizzy spells, strokes, or
cardiac problems and are unattended for long periods, electronic monitoring
with instant communication may be helpful. Wearing a small radio transmit-
ter allows assistance to be summoned if necessary, giving some measure of
security to both the older person and his or her families.

Other Options

At some point with elderly people living alone at home, issues of safety may
become paramount and difficult decisions may have to be made by relatives
about the proper environment for those individuals unable to do so for themselves. One option might be moving in with a child who can provide some
help and hire aides for whatever else is needed. Another might be remaining at
home with full twenty-four-hour supervision. An assisted living complex might
be another alternative, with or without special aides. And eventually, a nursing home might become a necessary choice. All of these possibilities entail
major loss of autonomy for older people whose independence had been

steadily shrinking previously and is likely to be resisted by these individuals who may not be able to realistically assess their own situations. Though ultimately the older person may be forced to surrender to the will of the family, there should be an effort made to accommodate to his or her wishes if it is at all feasible. Even without full insight into their own limitations, they still have their pride and know the way they want to live.

Society's Role

There are times when spouses, children, or other family members may not be part of the equation in determining the kind of assistance an elderly individual requires. This may be because there are no relatives for someone who never married or never had children. Or the person may, unfortunately, have outlived children and other relatives. And in some instances, the individual who needs help may refuse to call on children or relatives. The stumbling block may be ego, or there may be hostility and anger toward family members, the result of real or imagined slights that occurred in the past. (If the person is cognitively impaired, the family may be contacted by the physician, a visiting nurse, a social worker, or another professional over his or her objections.) Where there is no family, or the family is out of the loop, society has to assume responsibility for care through various governmental agencies or private charitable organizations that have been given this assignment. Home health care organizations and visiting nurses' services may be able to provide this type of care within the home setting, or a nursing home may be necessary.

Hired Caregivers

Assistance by hired caregivers presents a different set of problems for the recipient than dealing with family members. Without the emotional baggage of past relationships, in some ways it may be easier to accept the help, but in other ways it is more difficult. Though there is no love, hate, guilt, or anger toward the caregiver, and no manipulative behavior or power struggle with this unknown person (at least initially), there are still the issues of pride and self-esteem that must be considered. The type of care being given and the level of comprehension and insight of the recipient are important elements. For most people, having a stranger bathe and assist with hygiene and prepare meals and feed them may be quite upsetting. Or shopping for them and managing their finances. Or dressing them and dispensing medications. Even without the assistance, just having another person in their home, in their territory, may cause resentment or anxiety. (The more cognitively compromised the individual is, the easier it may be.)

Over a period of time, there may be greater acceptance as the recipient becomes accustomed to the care being given and the intrusion in their personal space. However, this is contingent to a large degree on the temperament and compassion shown by the caregiver. If this person is condescending, arrogant, overly critical, or insulting, time may increase hostility and resistence rather than assent. On the other hand, if the caregiver is kind, understanding, and patient, he or she may be able to establish a positive relationship with the recipient, which makes it more comfortable for both of them in the long run.

Unfortunately, public agencies may not always be able to furnish caregivers with the right demeanor and emotional state to deal with people who have different types of disabilities. These organizations do not have the time nor the funds available to adequately educate caregivers about their roles, not only delineating the services they will have to provide, but how to interact and respond to older people, especially those who require a higher level of care. Usually, professionals such as nurses, social workers, therapists, and the like are more cognizant of the problems of the elderly and are able to manage them better. The home health aides and nurses' aides, who are generally paid poorly and have less training, but provide more of the hands-on care, may not be as respectful or forbearing as their professional colleagues. (Home health aide is currently the fastest growing job category in the United States. Since 1989, their number has doubled to more than 500,000.[10])

Quite often an elderly client is treated as a child by a caregiver, who orders him or her about without explaining matters, even berating or scolding when things do not go as expected. In addition, there may be cultural differences or language difficulties between caregiver and client that make communication difficult, or make a caregiver less sympathetic to the person being cared for and less willing to extend himself or herself. Of course, it can be very frustrating dealing with some of the elderly who do not hear or see well, or move slowly because of strokes or arthritis, or have cognitive problems and do not fully grasp what is being asked of them. However, caregivers without patience and compassion often rob their already impaired elderly charges of the few remaining shreds of dignity they have left. These older people have limited power, or no power at all, and are completely at the mercy of the strangers who enter their homes to care for them.

Assisted Living Residences

Even with family participation, visiting nurses, and home health aides, at some point it may become too difficult for a person to remain in his or her usual home environment. Depending on the individual's needs, various options can be considered. If the person is able to take care of himself or herself to a certain degree, assisted living residences may be the answer. These relatively recent developments come in different sizes and shapes, and may be found in urban, suburban, and even rural areas.[11] The number of these assisted living residences has been growing dramatically: from 3,800 in 1994 to 7,500 in 2000.[12] Many have been constructed and are operated by large corporations, some of which are in the hotel or nursing home businesses, or are part of real estate investment trusts. It is important to remember that for the most part they are for-profit ventures that do not give anything away for free. (A small number of these are run by charitable organizations and are focused more on lower income people.) Based on how the project is structured, the individual units may be rented by the elderly, or purchased as condominiums, with additional services included for an annual fee, or paid for as required.

The services offered can vary greatly from complex to complex, or even to different people within the same development. Usually they will provide one, two, or three meals a day in a common dining area, or in the person's own apartment if he or she cannot get out for meals. Maid service is available to clean the apartment, change the linen, wash the clothes, and so on, as frequently as needed. Transportation is often furnished for shopping at nearby malls or shopping centers, with arrangements made to take residents for doctor's visits or other necessary appointments. A nurse may be on call to help with minor problems and sometimes there are also doctor's offices on the grounds. The larger complexes may have sections where people can reside to obtain skilled nursing care, either temporarily for an acute illness or on a longer term basis. (At times, a nursing home may be tied into the assisted living residence and be run by the same management.) It may also be possible to arrange for home health aides to assist the person in his or her own apartment for a short interval or for an extended period. The best developments are light-years removed from the "old age homes" of the past, having everything an older person needs, though the prices paid for various amenities can be steep.

When assisted living is chosen voluntarily by a senior, the transition may be quite satisfactory and not demeaning to the individual. But when people are forced into assisted living by family members, it can be devastating, as it signifies they are no longer autonomous and in control of their own lives.

Nursing Homes

For those people who are too impaired either physically or cognitively to live by themselves even with major assistance, nursing homes are a flawed though necessary solution. When there is no hope that an individual will be able to resume a functional existence in the future, he or she can be sent to reside in these warehouses of chronic illness and disability, where people are sequestered to await death in the company of others in a similar situation. (There are also a small percentage of patients with temporary disabilities who may utilize nursing homes for short stays to help them recuperate after hospitalizations.) Unlike a hospice setting, the patients in these institutions do not have a terminal condition with a limited life expectancy and death may not visit them for some time. So they linger in limbo, neither dead nor fully alive, sitting, eating, and excreting, with no dreams and no expectations of a better existence. No matter how dedicated the staff and how modern the physical plant may be, the conditions in these homes are generally repellent and dehumanizing, representing the ultimate loss of dignity for the elderly.

As noted in a *New York Times* editorial in April 1999,

> It is thought that as many as half of all women over 65 in the United States and a third of all men will spend some of their remaining time in a nursing home. . . . Nursing homes have acquired the sickest and most dependent of the old . . . less than 8 percent can bathe, dress, go to the bathroom, move about and feed themselves without help . . . as every study for decades has shown, great numbers of the old, many as helpless as babies, continue to be neglected and abused. Some die of accidents, malnutrition, dehydration, untreated urinary infections and bedsores that turn into toxic, flesh-eating wounds.[13]

In 1985, there were 19,100 nursing homes in the United States, with a total of about 1.6 million beds.[14] That same year, 5 percent of the 28.5 million people over age sixty-five resided in these institutions, that is, 1.3 million people. However, 21.6 percent of those eighty-five and over were in nursing homes, one-third of all nursing home occupants, though they were less than 1 percent of the entire population.[15] Proprietary nursing homes comprised 75 percent of the total, most of them organized in large chains for efficiency and economy of scale.[16] About 20 percent were run by hospitals or voluntary organizations and 5 percent by government. For the most part, nursing home facilities were small, averaging about 85 beds, with public units averaging about 132 beds.

Since 1985, the number of nursing homes is down 13 percent, though total beds have gone up 9 percent.[17] And interestingly, nursing home residents increased only 4 percent from 1985 to 1995, despite the fact that the population over sixty-five shot up 18 percent. (From these figures we can assume that either older people were healthier in 1995 than 1985 and less in need of nursing homes, or that other methods of care for the elderly were being utilized in place of nursing homes, that is, home care.) In 1995, there were about 1.5 million people in the 16,700 nursing homes in the United States, though nearly 1.8 million beds were available. While the number of for-profit homes decreased 23 percent during the previous decade, total beds in these institutions rose 3 percent, showing that there were fewer, but larger homes. About 90 percent of patients in nursing homes were sixty-five or over, while 35 percent were eighty-five or over. Eighty-eight percent of the residents were white and 72 percent were female.

Whether nursing homes are run by corporations whose goal is to make a profit, voluntary agencies whose aim is to provide a needed service, hospitals, or governmental bodies, there are certain common elements to their operations that make it inevitable that the residents' dignity will be compromised. First is the sheer mass of physically and cognitively deteriorated patients that require care. Second is the difficulty in attracting good personnel to work in a nursing home environment. Third is the fact that in order for these institutions to work efficiently, they must function like factories for the care of the elderly, with fairly rigid time schedules for the tasks being performed and specific assignments for the workers.

The vast majority of nursing home residents have significant cognitive deficiencies. This means that besides being unable to care for themselves, they cannot follow directions or retain admonitions regarding safety measures. Thus, they will get out of a chair or a bed, fall and injure themselves if they are not being properly restrained or observed every single moment. They will also neglect to ask for bedpans or urinals, or help in getting to the bathroom, instead defecating or urinating when the urge occurs. Because of this, they must be cleaned frequently in order to avoid bedsores and infections. Or a urinary catheter may be utilized to prevent them from wetting themselves. They may also be constantly demanding things from their caregivers, having forgotten that someone had recently provided it. And as they become more demented and confused, they may cry out or call repeatedly for no reason, disturbing everyone else around them. Eventually, it may reach a point where they make no sense at all, continuously screaming or spouting gibberish and responding inappropriately to various stimuli, having lost all connection with other human beings. It may be necessary to use heavy doses of medication to sedate these patients in order to care for them and to allow the other patients and staff some peace.

The physical problems that are ubiquitous in the nursing home population also complicates their care to a considerable degree. They are literally, as well as figuratively, on their last legs, with the preponderance having multiple medical problems and needing constant attention and assistance with all the tasks of daily living, such as feeding, dressing, personal hygiene, medications, and so on. For some of them simply to survive necessitates an almost heroic effort by their caregivers on an ongoing basis. They may experience pain from arthritis in various joints, limiting their mobility. Or they may have trouble walking and moving about because of strokes or Parkinson's disease. Or their activities may be restricted because of shortness of breath from emphysema, chronic lung disease, or congestive heart failure. Or they may have angina (chest pain) when they walk and this prevents them from getting around. Or they may have dizzy spells, diabetic neuropathy with or without amputations, osteoporosis, hip fractures, or lumbar stenosis, peripheral vascular disease, all requiring special help to execute various maneuvers. Virtually every patient in a nursing home has one or more of the above disorders in addition to cognitive impairment, continuously taxing the patience and skills of the caregivers who work in these institutions. And very often when patients are in pain and need medication for relief, they are ignored by the staff.[18]

Recruiting decent personnel to work in a nursing home environment is a major problem for administrators. Because of this, standards may be compromised at times and it is the elderly residents who suffer. The best nurses and aides want to be in acute care hospitals, busy medical offices, clinics, public health units, and the like where there are more challenges, more intellectual stimulation, and more excitement. They want to feel their work means something and that the patients they treat may possibly improve, and, if in a hospital, go home. In these other venues, there is also communication between patient and staff members, which can be emotionally satisfying for the caregivers. Nursing home work, on the other hand, is drudgery and unpleasant to boot, consisting of feeding, dressing and undressing patients, and cleaning up urine and feces. There is no excitement in caring for these patients, no creative energy unleashed, and little emotional interaction. Not unlike the residents themselves, there is little for the staff to look forward to in terms of the care they are rendering. None of their patients are going to get better and leave the nursing home. The only way out for them is to die.

Virtually all of the day-to-day care in the nursing homes is done by aides rather than nurses. The latter serve primarily in a supervisory capacity and dispense medications, rather than attending directly to patients. In general, the people who opt to work in nursing homes are not as ambitious as their hospital colleagues in terms of personal development, though most put in the hours and do what they have to do. Education and training of the staff in these institutions is also not as comprehensive as at most hospitals, even in areas related to their specific patient populations and chronic illnesses. This is in spite of the fact that caring for nursing home residents is more demanding in a number of ways than for hospital patients. (In fact, for nurse's aides in nursing homes, "there is often less required training than for a manicurist at a beauty parlor, and they may be paid less than a beginning caretaker at the zoo."[19])

It is also important to remember that in most nursing homes, the bottom line is the major determinant of the services that can be given and what can be spent on personnel. To make a decent profit for their corporations and to boost stock prices if they are public, the executives who run the nursing homes want to get the biggest bang for their buck, trying to get the most done with the least number of people and the lowest expenses. These executives are out to provide adequate rather than top-notch care. They want to meet minimum standards so the regulatory agencies will not crack down on them and lift their licenses, but do not want to spend extra money to obtain more and better personnel. This translates into lower salaries for their nurses and aides.

The bottom line is also the reason that nursing homes tend to operate as factories for care of the disabled elderly. With limits on the number of nurses and aides that can be hired, the staff must be organized in a way that will maximize its ability to deliver services. This means assigning staff members to tasks that are tightly scheduled and must be performed within particular time constraints. Unfortunately, it is not always possible to allot definite time slots in caring for cognitively and physically damaged human beings, as problems often arise that require special attention and extra moments (incontinence, falls, pain, shortness of breath, anxiety, and so forth). And not infrequently, a patient who is depressed or anxious may need verbal reassurance, or hand holding, which may also take additional time. However, if a caregiver is behind in his or her schedule and feels pressured to move on and complete his or her work, the patients may be shortchanged and not given the physical care or emotional support they require, further undermining any remaining dignity.

Because of the aforementioned problems, nursing homes should be a solution of last resort, reserved for elderly people who have major cognitive deficiencies and are unable to comprehend the degrading conditions to which they are being subjected.

LOSS OF CONTROL WITH VARIOUS TYPES OF LIFE SUPPORT

A number of diseases in older people can damage or destroy critical organs, altering the metabolic or physiologic parameters necessary to sustain life. Before the modern era of medicine, this always resulted in death. Currently however, with the use of drugs and tubes and electronic and mechanical devices, people can be kept alive, even after their vital systems have failed and are no longer performing the required tasks. But when artificial support mechanisms are used to preserve life, the recipients of this technology may wind up losing control of the decision-making process and be sustained in states they would not have chosen voluntarily. The type of support I am alluding to includes assistance with cardiovascular and pulmonary function, nutritional maintenance through feeding tubes, renal dialysis to forestall kidney failure, catheters for urinary drainage, and ostomies for bowel and urinary diversion.

When life is extended and the quality of life is not significantly diminished by these assistive devices, there is little controversy about the use of these aids. As examples we can cite cardiac pacemakers or artificial valves. Questions arise in other areas however. The use of a ventilator for pulmonary support in an acute situation is generally accepted. But it is another story when a ventilator is utilized to prolong life in a person with a terminal illness who has no hope of recovery. Similarly, questions can be raised about the placement of a feeding tube to keep someone alive who is severely brain damaged, or even in a persistent vegetative state, after a major stroke or devastating injury. Unfortunately, people usually are not able to approve the use of these devices because of their cognitive status. If they have a living will, or have designated a health care proxy who is attuned to their wishes, they may be able to escape this ultimate loss of dignity—being kept alive through artificial means with no mind or free will, and none of the attributes that characterize them as human.

The use of ostomies to prolong life is usually straightforward when there is a curable, life-threatening disorder that can be circumvented, or for palliative reasons when survival is extended. (Ostomies are shunts in the intestines or ureters that direct urine or feces to the surface of the abdomen where they can be collected in special pouches when the normal passages are blocked.) It is more questionable if survival will be short term or of poor quality, even with the use of this technique. Urinary catheters are generally not objectionable when incontinence or urinary retention is a persistent problem that cannot be solved in any other manner (though they do cause frequent urinary tract infections). Renal dialysis is used to forestall kidney failure resulting from several different disorders and can be continued for many years, unless a renal transplant can be performed to restore kidney function. Since it is an expensive, laborious process, in other advanced industrialized countries renal dialysis is rationed, with a cutoff in terms of how old a person can be and still receive it.

In determining whether to proceed with any of the above-mentioned techniques, increased survival should not be the critical factor, but rather the quality of the person's survival.

LOSS OF DRIVER'S LICENSE

The loss of a driver's license and the ability to drive is a development dreaded by many older people, seriously imperiling their self-sufficiency. In 1995, there were 24 million drivers over the age of seventy.[20] This is expected to increase to 40 million in the year 2020. Accident rates per mile driven rise after age seventy-five and even more significantly after eighty-five. And the use of medication can particularly compromise safety in older drivers.[21]

Though licenses may be surrendered voluntarily, often they are taken away by other family members, physicians, or the legal system. The reasons for this include cognitive decline, diminished visual acuity, various physical disabilities, and heightened anxiety. But the end result for those deprived of their licenses is the same: a loss of freedom and control over their own lives. And if the deprivation is involuntary, the loss of dignity is even greater. When driving privileges are removed, the elderly become aware they have reached a new stage in their lives and from that point on must rely on others to travel anywhere. These circumstances develop for many older people almost as the inverse of their situations as teenagers, when they were eagerly awaiting the granting of driver's licenses as further affirmation of their status as adults. Instead, the elderly await the forfeiture of their driver's licenses with apprehension, seeing it as further affirmation of their passage into senescence. It appears to be even more devastating for men than for women, perhaps reflecting on their masculinity.

Most people in the United States take their ability to drive for granted since it is so much a part of their everyday lives. Indeed, in those areas lacking reliable public transportation, driving is an absolute necessity for people to function within society. It is only when that power is taken away that we realize its importance to us, as like children we are forced to surrender our dignity and seek rides in order to visit someone, go shopping, or perform simple chores. In many elderly communities, a person who drives and has a car has a special standing, being envied by his or her peers, because he or she has the freedom that others lack, and can also provide a valuable service. It is similar to teenagers who bestow an elevated status on their friends with cars. For some older people the ability to drive may be closely tied to pride and self-esteem, and relinquishing that privilege may result in depression.

A male patient of mine, a former physician who was ninety-years-old, refused to give up driving even though he had a budding dementia, with poor balance and coordination owing to a number of strokes. He insisted he was capable and could not carry on his day-to-day existence without his car. After going through stop signs and red lights on several occasions and having near accidents, the local police took his license away pending medical clearance for him to drive. Being quite affluent and extremely stubborn, he was accustomed to having his way and continued driving without a license, a manifestation of his poor judgment.

In granting driver's licenses, governmental authorities want to protect other members of society from those who have insufficient skills or acumen to operate vehicles and also protect the deficient drivers from harming themselves. However, it is also important for society to help people maintain their independence and autonomy, and so, in withdrawing privileges, must balance competing mandates. Many elderly drivers with disabilities who lose their licenses may still be able to drive safely in certain circumstances: at low speeds, in daylight, and in local, familiar territory. Though their reaction time may be slowed, these drivers also tend to be very cautious and take fewer risks. Some states have already started moving toward providing restricted licenses for the elderly and disabled, with repeat testing required to renew privileges. But even more effort should be made to issue multiple categories of licenses, taking into account people's particular needs and functional abilities.

LOSS OF LOVED ONES

Throughout our lives, relatives and friends die, necessitating periods of mourning and adjustment. Sadly, as we age, we have fewer friends and peers to accompany us on our journey through the years, as our coterie of contemporaries dwindles. Those who survive with us become the last remnants of our generation—individuals who have had the same experiences and have lived through the same times that we have. And too often, it is difficult for us to communicate with people who were not there as our universe evolved— even our children and grandchildren. Indeed, some of the younger members of society view the elderly almost as historical figures, antiques, who are not really a part of the current world. At best, they are perceived as cute old men and women who are really not relevant.

The way we deal with these losses and the grief that is generated when we are older is also a factor in our ability to maintain our dignity and vitality. If we are unsuccessful in this task, as our peers die, we can wind up grieving for long periods, covered by a mantle of depression and unable to carry on with normal living. In some cultures this is the expected path, particularly when a spouse (male) dies. In many Mediterranean countries, wives dress in black and may spend the rest of their lives so attired, forever mourning their husbands. Perhaps they see themselves as figures of nobility and rectitude, though others view them as objects of pity. In Hindu cultures, suttee was a traditional practice among the upper classes. When a husband died, since the woman's life was essentially over, she would throw herself on the funeral pyre to die with him. But in modern, Western societies, all of us are encouraged to maximize our own potential and live our lives to the fullest, after coming to appropriate terms with the loss of our loved ones. This can only be done if we do not drape ourselves in black and allow grief to overwhelm us.

Accommodating to the deaths of relatives and close friends occurs at different times for each of us, with the impact depending on the strength of the emotional relationships (and the geographical proximity) that previously existed. The deaths of people within our households, or those with whom we interacted on a daily basis, affect us the most in terms of altering our routine, but the internal consequences are determined by the bonds that had been present. In a common pattern, grandparents might die while we are teenagers or young adults, with parents dying when we are middle-aged. At least this is the anticipated sequence and though painful it is felt to be the natural order of things. Then later in middle age, our peers begin dying, with more of them disappearing from our lives as we continue to grow older.

At some point we also lose our spouses and are forced to change the way we conduct our lives. Aside from the love and comfort that is no longer there, the loss of a spouse interferes most with our usual activities. Habits must be reshaped and shared responsibilities must be totally assumed by the surviving member of the couple. And there is the reconciliation to being alone, with no companion in the home and no one with whom to share one's thoughts. Living with someone for thirty, forty, or fifty years, people become complacent, believing this is the way it will always be, even though they realize at some level that change is inevitable. Then, after the loss, the survivor is immersed in a sea of depression and apathy that must be battled constantly. Sometimes, he or she simply gives up on life, particularly among the very old, who often die soon after their spouses.

Unfortunately, children sometimes die before their parents, which can be emotionally devastating for anyone, but is perhaps less well tolerated by the elderly. Severe depression and withdrawal often results. Some parents are never able to accept this loss and if recovery occurs, it may take many years.

The deaths of our peers moves us in a number of ways, whether these were friends, acquaintances, or simply people who existed in our lives. First, it brings home our own vulnerability and makes us examine the possibility of our own mortality. Second, it gives rise to feelings of guilt about our own survival, with someone else our age having died. Third, it heightens and extends our sense of isolation, as more and more familiar faces vanish and are replaced by those of strangers with whom we have no connection. And as our friends leave us, the emotional support system we have constructed over the years begins to crumble and often cannot be replaced.

LOSS OF IDENTITY AND SELF-IMAGE

Most of us must deal with a loss of identity and self-image as we age. Mired in the quicksand of cognitive decline and physical disabilities, there is a tendency for us to forget who we are, what we stand for, and what is important. Looking in the mirror, we see old people who cannot be us, disregarding the possibility that what we are seeing might merely be a veneer, an external surface that has aged, while the energy, dreams, and passions inside have remained youthful. But without knowing who we are, it may be difficult to accept the fact we are old and have limitations, while still carrying on and relishing our lives. Instead of concentrating on the strengths that are still there, we obsess over what has been surrendered to the onslaught of the years and become listless and indifferent to ourselves. We forget that being old does not mean that life is over.

There are a number of other factors that also contribute to the loss of identity in older people. For some who have previously worked, retirement itself can be profoundly destructive. Whether voluntary or forced, the loss of one's job with its status and demands, can cause significant pain while puncturing the balloon of one's ego. During most of our adult lives, our sense of identity is closely connected to our occupation. We are known as so and so the banker, the plumber, the attorney, the cabinetmaker, and so forth. Upon retirement, there is a severing of these bonds and a disassociation from what we had used as our credentials. In addition to that, the entire pattern of our lives is transformed. No longer do we go to work daily and adhere to a specific schedule. And no longer do we have to be concerned with our productivity and ability to get things done. We are now called on to establish new identities, to play new roles with different goals and objectives. In short, we are asked to "reinvent" ourselves, a task for which many of us are unprepared and unable to perform, at least not to the degree that makes us satisfied with our performances and content with the people we have had to become.

Similar situations arise with women who have stayed at home to raise children and run a household. As the children grow up and leave home, mom no longer has the same responsibilities and the same jobs to do. Living now in an "empty nest," she has time on her hands and has lost her previous identity as a mother. No longer needed in the same way by her children, she must also find a new uniform to wear and redefine who she is.

The diminished income that usually comes with retirement may also affect people's self-image, particularly if their feelings of self-worth were tied to their financial state. With less money available, they may have to restrict their spending and "conspicuous consumption." Less extravagant clothes, travel, recreation, and dining out may be necessary, along with a less expensive car and more affordable living quarters. Moving into a smaller home and perhaps keeping a car for a longer period may seem like common sense to most people, but for others it connotes a step down on the social ladder and a loss of self-esteem.

There are also those whose self-image may be damaged when they perceive themselves as no longer being productive members of society, not only in terms of generating paychecks, but in functioning in ways they consider important. It could be doing something, or making something, or selling something, or whatever, but it was significant to them and now it has been taken away with nothing comparable to replace it. If they fixate on this loss instead of trying to find a new focus for themselves, it may also lead to depression and they may be unable to move forward with their lives after retirement.

This period may also bring forth a great deal of introspection and self-analysis in some individuals. Having reached the end of the productive road, they may feel as if they did not do anything of value during their years of working and perhaps their lives were wasted. Or they may be reminded that they did not realize the dreams of their youth and now there will be no more opportunities for them. Of course, the situation had been like that for years, but retirement brings the reality home to them. Whatever they have already achieved, or not achieved, that is it forever. Most can accept this, but some see themselves as failures for not having accomplished more with their lives. However, for many others, this is not even an issue to be debated.

LOSS OF INITIATIVE

For the majority of people, aging is also associated with a loss of initiative and a loss of drive, which can be upsetting for those who previously thrived on activity. In general, this is not a time for new ventures, starting new businesses, or building new homes. Some of this may be based on physical and cognitive changes, and a drop in levels of certain hormones. And in some people, depression may play a role. Many people also feel burned out, perhaps having been in the same position, or having done the same thing for years. There is also a fatigue that sets in after decades of conflict and stress. But whatever the cause, a dwindling of energy is often evident.

It is also true that the familiar feels good to us as we age, and being in a comfortable and predictable environment is reassuring. No longer do we lust for excitement and take risks in the way we conduct our lives. For many of us, this conservatism goes along with support of the status quo in our personal worlds and in society at large. There is often an unwillingness to consider new ideas and new ways of doing things. However, those who are self-assured and unafraid of the future are more disposed to contemplate change, more open to new methods and new patterns of behavior, and also more amenable to new adventures.

LOSS OF MEANING

Many of us are aware of a void in our lives in our later years, as if something is missing, over and above our previous jobs and lifestyles. Although we might not be able to articulate what this is, perhaps what is missing is "meaning" on a spiritual level, as many of us have a yearning to understand what life is all about, including some comprehension of our role in the universe. This is different from the meaning that comes with working, with its focus on productivity and the goals that are intrinsic to a job. It also supersedes the need to establish a new identity and new goals that are part of retirement. During the years of employment, we may have been too busy to ruminate about the purpose of life, trying to do our work and earn a living, or manage the household and bring up the kids. It is only after retirement that these questions bob to the surface, nagging at us and demanding our attention.

In the past, religion gave most of us answers to our questions, or negated the need to ask. Since survival was an issue in antecedent societies, people worked until they died and did not wonder as much about life's meaning. If they did, religion was there for them and without the constant bombardment of information that raises questions for us. Even today, for those of us who are believers, there may be no emptiness and absence of meaning, but serenity instead. And among the faithful there is more likely to be an acceptance of what has been and what will be, making questions unnecessary.

Existence was also less complex in earlier times as we all had a place in an extended family, with defined roles at every stage of our lives. In addition, there was an attachment to the communities where we had spent our lives, usually remaining in the same town from birth to death. We knew our neighbors and shared the good and bad times with them, watching as the kids down the street grew up, married, and had babies. All of us felt we were a part of something greater than ourselves: our families, our communities, and also our nation. This changed with the mobility that became a hallmark of the last half of the twentieth century. People went wherever their corporations sent them, or wherever they thought there was work. Or they wanted a town with better schools for their kids, or nicer homes, or a better climate, or more recreational facilities. Always moving and seeking new vistas. The price paid was a rootlessness and anonymity, with strangers for neighbors. Then our kids became adults and moved away, leaving us alone as we aged to chart a new course for ourselves. And with this came an existential angst and emptiness that is difficult to describe. Thomas R. Cole notes in *The Journey of Life* that "[i]n our century, vastly improved medical and economic conditions for older people have been accompanied by cultural disenfranchisement—a loss of meaning and vital social roles."[22]

CONCLUSION

The clock cannot be turned back to assist us in our search for meaning, or for older people to regain the defined positions they once held. Instead, we must look elsewhere within the context of our own time to give our lives a purpose. We must empower ourselves. We must deal with our losses and carry on. And to do so, it is necessary that we have objectives we can pursue with passion, that give us a reason to awaken each morning, while blunting some of the pain that comes with living. (I will discuss some options in Chapters 7 and 8.) At the same time, we must continue to guard our autonomy and control of our lives however we can. It is important as well that we remain connected to our family and friends, and aware of what is happening in our local towns, our country, and the world. And to maintain positive feelings about ourselves, we must also find ways we can give something back to our communities.

6

AGEISM

Society's Attempt to Deny
Dignity to Older People

—————————————— • ——————————————

This policy and reverence of age makes the world bitter to
the best of our times; keeps our fortunes from us till our
oldness cannot relish them. I begin to find an idle and
fond bondage in the oppression of aged tyranny.

—WILLIAM SHAKESPEARE
KING LEAR

—————————

Many societies are biased against those factions that are less powerful, or with
different values, than the majority and work to suppress them with various
measures. This prejudice may be manifest as racism, sexism, or discrimination
against ethnic or religious groups. While some cultures respect and revere
their older members, in the United States there is a bias against the elderly,
that has been called "ageism," that is expressed in a number of ways. Among
the evidence confirming this is the disregard and marginalization of older
people, forced retirement at a particular age from many jobs, ghettoization of
the elderly, negative media coverage, crime directed against the elderly, and
ageist jokes. There are also more subtle actions against seniors that are more
or less accepted, even if they are hurtful to a minor degree.

Betty Friedan noted in her book *The Fountain of Age* that

[t]he blackout of images of women or men visibly over sixty-five, engaged in any vital or productive adult activity, and their replacement by

the "problem" of age, is our society's very definition of age. Age is perceived only as decline or deterioration from youth. An observer from another planet might deduce from these images that Americans who can no longer "pass" as young have been removed from places of work, study, entertainment, sports—segregated in senior citizens' "retirement villages" or nursing homes from which, like concentration camps, they will never return.[1]

AGEISM

Ageism may be based on an undercurrent of resentment toward the elderly that exists in our society at large, seen in young and even middle-aged people. Its origins date back several centuries. During colonial times, Protestant churches espoused the ideal of a hierarchical structure in the family, with the younger members serving and venerating the elderly.[2] However, the ideal was not always what was practiced. There was also a common belief that the debility and decrepitude of old age was punishment for sinning earlier in life and that those who appeared healthy in old age were the ones who were morally upright. This of course led to a detrimental view of the elderly, since the majority of them were impaired in different ways. (Though abuse of alcohol, tobacco, slothfulness, and sexual debauchery did cause disease and decay, most of the elderly were simply the victims of normal aging and the illnesses of later life.) Thus, there were ambivalent attitudes toward older people.

In the late nineteenth century, an American physician, Dr. George Miller Beard, propounded the idea that man's productivity was maximal by age forty and that there was a rapid decline afterward due to deterioration of the brain. He also contended that the economic power concentrated in the hands of old men was misplaced, as they were incapable of managing it properly. He chastised society for venerating the elderly, whom he felt were unworthy of respect.[3] Other prominent figures in America, including Dr. William Osler, supported some of these beliefs regarding the elderly, and by the turn of the century, they had gained a degree of general acceptance. Over the past seventy-five years, science and medicine have uncovered many of the mechanisms of aging and its associated diseases, showing that the previous characterizations were rubbish. However, some of the misperceptions persist, though they are frequently unspoken and may even be unrecognized by those who harbor these feelings.

The embers of hostility toward the elderly are fanned by the fact that they are, for the most part, nonproductive members of society (in terms of having a paying job and earning money) and have to be supported by its working members. In addition to individual responsibilities in caring for parents and grandparents, workers contribute to keep Social Security and Medicare solvent, which primarily serves the elderly, along with various other smaller government programs. And since the inception of Social Security in the 1930s, the ratio of workers to retirees has steadily declined, resulting in an increased financial burden for each worker and more money extracted from his or her paycheck. "In 1950, there were 16 workers for each Social Security beneficiary. Today, there are slightly more than three."[4] By 2020, when most baby boomers will have retired, it is projected that there will only be two workers for each person receiving benefits. And unfortunately, because of the lack of political will in Washington, the problem with Social Security has been passed along to future generations, instead of having been placed on a sound financial footing to lighten the load for those who will still be working.

Envy of the lifestyle of some retirees, who are seen boating, golfing, and playing cards, may also be an issue for some younger people. Not only does the rest of society have to pay to assist the elderly, but there is a belief that the group as a whole is fairly affluent and could afford to do more for themselves. While it is true that the grinding poverty once endemic among the elderly has been reduced by Social Security and Medicare, older people in general are far from wealthy and usually live in a moderate fashion. There are also medical expenses not covered by Medicare that decimate the finances of so many of the elderly, such as for prescription drugs and long-term care. The young and the middle aged may be prone to forget that in the future they themselves will require support from those who will then be working.

Some children also harbor controlled anger toward their parents for the care they must provide, as may other family members who consider themselves obligated to elderly relatives. These feelings may be repressed to some degree, but linger just below the surface. It may not even be the money they are sacrificing, but the time and the type of tasks required, with seniors seen as a physical and emotional burden, causing significant stress and aggravation. Many younger people may not even realize that a role reversal with their parents has occurred and that they are now functioning as the adults in the relationships. They just know they have responsibilities they would rather do without, directing various aspects of their parents' lives. This may contribute to the resentment they have toward all elderly, which is communicated to their peers.

Another element that fuels society's antagonism toward older people is a belief that much of the money that the government spends on them is unnecessary or wasted and could be returned to taxpayers, or spent on other programs of more generalized benefit. The elderly are perceived by some as being only a step away from death with their lives essentially over. Why should funds be disbursed on programs designated specifically for them? What do they need it for? Do they deserve it when they are unproductive? What value are they to society? These ideas may not be generally discussed and may be held by only a few, but may influence how the population as a whole views the elderly.

A dramatic example of Western society's indifference toward and devaluation of the elderly was evident in the summer of 2003 in Europe, most prominently in France.[5] The continent had been scorched by an extraordinarily severe heat wave continuing into August. Traditionally for the French, August is the month for vacations, when individuals and families leave the sweltering cities for a period of relaxation at the seashore or in the countryside. As the French departed for their usual vacation sojourns, elderly parents and other relatives remained behind in the heat, with no air conditioning and without special arrangements being made, or concern for their well-being. Unaware of the need to consume large amounts of fluids, or unable to do so, thousands of older people died alone in their ovenlike apartments of dehydration or heat stroke, completely unattended. Often constrained by pride, perhaps depressed by their situation, or unable to comprehend the danger, many did not ask for help. Only the stench of decomposing bodies alerted neighbors that something was wrong. Even after being informed that elderly relatives had died, many of those on vacation were unwilling to return home early to claim the bodies and the morgues were overwhelmed. It was estimated that 10,000 to 11,000 older individuals died prematurely in France because of the heat and the absence of precautionary measures, an indictment of the families as well as the whole social order. After the fact, the French government proposed measures to prevent a recurrence of this catastrophic event. This merely reinforces the esteem in which "modern" nations hold their elderly.

MARGINALIZATION OF THE ELDERLY

Whether younger individuals are hostile, neutral, or understanding in their attitudes toward older people, they still tend to disregard the elderly and ignore their opinions, marginalizing them with respect to their place in society. An eighty-seven-year-old patient of mine who was intellectually intact and quite bright expressed it to me in this fashion: "The worst thing about growing old is that nobody listens to you anymore, even when you have something important to say. Everybody's either too busy or doesn't care and most of your old friends have died." Some of the elderly even visit physician's offices with minor problems just to be able to speak to the doctor and his or her staff so they will have someone who will listen.

An unexpected factor contributing to the marginalization of the elderly has been the technological revolution since the mid-1980s, with the important role that computers and the Internet play in people's lives. Older individuals for the most part are not particularly skilled in the use of these tools, not having grown up with them and never having had the opportunity to learn about them. (However, there are many older people who have educated themselves in one way or another about the use of computers.) In our world, unfamiliarity with computers and the Internet puts a person at a disadvantage in terms of acquiring knowledge and the ability to communicate. With well over 50 percent of our households now having personal computers, buying things online, searching for data and participating in chat rooms, it is rare for a middle-class person not to be sending and receiving e-mail and utilizing their computers for various tasks. These deficiencies make the elderly less relevant in other people's eyes and is another negative they must overcome.

However, certain aphorisms that have circulated in our society for generations attest to the fact that ageism is not a recent development and that marginalization of the elderly occurred in the past. One example is the saying "There's no fool like an old fool," which suggests that old people appear even more foolish than the young when their actions are outside of accepted boundaries. This can apply to an older man pursuing a younger woman, but also to any type of behavior that is different and does not conform to what is expected for older people. It is as if society has a different set of standards for older individuals than for the young.

Another classical maxim is "You can't teach an old dog new tricks," which implies that all old people are fixed in their ways and unable to adapt to new developments. Thus, as the world evolves and changes, they are left behind, acting as they always had and existing in the past. If this were correct, it certainly could be cited as a rationale for the marginalization of the elderly, who could not function successfully in a new environment. But though this adage has been around for many years, that does not make it true. In reality, the elderly can learn and retain new information (even how to use computers). It just takes them longer. And although they may be more resistant to change and conservative in their outlook, this does serve a useful purpose in a society that is all too willing to discard old ideas and values that previously worked well. Older people serve as a repository for these ideas and values and assure that they will be considered carefully before any change takes place. And the elderly can transform their mind-set when it becomes necessary and act appropriately in any new circumstances that emerge.

JOB DISCRIMINATION

Older employees are not respected in the workplace in the same way that younger workers are. Though the federal government and many state governments have passed legislation prohibiting age discrimination in employment, it is difficult to enforce and there is an obvious bias related to age. This is evident in forced retirement and buyouts of older workers, and the desire of many corporations to have a younger workforce. Whenever there is downsizing, a disproportionate number of older employees are usually involved, both blue collar workers and lower level executives, particularly those past fifty. There are several reasons for this. With seniority, older workers have higher salaries and hourly wages than their younger peers, though they may be performing the same or similar tasks. It is always cheaper to replace them with younger people who are making less money. There is also a perception that younger workers are faster and more efficient than older ones, and it is believed that older individuals are more difficult to train for new jobs and to use new technology. Because of this bias, they are often not afforded the chance to compete with younger people to determine whether they can perform.

There are also various unwritten job restrictions on many employees who have reached their late forties or fifties and have not attained the upper echelons of management. They are no longer provided with the same opportunities for advancement as their younger colleagues and are not promoted to higher positions, though many of them may be quite competent. Once a particular age is reached and employees are at a certain level, they are seen as not being able to go further on their career paths and are often relegated to dead end work. Thus, it is easier to lay them off in any restructuring, as they were not perceived as being important to the corporation in any case.

And once they have been laid off, it may be even more difficult for these people to find jobs because of ageist bias, though placement of older job seekers is dependent to a large degree on the state of the economy. (If unemployment is low and workers are in demand, it is easier for individuals to get jobs, even if they are older.) However, employment agencies and corporations that are hiring are usually not interested in older workers to fill positions similar to those they previously held, wanting them to function instead at a lower level with less pay. Trying to find a different type of work or a new career may be equally frustrating, as there is a reluctance to retrain older people. Many of these individuals have to become self-employed if they want to continue working, going into business for themselves as consultants, freelancers, entrepreneurs, franchise holders, small shop owners, and so forth. This may entail investing some of their own money to get started and may also mean having to forego benefits like health insurance and pension plans.

Of course, the situation is different for the top executives or chief executive officers of large public companies. Not only are they retained after fifty, but their remuneration continues to escalate as they grow older. And they are given greater responsibilities with challenging tasks and a vital role to play. Still, with many corporations, sixty-five remains the end point, after which retirement is mandatory. Only under special circumstances (such as partial ownership or control of the board of directors) will an individual be allowed to continue working.

The story regarding age also changes if a person owns a business, or has a major interest in it. Then he or she can continue working as long as desired, occasionally into his or her eighties or nineties. These people are also able to set their own schedules, working as hard as they want and tailoring their hours to meet their own needs. The viability of this kind of arrangement is affirmed by the fact that these businesses continue to be successful when run by older people, as age does not preclude the possibilities of hard work, innovation, and success. The same outcome is seen in both small and large businesses, retail outlets, and in the professions—law, medicine, accountancy, and so on. And in the arts, there have been numerous writers, artists, composers, performers, actors, and so on, who have been productive in their sixties and seventies, and even for decades afterward. As examples, Arthur Miller, who is in his eighties, is writing plays. Toscanni and Picasso were also in their eighties and still conducting and painting, respectively.

Because of the bias against older workers, not enough weight is given to the positive aspects of their performances in deciding whether to advance them, keep them when corporate restructuring occurs, or hire them when they are seeking new jobs. The work records of older employees generally shows less absenteeism and more reliability than those who are younger, and a greater loyalty to the companies for which they work.[6] They are usually more willing to go out of their way to help out when a crisis develops, for example, by working longer hours or overtime. In addition, they are better able to deal with other people than their younger counterparts, being less confrontational and more compassionate, understanding, and respectful. This is important in any position where they have to interface with the public, consumers, or other workers. Experience counts and should not be overlooked, whether it is in doing a specific job, or merely living one's life.

It should also be remembered that with the retirement of the baby boomers in the near future, there will be a shrinking workforce without enough younger workers. Corporations will have to turn to retirees and older workers to fill positions in order to maintain growth and profitability.[7] Companies perceived to have had an ageist bias may not be successful in their attempts to retain or attract seniors.

Rather than pushing them into retirement, corporations should value older workers and change the way they use them. Besides shifting them to positions that are less physically demanding and where they seem to function better, there could be more flexibility built into work schedules, according to the needs of the companies and the employees. This could lead to less time spent commuting and part-time work when desired.

Though forced retirement may be detrimental to the individuals involved, the question arises whether it benefits society in certain circumstances. For instance, in the universities there are a limited number of tenured positions. If these are held by professors past a retirement age, it does not allow junior people to develop and reach their full potential, and new ideas may not get as vigorous a hearing. A turnover of those at the top tends to stir up intellectual debate and is worthwhile for academic disciplines. Younger people have to know that opportunities will be there for them to move up the ladder. Similarly, corporations need to be invigorated periodically by new blood and new ideas. And that may entail appointing younger people to leadership positions, sometimes replacing older managers and bypassing other older employees. However, it is important for all to recognize that advancement will be on the basis of merit, and not because of either seniority or youth. Older workers must feel that opportunities are there for them as well, if they are up to the task.

In politics and government at least, age does not appear to be as much a liability as it is in other fields. Many politicians are elected to office in their sixties, seventies, and even occasionally their eighties. Rarely, some even play a role in their nineties, as did Strom Thurmond in the U.S. Senate. Actually, most of these people are reelected, rather than elected for the first time. It seems that in legislative positions, where seniority is an important determinant of power, the public is more willing to support older incumbent candidates. This is true in state and local governments as well as on the federal level. However, the movement toward term limits may prevent many older politicians from continuing in office, though the impetus behind this seems to be waning. In the executive branch of the federal government, many cabinet members serve and have served in their sixties and seventies, with their expertise overcoming any qualms about their ages.

Senator John Glenn is an example of what older people are capable of doing if they have the proper drive and attitude. In addition to being actively involved in the day-to-day business of the U.S. government in his seventy-seventh year, he became an astronaut again and was launched into space with the younger members of his team.[8] He was excited by the challenge of doing what no one else had done before, but also felt it was important to learn what effect space flight and weightlessness had on the physiology and bodily processes of an older person.[9]

GHETTOIZATION OF THE ELDERLY

Another way ageism manifests itself in our society is through the ghettoization of the elderly. While it is true that the desire of older individuals for separate housing has advanced this trend, it is at least partially because they are not made to feel comfortable living with younger people, who are likewise ill at ease with the elderly. Thus, both segments of society are responsible for segregating people on the basis of age and both segments lose out because of this. Some might say there is nothing wrong with this ghettoization since it is mostly voluntary, but it lessens the diversity in many communities and does not allow for enough discourse and interplay between generations. This leads to a lack of understanding of the hopes and needs of each group, and a tendency for each to stereotype and denigrate the other. Conflict thus becomes inevitable and more difficult to resolve.

By ghettoization, I am talking mainly about the huge retirement villages that have sprouted up in various areas, not the smaller complexes for older people in cities and towns that remain a part of the general community. The retirement villages contain hundreds or even thousands of homes or condominiums that cater exclusively to seniors. Because the elderly seem to be drawn to warmer climates, these are particularly prevalent in the Sun Belt (Florida and the rest of the Deep South, Arizona, New Mexico, Southern California), though they can be found everywhere. Their common characteristic is that younger people are not welcome to live there. The usual cutoff age for residents is fifty-five, though some may raise the bar even higher. (A younger spouse is acceptable, as long as one-half of the couple meets the age requirement.) While adult children of residents may also be allowed to live in these developments, younger children are prohibited. As an example of the ultimate in segregation by age, in March 1999, the residents of the Leisure World retirement community in California voted to turn their gated community into an incorporated city, with its own mayor and city council.[10] This city of 18,000, called "Laguna Woods," had an average age of seventy-seven, with more than 90 percent of the population over fifty-five.

The majority of the inhabitants of these retirement villages are white and middle-class, this usually occurring without any overt discrimination on the part of management. However, some do try to attract specific ethnic groups, or people from particular areas of the country, believing that their clients will be more comfortable with other people having similar backgrounds. Some complexes are also geared mainly to affluent residents, offering more luxurious homes or condominiums with other special amenities and pricing their products higher to ensure economic selectivity. There are also developments that aim their pitch at retired professionals like teachers, administrators, and the like who may not be wealthy but want to live in a nice community in a warm climate and are willing to forego some of the frills.

The actual physical and financial structure of these complexes varies. The living units may be in apartment houses, detached homes, or attached townhouses of one or two stories. Though the apartment houses have elevators, the two-story developments may contain walk-up units on the second floor (a potential problem as retirees get older).[11] Many of these communities are also gated and have guards. Residents may be required to purchase their units and then pay monthly maintenance charges, or they may have to rent the units, though other arrangements also exist. The corporations that have built these retirement havens are out to make a profit and generally charge whatever the market will bear.

The facilities in each community also differ widely. Many of them have swimming pools and tennis courts, while some of the larger and more expensive ones have private golf courses. Shuffleboard, bocce, and other similar games may be provided. A community center on the grounds that the residents can utilize is usually included as well, with meeting rooms, card rooms, and game rooms. In addition, small medical offices with a nurse and occasionally a doctor may be available, either around the clock or at specific hours. Lectures, movies, and concerts may be scheduled by the management or under the direction of an elected council of the residents. Some of the larger complexes have stores on the premises, or there may be shopping nearby that can be reached by car or private bus. With everything that is provided, many of these developments are self-contained to a great degree, so residents rarely have to venture into the outside world. This isolation translates into little interaction with other age groups or other social segments.

One may ask why these retirement villages continue to entice the elderly when the atmosphere appears to be so constricting. Notwithstanding the negative aspects, there are a number of reasons for their success. First is the attraction of warm climates for many older people. Moving to a strange part of the country, it is reassuring being in an environment with other individuals who are in the same circumstances. And as people age, they become less tolerant of chaos, noise, traffic, and so on, which makes the retirement communities more desirable. The protection offered by gating and security guards is also important for some seniors, with the recreational facilities and the breadth of activities as additional lures. Given the demise of the extended family and the fact that parents no longer live with or near their children, retirement communities offer a reasonable alternative. Here, people can form instant friendships with others their own age who have similar interests. And the ubiquity of modern transportation also makes communities in different areas of the country acceptable choices for the elderly. If they want to visit children, relatives, or old friends, they can hop on a plane and be anywhere in a few hours, or even drive to many regions of the country.

Though retirement villages are often appealing places to live for late middle-aged people, or the young-old, the luster may be lost as these individuals age further.[12] Some of the communities are really planned for healthy residents, and as people become more infirm, it may be difficult for them to live in this milieu. Climbing stairs, which was not an issue ten years earlier, may become a problem. There may be great distances between parts of the complex, and when a person is no longer able to drive, it may not be as simple to get around. Also the draw of golf, tennis, and other recreational activities disappears when chronic illnesses and disabilities must be dealt with; when vision fades, arthritis limits movement, and balance is impaired by cerebrovascular disease. In addition, there may not be adequate assistance provided for the tasks of daily living, when a person cannot manage alone because of disabilities. Many elderly people move out of these retirement communities in their later years, returning to their home towns where help may be more readily available, or they end up living near their adult children who can lend a hand when it is necessary.

In fact, there are many seniors who never consider retirement communities in the first place, but remain in their own homes. It is often the most affordable option for them, as well as a familiar, comfortable environment. Augmenting their decision, it is usually close to family and friends, and the support apparatus they have built up over the years. Many are also unwilling to endure the process of moving, with all the hassles that entails. And a significant percentage of older people want to remain part of the general community, rather than being segregated by age in a huge complex.

Perhaps more desirable than the major retirement villages are the smaller developments designed for seniors that are not as self-contained as the larger ones, with ten to perhaps one hundred residents. Being modest in scale and located within conventional cities and towns, they are not meant to be separate from the surrounding communities, and their residents are not as isolated from the rest of the populace. Shopping, recreation, and entertainment occur off the premises and there is communication with different social groups and individuals of every age. In these smaller facilities, the elderly get to live with others who have similar needs and problems, which can be addressed by the management and staff, yet they are not sequestered from the outside world in an age-based ghetto. Both older people and society win in this type of arrangement.

A type of retirement community that has been overlooked by many people though it meets the needs of seniors and society at large is the so-called NORC (naturally occurring retirement community).[13] These are mostly large developments or apartment houses that were built decades ago as affordable housing in urban settings, where the population has remained in place as it aged. Now, a considerable proportion of the residents of these developments are older and retired, many with special needs. Programs have been devised in some of these complexes to meet those needs, providing various services. These include community centers for seniors with recreational facilities, help with transportation, nurses, Meals on Wheels, and social services. Remaining in familiar, comfortable settings, people can go from youth to middle age to old age in these NORCs, with appropriate care as they grow older.

There are many suburban towns, particularly affluent ones, with policies that are destined to drive seniors away. Older people who have lived in these towns for decades, often with their mortgages paid off, have been seeing their taxes rise astronomically to pay for the rise in education budgets because of additional children in families who are recent arrivals. These seniors on fixed incomes are subsidizing the school systems with their taxes, with education frequently the preponderant part of the town's expenditures. Even those older people who are moderately well-off may have difficulty handling the new and onerous financial burdens. Thus, they wind up selling their homes and moving to condominiums or homes in less expensive areas. In their stead, more new families with children move in, pushing more older people out. But the majority of townspeople seem indifferent to this pattern.

On the other hand, in the last few years, some suburban towns with the opposite philosophy have been trying to enjoin seniors from moving away by reducing their taxes, providing free or discounted public transportation, medical screening, senior centers, and so on.[14] The administrators of these towns realize that seniors are an asset to their communities and that it is important to have age diversity in their population. But the major reason for trying to retain older people is economic. There is understanding in these towns that the cost of tax abatement and services to seniors is cheaper than having additional children in the school system.

THE MEDIA AND THE ELDERLY

The media has reinforced ageism in recent years by portraying seniors in an unfairly deprecatory manner. As an example:

In 1988, the image of the "Greedy Geezer" was born. Depicted on the cover of the *New Republic* magazine, the advancing army of angry-faced older persons wielding garden trowels, fishing poles, and golf clubs looked menacing, poised to assault America. The essay inside by Henry Fairlie described what the cover expressed visually: Older people are selfish and drain the country of resources that might otherwise be chan-neled elsewhere, especially to children. There have been other similar negative attacks on older people in this country.[15]

The media both reflects society's bias against the elderly and contributes to the perpetuation of offensive stereotypes that reinforces this bias. Aside from celebrities, or special achievements by senior citizens (including just living to a very old age), the news media, both in print and on television, tend to focus on the problems of older people, depicting them as feeble, demented, ill in various ways, and unable to manage their own lives. The elderly are almost never shown in a favorable light and there are few stories about older indi-viduals who have dealt successfully with aging, perhaps living a mundane but independent existence. News reports may describe scandalous conditions in the nursing homes, where helpless elderly patients are mistreated. Or may present the details about an injudicious older person who was a victim of a crime, or some sort of scam. Or show old people who died of dehydration during a heat wave. Or a senior who had an auto accident because the wrong pedal was pressed. Or a new treatment for Alzheimer's disease or Parkinson's disease that may help the afflicted, with images of these patients tottering about. All of these reports show the elderly as pitiful, helpless, or foolish, and certainly not worthy of respect, or admiration. And there are few salutary tales to counteract these characterizations.

There are also scarcely any films or television programs made for or about older people.[16] If an older person is seen in a film it is generally in a peripheral role, not as a central character. Whereas young children, teenagers, adults, or even animals are depicted performing heroic acts in the movies or on television, seniors are almost never presented in this fashion. In fact, when they are seen, it is often as fools, or comic figures, or being out of touch and not understanding the situation at hand, or even as evil schemers, again reinforcing society's biased view. The target audience for movies and television are teenagers and young adults, and the content of these productions is what the media executives believe this audience likes. Thus, action, violence, sex, and visual effects are favored over coherent stories, and the elderly rarely have roles to play. Part of the problem may be that the people who make the movies and television shows and those who control the purse strings—the writers, directors, producers, and advertising and network executives—are rarely in their sixties and seventies, with the sensibilities and perceptions common to this age group.

Older people do have money to spend and would go to the movies more frequently and be more interested in television programs if the offerings had themes that were more appealing to them, perhaps even about some of them and the lives they lead. They would also be more likely to respond to media advertising promoting fashionable clothes and other items if older models were used instead of the characteristic unblemished bodies of the young. Some leaders in the fashion industry are beginning to understand this and have been displaying their clothes on senior models, receiving favorable publicity for their "innovative" stances.[17]

CRIME AND THE ELDERLY

The prevalence of crimes against the elderly, who are our most vulnerable citizens, is a further sign of the insensitivity, lack of respect, and lack of caring by the rest of society toward older people. Because some of them are disabled in various ways and slow to react to unexpected attacks, or not as discerning as they once were and, thus, more trusting of strangers, the younger criminal element views them as "easy pickings." And because of society's ageist bias, the predators can almost rationalize their behavior, seeing their victims as not needing their money or possessions because they are old.

Crimes directed against the elderly can either be physical in nature, or fraudulent and "white collar." The usual physical crimes that the general public encounters, such as robbery, burglary, muggings, and the like, are also common among seniors, perhaps occurring with even greater frequency in this population. The felon knows that old people generally will not fight back and does not see them as any sort of threat, or deterrent, knowing that they are afraid of even minor trauma. Two types of physical crimes are visited more often on the elderly than the public at large and usually occur in urban settings. The first are purse snatchings where the thief will suddenly rip a purse from an unsuspecting victim and run away, sometimes disappearing into a crowd. The thief realizes that once he is out of sight he is home free, since an old woman cannot give chase. This ordinarily does not result in any harm to the victim unless she offers resistance or will not give up the purse. At times however, the victim can be thrown to the ground as the purse is wrestled away and this can cause a serious injury or even death to a feeble individual. The second type of crime has been designated as "push-ins." In this kind of assault, the perpetrator follows the elderly person home, usually into an apartment building or walk-up. As soon as the victim takes out the key and opens the door to his or her apartment, the felon pushes him or her inside and follows, closing the door behind them. The victim is terrified as he or she is threatened with physical force, a knife, or a gun, as cash and valuables are demanded. With just the fall from the initial push-in, a hip, wrist, or ribs may be broken, but the person may be beaten as well, even if he or she complies with the demands. This is the most cowardly of acts and robs people not only of valuables, but of any feelings of security they might have had in their homes and neighborhoods.

Fraud and scams directed at seniors take a number of different forms, with the realization by the criminal that many older people are not knowledgeable about economic matters. Because they are trusting and unable to analyze financial claims properly, Ponzi schemes and con games are frequently accepted at face value when pitched at the elderly. Some have been known to give away part or all of their life savings to strangers in response to promises of impossible returns. Worthless penny stocks and phony home improvement schemes have also been used to flimflam them, and sweepstakes companies and telemarketing pitches offering extravagant prizes have preyed on the elderly for years, bilking some individuals out of thousands of dollars.[18] The devastation wrought by these unscrupulous criminals on the elderly is immeasurable, since these people no longer have the opportunity to recoup their losses, and it is usually the less affluent and unsophisticated who suffer the most. And irrespective of their own feelings of inadequacy and stupidity, they are also made to feel quite foolish by others around them for what they have done. In addition, they may not know what steps to take to seek redress, making it more likely the criminal will go unpunished.

Whether the crime is physical or white collar, it takes a tremendous emotional toll on the victims, stripping away people's dignity and self-esteem. And society does not take the necessary measures to deter these types of incidents and offer the elderly sufficient protection.

AGEIST JOKES

Social attitudes toward the elderly and the bias that is endemic in our culture is reflected in the ageist jokes that are delivered by stand-up comedians, imparted in the movies and on television sitcoms, passed from person to person, and circulated on the Internet. These anecdotes generally denigrate and ridicule the elderly and their infirmities, focusing on the problems that are inherent in growing old. Characteristics are usually exaggerated and the incongruity of the situation makes it seem funny, but it is also an attack on the dignity of older people. This type of distasteful humor is similar to racist, ethnic, or sexist jokes and is hurtful to those who are the butt of the jokes. However, since aging is a universal condition and everyone will pass through the same stages of life (unless they die prematurely), young people should consider that they too will have the same infirmities as the elderly at some point and think twice about disparaging seniors with their ageist jokes. On the other hand, if an older person tells a joke about aging, it should not be discouraged. Joking about one's problems is a way to deal with pain, and it is good to be able to laugh at yourself and be self-deprecating.

Many of the ageist jokes focus on the sexual difficulties of the elderly, their bowel or urinary problems, hearing loss, or their memory and cognitive decline. Though many books could be filled with these jokes, a few examples will be illuminating.

Jack and Lucy have been dating at their assisted living residence and Jack thinks it's time to make a move.

"Lucy, why don't we go upstairs and have some sex," he asks her at dinner one day.

"Jack, at my age we can only do one or the other."

Jim who is 92 and Margaret who is 89 are excited about their decision to get married. They go for a stroll to discuss the wedding and pass a drugstore. At Jim's suggestion, they go in and he addresses the man behind the counter who is wearing a white coat.

Jim: "We're about to get married. Do you sell heart medication?"

Pharmacist: "Of course we do."

Jim: "Medicine for circulation?"

Pharmacist: "All kinds."

Jim: "Medicine for rheumatism?"

Pharmacist: "Definitely."

Jim: "How about Viagra?"

Pharmacist: "Of course."

Jim: "Medicine for memory problems, arthritis, Parkinson's disease?"

Pharmacist: "Yes. A large variety. The works."

Jim: "What about vitamins, sleeping pills?"

Pharmacist: "Absolutely."

Jim: "You sell wheelchairs and walkers."

Pharmacist: "All kinds."

Jim looks at Margaret, then addresses the pharmacist again. "Can we register here for our wedding gifts?"

Young child pointing to old gray-haired woman approaching her and her playmate. "Here comes my grandma."

Second child. "She can't be your grandma. Grandmas are blond."

An elderly man is at home in bed dying. He smells his favorite chocolate chip cookies being baked and wants one last cookie before he dies. Falling out of bed, he crawls to the landing, rolls down the stairs, and crawls into the kitchen where his wife is baking. With waning strength, he is barely able to lift his arm to the cookie sheet. As he grasps a warm, moist chocolate chip cookie, his wife suddenly wacks his hand with a spatula.

"Why?" he whispers as he drops the cookie. "Why did you do that?"

"Those're for the funeral."

An older couple is playing golf in the club championship. They are in a playoff and the wife has to make a six-inch putt. Trembling, she takes her stance, putts and misses, and they lose the match. On the way home in the car, her husband is fuming.

"I can't believe you missed that putt," he snarls. "It was no longer than my willy."

His wife looks over at him and smiles. "Yes dear," she says. "But it was much harder."

Acquainting himself with an elderly woman who was a patient in the hospital, the young doctor asked, "How long have you been bedridden?"

The woman looked confused and flustered. "Why not for twenty-five years when my husband was alive," she answered.

Perhaps there is an element of denial in the young people who tell these ageist jokes, with the belief that if they laugh about these situations, it won't happen to them. However, age and its problems are inescapable, and whistling in the dark offers no protection. On the other hand, a positive attitude and behaving in certain ways can make a difference.

7

TAKING CHARGE

Strategies in the Quest for Dignity and Vitality

•

Chase after money and security
and your heart will never unclench.
Care about other people's approval
and you will be their prisoner.

—LAO-TZU
TAO TE CHING

Keeping our dignity and spirit as we age is not easy given the multitude of factors arrayed to destroy self-esteem and self-respect in older people, tearing down those protective walls constructed brick by brick over the years. Nonetheless, most older people can retain their dignity and control their lives if they are willing to work to preserve them. To make success more likely, there are issues that should be understood and steps that should be taken.

ACCEPTANCE OF THE AGING PROCESS

On some level, each of us tries to deny our own aging, thinking that somehow it will be different for us, while knowing it will not be. One of the essential elements for all of us in holding on to dignity is to accept the aging process as inevitable; not doing things that make us seem foolish as we attempt to ward off the hands of time. That does not mean we should remain passive and allow age to conquer us without resistance. Instead, we should choose our battles selectively, in places where the terrain is favorable to us and we have some advantages. We should also have realistic goals and, preferably, act in ways that are consonant with nature's methods.

In our society where youth is inordinately favored and age stigmatized, it is little wonder that people will go to great lengths and spend large sums of money to look young. On television, radio, and in the print media, we are constantly bombarded by pitchmen (usually handsome or beautiful specimens) telling us to buy this or that product—from vitamins and dietary supplements to exercise machines to skin care oils and creams to items of clothing—to help us appear and feel young. Advertising agencies know there is a strong market for any merchandise that claims to help people remain youthful. In recent years, we have also seen numerous advertisements that advocate different types of cosmetic surgery and special procedures to reverse the aging process, like BOTOX and collagen injections to eliminate wrinkles. What are reasonable steps for us to take in the pursuit of youth and where do we step over the line and invite ridicule? Of course, the decisions must be personal depending on each man and woman's insecurities and needs, and there are no right or wrong paths. But sometimes we make choices that cause others to question our actions and that we ourselves may question later on.

In general, it is important for each of us to look as good as we can, for that promotes healthy feelings of pride and self-worth. And our looks are also our introduction to other people, even before we speak. While the substance of a person is not necessarily reflected in what we see superficially, dress and appearance do tell us something about that individual and we do make judgments on that basis. Both for ourselves and others, we should be clean and neat and dress well. However, we should not go to extreme lengths in an attempt to seem younger than we are. Looking good does not necessarily mean looking young. Ideally, it means being as physically fit as we can be, with our weight within a moderate range, neither too obese nor too thin, with appropriate hairstyles and dress for our age. The question then arises, What is appropriate dress or hairstyle in relation to age? The answer is that there is not a specific mode or fashion we should adhere to, but a range of dress in terms of what seems right from an esthetic standpoint. For example, a woman of seventy with wrinkled skin and prominent veins in her legs should not wear short skirts like a twenty-year-old, but could buy pants that might also appeal to a younger person.

Though one should not be a slave to fashion, there is nothing wrong with being stylish if one enjoys it and it has always been part of one's life. It is also okay to have your own unique style and make a statement about who you are, as long as you do not take it too seriously and denigrate others who are less stylish. And it is not necessary to spend huge amounts of money on clothes in an attempt to be fashionable, as style is merely putting things together in a way that makes people look interesting. Of course it is more of a challenge to cultivate style when you have less money; where creativity and innovation become critical. (I have a woman in my practice in her seventies who barely gets by on Social Security, but always looks like she just stepped out of the pages of *Vogue*, with chic haircuts and creative ensembles.) There are numerous women over sixty, or even much older, who are interested in dressing well but bemoan the lack of options available to them, as designers seem to ignore this demographic group.[1] There are 32 million women in this market, many of them affluent and willing to spend if they can find clothing that appeals to them.

The use of makeup by women is also a subjective choice, including whether to use it, what type, how much, and where. Unfortunately, makeup is not always applied properly. Excessive facial powder in some circumstances accentuates wrinkles rather than hiding them, bringing about the opposite effect of what was intended. Older women may also have problems with vision that result in difficulties in utilizing makeup. Lipstick and eye shadow may be smeared or wander onto adjoining areas of the face, which can be unsightly.

Most measures that have been promoted to retard the effects of aging, such as special skin creams, oils, or nutritional supplements that are sold over the counter, have not been shown to be of particular value. However, the application of retinoic acid to the skin does seem to reverse some of the changes of photoaging, though it also can produce an inflammation that usually improves over time. Other compounds are available as well that appear encouraging in counteracting the consequences of aging on the skin, but all need to be used under a physician's supervision.

There are no exercise machines that have been proven to have special merit in reducing abdominal paunches, heavy thighs, and so forth as we grow older. However, any aerobic exercise in itself is worthwhile. There are also no pills promising "girth control" that do not have unacceptable side effects.

Cosmetic Surgery

As techniques improve and the downside risks lessen, cosmetic surgery is being enlisted as an ally by more and more seniors (and younger people) in the battle against aging. Asking the question again of what is sensible and what is not, again it must be answered on an individual basis, influenced by our desires and expectations. The procedures offered include face lifts to erase wrinkles, removal of redundant skin in the eyelids and around the eyes, removal of excess skin underneath the chin, cutting away skin and fat in the abdomen and thighs, removal of age spots or other blemishes, liposuction to reduce fatty tissue, stripping away varicose veins from the legs, and hair transplants. BOTOX injections and collagen injections can also eliminate wrinkles, but must be repeated periodically. Chemical peels, dermabrasion, and laser surgery can be employed as well to improve the skin's appearance.

There is little criticism of those procedures that remove a disfiguring blemish, but others that attempt to reverse the tide of aging, where vanity alone may be the motivation, are more controversial. However, for those people whose self-esteem is related to their physical facade and who suffer greatly when they look in the mirror and see the ravages of time, cosmetic surgery may provide relief. Some may argue that the positive effects of the procedures are only transient and that the advances of age are inexorable. So why go through these painful operations when age will ultimately eradicate the results and possibly even make things worse. Then a second or even third operation may be necessary, with the outcome a little bit less satisfactory each time. And even the initial procedure may not produce the anticipated results, leaving facial features that seem artificial and skin that is stretched too tight. But it may be worth it for those who are emotionally distraught over the consequences of aging and willing to take the risks. Another caveat is whether the person is able to afford the procedure, for the exorbitant cost is another aspect of cosmetic surgery that must be factored into the equation. In addition, the fees must be paid out of pocket, as health insurance will not cover these types of operation. There are people who will borrow thousands of dollars to have one of these procedures in the hope it will make them look younger. There are even loan companies who specialize in this type of financing, if adequate collateral is available.

Inappropriate Behavior

Our actions may also indicate whether we have come to terms with growing older and, if inappropriate, can lead to a loss of dignity. Again, there is a range of behavior at various ages that is considered acceptable and if one wanders too far out of that range, eyebrows may be raised, snickers may be heard, and one may look ridiculous. Age is not, however, the sole determinant of behavior; geographic region, urban or rural locale, educational status, and ethnic background are among other factors that help set the norm.

The area of greatest conflict in terms of behavior as we age revolves around sexuality. (This subject will be discussed further later in this chapter.) To a large degree, our society expects its older members to be asexual and when they act out in various ways that would be sanctioned in a younger person, they are castigated. If a single older man and older woman somehow connect and become a couple, the rest of society sees them as "cute" when they hold hands or hug each other, even though it is perfectly natural activity that would not warrant a second look if they were in their twenties or thirties.

While sexual indiscretions and affairs are common patterns of behavior in the young, they also occur in the older population, more frequently among middle-aged married men and women, and rarely in the elderly. For some, it is a last fling; an attempt to affirm youth, sexual attractiveness, and virility. But it is not only about sexuality and youthfulness. Some men also see it as a validation of their power, and proof that they have "made it" and are successful. The affairs may be a passing need during a particular period that a strong marriage can weather, or they may lead to separation and divorce, depending on the circumstances. Even if the marriage survives, strains in the relationship, including a lack of trust, inevitably result and may persist for years.

Some people are also surprised when they see older couples dancing, particularly when they are doing a fast number, or their bodies are moving sensuously during a slow piece. Society's vision is still of old people who are feeble and infirm, and do not participate in "youthful" activities. But many seniors find dancing a lot of fun and almost liberating in some ways. Ballroom dancing, square dancing, and even competitive dancing are increasing in popularity and gaining more and more adherents among the older crowd, notwithstanding the raised eyebrows of the young.

Exercise or competitive sports by older people may also be derided by those who are younger, who may be unsettled by seeing sagging bodies in shorts and tank tops, and do not see it as normal behavior for seniors. Not only is it healthy for older people to be active physically, but being fit enhances their pride and self-esteem, and should be encouraged. (This will also be discussed later.)

Alcohol and Drugs

Abuse of alcohol by middle-aged and elderly people, both men and women, is a potential recipe for forfeiture of dignity. Often, the intemperate use of alcohol began earlier in life and continues with aging. Older individuals may drink in secret and keep their addiction hidden, may drink openly and deny their dependence, or may not care about society's reprobation. For some, excessive drinking may be a sign of depression and a general unhappiness with life, an unwillingness as well to acknowledge that they are growing older. It may also help the drinker escape feelings of inadequacy and failure; the realization that life has not turned out as he or she had hoped. In addition, it allows him or her to escape dealing with various problems. Escape is the key word for alcoholics, who want to avoid facing reality. But once a person is addicted to alcohol, there are two problems to solve instead of one: changing the reality he or she tried to escape and coping with the addiction itself. Some seniors who were not problem drinkers, become so after the loss of a mate, when living may not seem worthwhile to them and they literally try to drown their sorrows. Other changes in life situations, such as retirement, or children moving away, may increase drinking as well.

Many elderly alcoholics also have difficulties bonding with people and are unable to express their feelings, or get close to others. Drinking alienates them from their families and friends, allowing them to avoid the intimacy that is part of normal relationships. While alcoholism is often blamed for the breakup of marriages and the end of relationships, at times it may be a symptom of preexisting problems, rather then the cause itself.

Drinking wine or other alcoholic beverages in moderation is a pleasurable experience for many individuals and can be beneficial in terms of decreasing stress levels and coronary artery disease.[2] It is the abuse of alcohol, not social drinking, that is dangerous. However, older people must be vigilant even when drinking moderately if they are taking medications, as harmful interactions may occur.

As previously mentioned, the misuse of prescription drugs, particularly sedatives and minor tranquilizers, occurs not infrequently among seniors. Most of those who take excessive amounts of these drugs deny their addiction to themselves and to others, though some are quite aware of what they are doing. The reasons for their drug abuse are the same as those for alcohol.

Detoxification and rehabilitation for either alcohol or drugs is usually quite difficult for older people (as well as for those who are younger). Special medications may be necessary during withdrawal to prevent seizures and DTs (delerium tremens). To be successful in the long run, individual and group therapy is important, including support groups such as Alcoholics Anonymous. Families must also learn how to deal effectively with this condition and organizations such as Al-Anon may be helpful in this regard. However, a person must be properly motivated and truly want to stop in order to achieve abstinence.

Marijuana, although illegal, is used at times by some seniors, particularly those influenced by the culture of the sixties. It helps people relax, improves socialization, and can heighten sexual pleasure. If tried occasionally, it appears to be safe, though intemperate usage may affect memory and can also lead to pulmonary problems.

Inappropriate behavior by those who are cognitively impaired or psychotic and also abusing alcohol presents a different type of dilemma than in intact individuals, since they may be unable to control their actions. Substance abuse in these people may be even more refractory to treatment.

PHYSICAL FITNESS AND HEALTH

Achieving and maintaining a decent level of physical fitness and remaining as healthy as we can are extremely important factors in preserving dignity and vitality as we age.

Exercise

The evidence supporting the value of exercise in terms of reducing various diseases and overall mortality is overwhelming to the point that people who avoid physical activity do so at their own peril.[3] Exercise greatly reduces the chances of becoming diabetic as well as developing atherosclerotic vascular disease and hypertension. And not only is survival enhanced by exercise, but disability rates are lessened and overall quality of life is improved. While any level of exercise is beneficial, a graded inverse relationship has been shown to exist between physical activity and all-cause mortality; that is, the more a person exercises, the lower his or her death rate.[4]

Everyone's capabilities vary as far as exercise is concerned, depending on genetic predisposition as well as past illnesses, accidents, and so on. But within the constraints imposed on us, we should all try to be physically fit. By this I do not mean training to become world-class athletes in seniors' or masters' competition, but rather seeing to it that we stay in shape aerobically and do not have limitations in our daily activities because of neglect and indifference. Exercise and sports are used by many older people in an attempt to improve their appearance, but the benefits are far greater than that and should be part of everyone's daily regimen. The actual routine followed can be individualized and changed at will, but should never be omitted, for otherwise, physical deconditioning invariably occurs.

I advise my patients to engage in aerobic activity for a minimum of thirty minutes each day, though an hour, or even more, is preferable. In fact, the guidelines issued by the Institute of Medicine, the medical division of the

National Academies, is for everyone to exercise for at least an hour every day.[5] Of course, for those who are working, time can be a major hindrance. Repetitive, mindless exercise is the desirable mode, where one does not have to think about what is being done. (Competitive sports, while enjoyable, serve somewhat different purposes. They are more likely to cause injuries and increase stress levels for many participants. This is not to suggest that competitive sports be eliminated for older people, but it should be done in addition to aerobic exercise, dispensing with the latter on the days one competes in athletic contests.) Weight training, or musculoskeletal resistance training is also beneficial in terms of improving strength, balance, and coordination, and reducing osteoporosis, but this does not negate the need for aerobic workouts.[6] When initiating any type of exercise program at an older age, it is a good idea to have a medical checkup first to be sure there are no contraindications. It is also prudent to begin any activities slowly, gradually advancing both distance and speed until your objectives are attained. Then occasionally, you can try going a little bit faster or a little bit farther just to test yourself.

Exercise equals empowerment for all of us. It gives us an opportunity to exert some control over our lives and our health; doing something we know is good for us. Feelings of pride and self-worth are also generated when we exercise, knowing that many people are incapable of willing themselves to work out regularly as we are doing.

Brisk walking is an excellent exercise for most individuals. The potential for injury is minimal, as there is little impact and your feet barely leave the ground. The speed at which you should walk depends on your overall physical condition, not your chronological age. Walking a mile in fifteen to seventeen minutes is excellent, but any rate is beneficial. (Some seniors are able to cover a mile in twelve minutes while others may take twenty or more.) It is helpful to find a course that interests you and measure it with your car's odometer or a pedometer. You can go in a circle, or return on your original route to get back to your starting point. Some people like to walk the same course every day, while others constantly change their itinerary. Four miles daily is a worthwhile goal, but not feasible for everyone. If you have the time and discipline to do more, so much the better. The key word is discipline.

Running or jogging is also a good aerobic activity, though it results in more injuries than walking. Many people who were runners when they were younger switch to walking as they age because of musculoskeletal problems. The main advantage of running is that you can achieve the benefits of walking in less time. The same amount of calories is burned per mile and the cardiovascular protection is the same. (A 154-pound person will expend about 110 calories for every mile traveled, walking or running, no matter the speed at which the distance is covered.) As with walking, when running, it is helpful to find a route, or routes, you like, perhaps adding or subtracting distance here or there. Some people prefer to utilize a treadmill indoors for their workouts, watching television or listening to the news while they exercise. Others use a treadmill only when the weather precludes outdoor activity. It makes no difference where the exercise is done, as long as it is done regularly.

I personally prefer walking outside, unless the weather is really miserable. Heavy rain, snow, or ice, or the extremes of heat or cold keep me indoors. Being outside in the fresh air is invigorating, with the changing environment stimulating all the senses. It is wonderful watching the evolution of the seasons and the transformation of the trees and vegetation, as they are clothed and unclothed, going from green to pastel colors to bare, then starting the cycle all over again. I also like the early morning, before the day begins for most of the world, being part of the cold darkness in the winter and the sunrises that come earlier and earlier until the heat of summer, then recede again. When you are outside, it also provides an opportunity for brief interactions with other people, as you pass one another on the road, comrades-in-arms fighting the same good fight. Finding a partner who will share the time with you also makes the miles pass more quickly.

Bike riding is another form of exercise that meets the necessary criteria. This also can be done outdoors, indoors, or both. (Three miles biking is roughly equivalent to a mile walking or running.) Other types of mindless, repetitive activity include swimming, jumping rope, rowing, and cross-country skiing. There are also various kinds of machines that have been devised to enhance cardiovascular fitness and burn calories, which can be used only inside. In-line skating is very popular with younger people, but more dangerous for those who are older, with a greater predilection for broken bones.

Resting a day each week is suggested by many exercise physiologists, but cutting down on mileage and slowing your speed for a day may also be restorative. Cross training, that is, trying different exercises on a regular basis, such as walking four days a week and bike riding three days a week, may also be worthwhile in terms of utilizing different muscle groups and limiting injuries.

To derive the most benefit from an exercise regimen it is necessary to have an ongoing commitment and be disciplined. Without these elements, success will be elusive. Having a hard and fast daily schedule that is followed fairly rigorously is a significant step forward. If you exercise at the same time every day, it becomes easier after a while and eventually becomes almost automatic. For a number of reasons, I believe early morning is the best time. You are less likely to be fatigued, since you are just awakening from sleep and other activities are less likely to interfere. Later in the day, things frequently come up that must be dealt with. An additional reason is that the brain produces endorphin in response to sustained physical exertion and the levels of this chemical remain elevated for a number of hours after exercise. Thus, by exercising earlier in the day, we reap the benefits of endorphins while we are awake. (This will be discussed shortly.)

Another way to improve conditioning is to alter normal patterns of activity and do small amounts of exercise whenever possible during the day. By this I mean walking up the stairs instead of taking the elevator if it is feasible. Also walking or riding a bike to do errands instead of using a car. If you play golf, walk and carry or pull your golf clubs rather than riding in a cart. All of these add up to improved physical fitness.

You may be still asking the questions, What do I get by including exercise in my daily routine? Is it worth my commitment? The answer is a resounding *yes* for every moment devoted to physical activity for the reasons I will discuss.

From the standpoint of health, cardiovascular disease is significantly diminished by regular exercise. It can lower blood pressure and cholesterol, as well as control or prevent diabetes in some people. A sedentary lifestyle and obesity are risk factors for heart attacks, strokes, and peripheral vascular disease that can be reduced by physical activity. Osteoporosis is also delayed or prevented in individuals who do weight-bearing exercise and immune function may be enhanced. Interestingly, there is some evidence that suggests that various types of orthopedic problems are lessened by frequent exercise, though one would expect the opposite to be true. And there are even some reports that the risk of dementia is reduced by exercise.

Emotional health is also improved by exercise. The endorphins that are generated act as a natural tranquilizer, painkiller, and possibly antidepressant as well. Because of this, stress and anxiety can be reduced by aerobic activity, which may be similar to meditation in terms of its relaxant effect. Studies have also shown that mild to moderate depression can be alleviated by exercise, with response rates comparable to or better than psychotherapy or medication.

Weight training should supplement aerobic activity in all older people. This can be done with free weights or with resistance machines.

The Surgeon General recommends the following strength training routine for people over the age of 50:

- 8 to 12 exercises engaging the major muscle groups;
- 8 to 15 repetitions performed to fatigue or a level perceived as "comfortably hard";
- 1 set;
- 2 times per week.[7]

Strength and stamina can be built up over a short period of time and the program should only require twenty minutes or so twice a week, a good investment in maintaining health. There are other exercises aimed at improving posture and balance that can also be performed regularly, with directions available from physicians, physical therapists, and the like. By working out in a gym or fitness center, both aerobic exercise and weight training can be opportunities for socialization and companionship, which is important for some and makes the process more enjoyable.

Exercise empowers older people, improving their ability to care for themselves and allowing them to remain independent longer. And contrary to what many people believe, it is never too late to begin a conditioning program, no matter how old you are and how sedentary you have been. In an interesting research study, frail nursing home residents with an average age of 87.9 years were started on a schedule of strength training for an eight-week period. There was a dramatic improvement in strength, walking, and functional ability by the end of the program.[8]

People who are physically active look better than their peers and generally feel better about themselves. The burning of extra calories helps keep their weight down and allows them to enjoy eating without feeling guilty. With more discretionary time available to us after retirement and our children gone, it is certainly possible for each of us to devote an hour daily to our bodies for physical fitness. Though it may be harder to exercise as we get older (particularly for those who have not done it before), it is important for all of us.

Masters' competitions are only for those who are fanatical about their training regimen and enjoy competition. If it adds excitement to someone's life and is not dangerous, there is no reason not to do it. (Medical clearance is particularly important for seniors who push themselves to their upper limits in competitive events.) Aside from the various racquet sports, track and field events and swimming have regular masters competitions. The training for these events ensures a high level of fitness and is even more important than the competition itself. While most people feel golf is also a sport, conditioning and aerobic training play no role in performance on the golf course and it is really more of a game than a sport. This is not to negate the skill involved and the pleasure derived by those who love golf, but it is not a substitute for daily physical exercise.

Nutrition

Many older people neglect their diets, eating haphazardly and not always adhering to an adequate, balanced food intake. This occurs more often when a person lives alone and either does not want to be bothered with shopping and cooking, or is simply unable to manage it because of physical, cognitive, or emotional problems. Sometimes, older people get by with cereal, candy, or snack foods for every meal, which requires no preparation and alleviates hunger, but does not provide essential nutrients. Whatever the reason, if the dietary depletion is severe enough, it can result in malnutrition and damage to various organ systems as well as a greater susceptibility to a number of different diseases. This is why Meals on Wheels and similar programs that cater to the homebound elderly are vitally important to the recipients' well being.

As the converse of dietary deficiency, overeating and obesity are also major health hazards in America where a high percentage of the population is overweight and sedentary.[9] The increasing popularity of fast foods and greater intake of foods with high fat and carbohydrate content play a major role. Because many people reduce their levels of activity as they age, the vulnerability to obesity becomes greater with the same or increased caloric intake. And obesity is a major risk factor for diabetes, atherosclerosis, and some cancers, reducing life expectancy significantly.[10] In addition to heightened risk for illnesses, obesity also exacts an emotional toll, with poor self-image and loss of self-confidence in those who are overweight. It also causes greater difficulties for people who may already have impaired balance and lack of energy and stamina. There are only two ways for anyone to shed pounds: either reduce caloric intake by eating less or burn up more calories through increased exercise.

Dietary supplements have become increasingly popular in recent years for older people, purporting to provide more energy and vitality for those who are fatigued or weak. There are also formulas to enhance sexual performance, cognitive ability, or just about any function that declines normally as part of aging. Some of the supplements are food substitutes, others are herbal mixtures, special vitamins, vegetable derivatives, and other types of nutritional additives. There is no persuasive evidence that these are of any value for those who eat a well-balanced diet, though taking a multiple vitamin, folic acid, and moderate doses of vitamin E are probably worthwhile. (Vitamin E is an antioxidant and is thought to be of possible benefit in retarding the development of atherosclerosis, some types of cancer, Alzheimer's disease, Parkinson's disease, and the effects of aging.) Vitamin D and calcium may also be required for those with osteoporosis. While food supplements under medical supervision may be helpful for individuals whose nutritional intake is deficient, they do not appear to be necessary for the population at large.

Medical Care

Medical checkups with appropriate treatment and follow-up for illnesses also aids in maintaining health and fitness as we grow older. The utility of a routine physical examination itself is somewhat controversial, but there are some elements of a checkup that are important. These include measuring blood pressure, lipid and cholesterol profiles, blood sugar, and hemoglobin levels on an annual basis, along with a PSA and a digital rectal exam for men. Colonoscopy should be performed periodically in both sexes in addition to mammography in women, though the frequency of these procedures remains in question. The need for pap smears in older women is also a matter of debate. A flu shot should be obtained by seniors every year prior to flu season, as deaths from influenza have increased significantly in the past twenty-five years in those who are sixty-five and older.[11]

Another aspect of the regular physical is establishing a relationship with a physician. You must be certain you are comfortable with your doctor and can discuss the intimate details of your problems with this person. If you are uneasy in any way, you should try someone else since this individual is going to be responsible for critical decisions involving your life. Your physician should also be familiar with your wishes about death and dying, and should possess your advance directives. You must have confidence in your physician's intelligence and knowledge, respecting the way his or her practice is conducted. Once you are ill and under his or her care, like changing horses in midstream, it is much more troublesome to make a switch.

Aside from well-care and routine examinations, your physician is there to investigate and treat your illnesses, perhaps with the assistance of specialists in particular areas. He or she may order tests and then initiate therapy when a diagnosis has been made. Dealing with any disorder entails a continuous dialogue between doctor and patient, with the latter not only detailing the symptoms of the disease, but also the response to medications and any side effects that may develop. Too often difficulties occur because of denial of illness by an individual, or noncompliance with the regimen prescribed. To maximize any doctor's effectiveness, the dialogue must go on and if the patient does not follow instructions, he or she must discuss that failure with the physician and agree on a course of action. Lying to the doctor or ignoring the problem with the hope it will go away are not acceptable alternatives.

If communication is not there, or a person is unwilling to engage in a frank exchange with his or her physician, there is no point in wasting the doctor's time and that person's money.

SEXUALITY

That older people have sexual needs and desires is not an issue our society is yet willing to address openly, though there is some work in this area by medical professionals and therapists that is starting to disseminate to the lay public. For the most part, all religions ignore this subject, while emphasizing the prohibition against adultery and sex outside of marriage. Hollywood and the entertainment media do not feature stories about romantic love between septuagenarians, nor do they show older men and women engaged in any type of sexual activity. Unlike the sexual habits of younger people (particularly celebrities), it is not something the news programs on television want to investigate and is not a frequent topic of discourse at dinner parties. (However, the introduction of Viagra has made the news media at least look at sexuality among older people and has made it more acceptable for discussion sans snickering.) But because society has chosen to keep the subject in the closet, the pursuit of sexual gratification by individuals who are felt to be "too old" for that sort of thing, can be embarrassing or painful for seniors in many circumstances.

Being old does not mean you should not be having sex. There is nothing dirty about it at any age and nothing wrong in doing something that is enjoyable and healthy. Sex is a normal part of life, though how sexual drives are fulfilled is an individual matter, or something for each couple to decide, whether young or old. In itself, sex should be fun, perhaps even more so once the time of reproduction has passed and the possibility of pregnancy is no longer a concern. Interest in sex is also a reason for people to take care of themselves, to remain physically fit and to try to look as good as they can.

What individuals expect in terms of sexual gratification is as varied among the old as it is among the young. For some, hugging and kissing may suffice. For others intercourse and orgasm are necessary. If intercourse is desired, the frequency can run from daily to once a year. And the type of foreplay and the positions used are different for every couple. There is also the delight of love and intimacy between two people that is a part of sexual relations—touching, caressing, and just lying together. How people meet all of these needs as they age can affect their feelings of self-esteem and dignity. Being married and having a partner certainly makes it easier, if both partners love and respect each other.

A survey on sexuality in seniors conducted by the AARP and Modern Maturity several years ago revealed that "more than 70% of men and women who have regular partners are sexually active enough to have intercourse at least once or twice a month," the frequency decreasing with age. "About half of 45- through 59-year-olds have sex at least once a week, but among 60- through 74-year-olds, the proportion drops to 30 percent for men and 24 percent for women." Confirming that frequency was not the most important factor in gratification, "about two thirds of those polled were extremely or very satisfied with their physical relationships." The survey also suggested that the younger generation (age 45–59) may well have more active sex lives as they age than those currently over sixty, espousing a more liberal attitude toward sex between unmarried partners, and engaging in oral sex and masturbation. They were also more likely to disagree with the statement that "sex is only for younger people."[12]

Studies have shown that a vigorous sex life may have health benefits. There appears to be a reduced incidence of heart attacks in men who have frequent intercourse and less depression in both men and women who have regular sex. However, the lower rate of heart attacks may have merely been a confirmation that these men were in better shape and more physically fit to begin with, which allowed them to engage in sex more often. Also men and women who are more interested in sex tend to have better relationships and less emotional problems than others in their age group and may have been less depressed initially. People who are physically or emotionally ill tend not to care about sex and are less able to perform when engaging in sex. But whether improved health results, and whether it is cause or effect, most geriatricians would agree that older people who are sexually active are better off both physically and emotionally, and have a better quality of life.[13]

One of the reasons for marriage is the formation of a sexual alliance and that is valid later in life as well as when we are younger. To have a satisfying sex life at any age requires a caring partner, perhaps even more so as we grow older, when various physical infirmities may interfere. These may be relatively minor, or quite serious, but have to be addressed if the inclination is still there. Included are musculoskeletal disorders like arthritis or back problems, cardiac or pulmonary conditions that restrict exertion, weakness from strokes or injuries, and so forth. Because of these difficulties, different positions and more restrained movement may be necessary. With age, men may also have more trouble achieving or sustaining an erection and may be too embarrassed to talk about this with their partners or physicians, instead simply refraining from sexual contact. And women as they age after menopause may experience vaginal dryness.

Both men and women should be able to discuss sex with their mates and, if there are any problems, with their physicians as well. This is an area many people avoid for various reasons and may not have been broached during decades of marriage. But if their needs, desires, and possible impediments to success are not shared with their sexual partners, they are much less likely to have their needs met. Any discourse however should occur during a dispassionate time, not related to an immediate goal of sexual satisfaction, or just after advances have been rejected and there is an aura of tension still about. There should be frank exchanges about any physical limitations and any activities that produce discomfort, and ways should be explored to eliminate these obstacles. There should also be discussions about what increases excitement and maximizes pleasure. Because sexual reactivity is reduced with aging, a greater effort may be necessary to attain a response. This may include heightened foreplay and increased manual or oral stimulation of the genitals. Excitement may also be augmented by approaching sex differently at various times and changing scenery. Using different rooms in the house and different times of the day may be helpful, as could going to a hotel or a motel. Sometimes pornography may also enhance excitement. Whatever works should be used as long as it is acceptable to both partners and does not cause physical or emotional injury.

Physicians should also be consulted when there are difficulties that cannot be managed by the individuals themselves. There are medical solutions to many of these problems and it is at least worthwhile to know what is available. Erectile dysfunction can be treated with Viagra, the anti-impotence drug, quite successfully in a large percentage of older men.[14] New compounds have also been recently approved for this condition and different mechanical aids are available. Testosterone (the male sexual hormone) therapy may be useful in selected cases. Women as well may be helped by hormone therapy to combat vaginal atrophy and increase lubrication if there are no medical contraindications. In addition, artificial lubricants may be beneficial for many women. When a couple has sexual problems, it may also be helpful for them to go for counseling with either a religious or lay therapist, as some people need guidance to prevent this issue from becoming a festering sore that can infect their marriages.

Having a good sexual relationship within a marriage is merely part of the total relationship and requires both partners to love and care for each other. If a marriage is devoid of love and affection, there cannot be satisfactory sex. However, when there is apparent love and one partner is not interested in sexual activity though physically able and it is important to the other partner, the situation may be a source of conflict. If there is a disability or medical reasons for an individual to avoid sex, his or her partner may be more under-standing, but it still may engender hostility. In general, clashes involving sexuality are more prevalent among middle-aged couples and the young-old, and are seen less among the old-old whose drives are considerably diminished. Sometimes the professed sexual interest may be more for psychological reasons than physical need, but still has to be addressed.

It may seem strange to younger observers that the elderly remain so concerned with sex, but it is a force to contend with, even in later life. I remember an office visit by a couple in their late seventies just after Viagra was approved for use. The man, who was my patient, had Parkinson's disease of moderate severity and was doing fairly well on medication. His wife appeared healthy on observation. Just as the visit was concluding, the man asked me if I would prescribe Viagra for him as he was having difficulty maintaining an erection. As I started to question him further, his wife, who was sitting behind him and off to the side, stood up and began waving her hands and shaking her head frantically, to try to stop me from giving him this new drug.

At times, because the predicament seems so intractable for a couple, one partner will suppress his or her sexual desires for the sake of peace. But there are several options available to the person who is unwilling to accept the status quo and wishes to continue sexual activity. One is to attain release through masturbation. Though this is not a satisfactory alternative for everyone, it does leave the structure of the marriage intact and may be the least traumatic way of dealing with the problem. Another possibility is to find a different partner for a sexual relationship. This can mean having an affair with someone while remaining married, or getting divorced and marrying someone else. For some people, it is simpler to see a prostitute or gigolo occasionally and pay for sex, though this is illegal and can lead to AIDS and other sexually transmitted diseases. (There was a report recently detailing an outbreak of AIDS and syphilis among a group of elderly men in a retirement community in Florida who had been going to prostitutes, many of whom were intravenous drug users.) What a person does may depend on the intensity of his or her sexual drive and the moral considerations of his or her choice. Again, counseling may be beneficial with a religious figure or a secular therapist.

Single older people without partners face similar problems in seeking sexual outlets. For those who have been single all their lives, it is usually easier, as they have dealt with this dilemma over the years. But for those who have been widowed, it may be more difficult to devise a solution. (Of course, sex itself may not be an important issue with them, as they may be more concerned with companionship, or merely learning how to survive and thrive on their own.) The options for sexual release for single people are the same as those listed above. However, when and if a new partner is found and a relationship of any sort is established, it is good at some point when both people are comfortable to discuss sexual needs and expectations to avoid future disappointments. This is especially true if marriage is being contemplated.

The negative stereotype of older people with an interest in sex is that of "the dirty old man" who leers at younger women, or makes overtures to them while looking for a partner. As mentioned before, there is nothing dirty about an older man with sexual needs, even if he is drawn to someone younger. For a number of reasons, it may not be appropriate for a seventy-year-old man to pursue a twenty-five-year-old woman and it may certainly impact on the man's dignity, but there is nothing illegal or immoral about it, if it is done within the constraints of accepted behavior. Two consenting adults can act as they please. However, there are circumstances when an older person is cognitively impaired or disinhibited and his or her actions in terms of sexuality may be outside the bounds of what is acceptable. Though this occurs infrequently, these people may need to be medicated and watched carefully, particularly if children have been approached.

RELEVANCE

In trying to preserve our dignity as we age, we should be knowledgeable about the world around us, and both intellectually and socially relevant. Past events and the cultural milieu that flourished in our youth may be important to us, but to be respected and connect with other people, we also have to be attuned to what is happening in the present. We can concentrate on those elements that affect us directly, but should still have a broad understanding of the issues.

Information on current events can be gathered by reading newspapers and news magazines, as well as watching news programs on television. The newspapers provide exposure to local news in addition to national and international events, and it is essential to know what is occurring in all of these areas, at least with the major stories. Having a viewpoint we can defend and discuss intelligently gives us more credibility among our social group and the general population. We must not be afraid to have opinions and express them. It becomes difficult for younger people to dismiss us if we know as much or more about what is happening than they do.

In terms of awareness from a cultural standpoint, it is impossible for anyone to encompass developments in every field of activity. The kinds of things we should stay abreast of should be determined by our own interests and the social circles in which we move, including our friends and relatives. This may mean reading the latest books, going to the movies, watching television, listening to music, attending the theater, and so on, but should focus on doing the things we find stimulating and enjoyable. (I am not dividing activities into pop culture and high culture, but speaking of the collective creative output of our society and the need for older people to participate and comprehend what is going on.)

Seniors do read more than the young, since this was a major source of their entertainment when they were children and the habit has remained with them. They are also able to sit still for longer periods than younger people. If we like reading, our subject matter (romance novels, mysteries, best sellers, biographies, general nonfiction, self-improvement books) should depend on our personal tastes. Of course, there is no reason to confine ourselves to one sector and we can try anything that kindles our curiosity, even topics we are not familiar with. Though the primary reasons for reading are pleasure and learning, it is also valuable for us to get feedback about the books we read from other people, as that heightens our critical powers and understanding. Conversations with friends may suffice, but discussion groups and book clubs may sharpen our minds as we debate the issues that books raise. Magazines geared toward older people, such as *Modern Maturity* and those that special-ize in areas that concern seniors, such as *Prevention* and *Today's Health*, as well as those of general interest, may also be worthwhile reading.

In America, if we want to be in touch with the times in which we live, it is good to be knowledgeable about the latest films. Putting forth our views on these movies also hones our thought processes and powers of perception, and helps us to remain relevant. We should see movies that are purely entertaining, but it is also beneficial to sit through some that are controversial or even dis-agreeable to expose ourselves to different ideas. Renting DVDs or videos or watching films on cable allows us to see those movies we might have missed, or that might have had a limited commercial run, but were critically acclaimed. This is less expensive than going out to see a movie and it also permits people who are housebound to enjoy a movie they otherwise would not be able to see.

In some social circles, television programs are also topics of major inter-est. Being able to discuss the latest developments on these shows is an easy way to reach other people and always engenders lively discourse with friends and family members who watch television. Many individuals follow the soap operas avidly, or are mesmerized by sitcoms or dramatic programs. We should watch whatever we find exciting or enjoyable, but should not spend an in-ordinate amount of time in front of a television screen. Being an inactive couch potato is not a healthy way to conduct our lives.

Going to the theater and seeing live performances helps expand our horizons. Either the classics or contemporary plays may raise issues that require thoughtful analysis, besides being entertaining. Musicals usually provide a shared experience with family and friends, as this is the most popular form of theater for Americans. The opportunities to attend the theater vary greatly depending on geographical location and the cost of tickets, but there are numerous fine regional companies and university and local community theaters around the country that mount excellent productions. And many offer senior discounts, so that prices will not be prohibitive for those on limited budgets. Other cultural events that should be considered are art and photography exhibits, dance, opera, and orchestral performances when the possibility arises.

Though music is also a large part of our culture, older people may find it difficult to appreciate the sounds that are lauded by the young, as tastes among the generations are very different. There are not many of the elderly who can "get into" rap, hip-hop, heavy metal, or grunge music, or their purveyors. But there is nothing wrong with rejecting creative work we find unpleasant or do not agree with. Instead, we should listen to music to which we can relate, whether it is pop from the 1940s and 1950s, early rock and roll, folk or folk rock, jazz, country-western, or classical. There are usually radio stations in most locales that play the type of music that older people prefer, and CDs, tapes, and live concerts are other ways to keep the melodies flowing.

In terms of cultural exposure and understanding, it is important for us to pursue those things we enjoy, but also to try to broaden our experiences, whether passively or actively. At every age, we should always try to grow and learn, and be stimulated in whatever ways we can. This keeps us vital and engaged with the world around us, allows us to interact better with others, enhances our self-esteem, and makes our lives more exciting. This is true as much for an older person as for a young child. It is just done differently, with information absorbed and digested at a slower rate.

Besides keeping abreast of current events and remaining attentive to cultural matters, older people should converse regularly with friends, acquaintances, and relatives. Having acquired a body of knowledge that is constantly expanding may be good in itself, but is of greater value if it is shared with others. It is also important to be cognizant of the latest news involving friends and relatives to maintain decent relationships. Who had a grandchild recently? Whose child just finished graduate school and what is he or she doing now? Who just retired? Who is moving away? These may seem trivial, but they are the changing facts about the people in one's life, and to relate well to others, it is important to know what is happening with them. This is called "being socially relevant" and is necessary if one's own voice is to be heard. Many people have a need to talk about their families and the milestones they have achieved, and it is important to be a good listener as well as a good conversationalist, showing interest in what others have to say and reacting appropriately.

To remain relevant in this day and age, older people should also try to be familiar with computers and be capable of going online, utilizing the Internet, and having an e-mail address. Many older people are learning about computers by attending classes at community centers, colleges, and libraries around the country, or are taught by children or friends.[15] Though it may take a while for seniors to feel comfortable dealing with computers, anyone who has the patience can do it.

INDEPENDENCE

Independence is of major importance in the battle to hold on to one's dignity, though it often can be taken away by factors beyond one's control. The degree of autonomy possible for each of us as we grow older is determined by physical ailments, emotional illnesses, cognitive compromise, and our level of affluence. However, within the limits imposed on us, we should all try to manage our lives by ourselves as best we can (or in an arrangement of mutual dependence with a spouse or a person we love). This is not to downplay the obstacles we might encounter, realizing that for some of us, circumstances may make autonomy impossible. But for many, like Esau who sold his patrimony to Jacob for a bowl of porridge, independence is virtually given away for ease of living.

If an older person has degenerative hip disease or a bad back, it is much simpler for them to ask someone to get them a glass of water than to get up and get it themselves, which may require considerable effort and some degree of pain. With Parkinson's disease, it may be faster to have a spouse or other family member get the mail than going for it ourselves. As well, if an older person has had a heart attack and is fully recovered, but relatives are overly concerned about his or her condition, he or she may allow them to do the shopping even though there is no reason why he or she cannot handle it alone. When the elderly try to accomplish all they can for themselves, they affirm that they are in command of their own lives and do not need others to care for them. This may necessitate doing things more slowly, or enduring temporary pain because of a physical condition, but it is a small price to pay to maintain one's independence. Whenever feasible, disabilities should be approached as a challenge to be overcome.

I am frequently amazed by the way patients of mine with multiple medical problems are able to brush them aside and lead active, rewarding lives. An eighty-two-year-old widow of an investment banker that I have been seeing for degenerative cervical spine disease and severe neck pain has been alone for eighteen years, living in a large house on the Connecticut shore. She also has cerebrovascular disease, a neuropathy, and ocular myesthenia (a muscle disease restricted to the eyes). A number of medications taken regularly have helped these various conditions. As a devotee of the theater and opera, she travels into New York City three or four times a week with a driver, going to plays and her series at the Metropolitan Opera. She also sits on the boards of several philanthropies and is making an earnest effort to give most of her money away. Her energy and vitality given her age and illnesses is inspiring. Though being wealthy may make it easier, it is not required.

Though preserving our independence should be a goal for all of us as we age, there are certain situations that may require us to relinquish it. We should not take any actions that countermand medical instructions, without first discussing our desires with our physician and obtaining his or her approval. There may be reasons for the restrictions that we are unaware of, and injury may result from disregarding the advice we have been given. Sometimes, we may deny illness or disability, because we want to be well and function the way we had previously, and that can have disastrous consequences.

In an attempt to remain independent, activities that are potentially dangerous, to oneself or to others, should be avoided. Sometimes one's judgment or wishes to direct one's own life and not be beholden to other people may be clouded by false pride. If there is ever any question about what one has in mind, ask someone who has no emotional investment in the outcome (a physician, a nurse, a friend, and so on) for an opinion on that activity. As examples, driving a car with poor vision, lifting something heavy with a bad back, or working on a roof when one has dizzy spells. At times, medical consultations and various tests may be necessary to determine whether certain roles are prudent and safe.

Independence should also take a temporary backseat if it means inconveniencing others. The desire for autonomy should not hold anyone else back unreasonably. For instance, if a group is leaving to go somewhere and a sweater is needed from another area of the house that will take a while to get because the person has arthritis in the knees, allow someone else to retrieve it to save everyone time. Or if cutting food is a laborious process because of a previous stroke and one is at a family dinner, request help from someone so the dinner can proceed. Under these conditions, if others want to assist and it will be faster, allow them to do it to accommodate the group. But do not let it become a common practice, particularly if it is just to make things easier.

Most of the issues I have discussed regarding independence involve physical problems and physical disabilities. However, when cognitive impairment and emotional illness is involved, the situations are different. As previously mentioned, not all memory problems are the result of dementia and one should not automatically surrender independence because of minor difficulties with recall that are a normal part of aging. Keeping one's life organized with lists and calendars can be helpful in this regard to supplement memory, with a schedule to be followed and an established daily pattern. As an example, one might arise at the same hour each day, perform chores, have meals, and exercise at set times. Pocket organizers to remind one of appointments, phone numbers, and so forth, can also be utilized effectively if the technology is not threatening and can be mastered without significant stress.

Clouded judgment and lack of insight are usually found in people with dementia at an early stage of their disease. Although they may be incapable of full independence at that point, they can make decisions with some oversight, hopefully from a caring family member, allowing them to have some amount of freedom. Then, as the dementia progresses, the circle of their autonomy shrinks, until eventually it is gone and their lives must be completely controlled by their caregivers. When people are affected to a moderate degree, the greatest areas of conflict with family appears to be over driving and going out of the house alone.

Independence in the face of emotional illness is a more complicated matter, lacking a scripted solution, since a different approach may be required for each individual. That said, anyone who is psychotic needs to be maintained on medications and monitored carefully, and can never really be fully independent while ill. (However, this is uncommon among older people, unless a consequence of dementia.) Obsessive compulsive disorders and phobias certainly restrict the freedom of those who have these conditions, interfering with autonomy. (Phobias are irrational fears of certain situations or objects that direct behavior.) Medication and psychotherapy may help somewhat, but limitations often remain.

Of course, the two most common psychiatric problems seen in the elderly are anxiety and depression, and the amount of independence desired and sustained by those afflicted with these conditions varies according to the severity of involvement. Those with major anxiety or depression need medication and therapy in order to carry on their lives at a minimal level, and independence is usually not a concern for them. On the other hand, individuals with mild anxiety or depression are able to act in a fairly normal manner, and usually try to maintain their autonomy. However, some may use their illness in a manipulative fashion, employing their symptoms to get people to do their bidding. This makes it hard for friends and family to know how to deal with them— whether to give them assistance or make them fend for themselves. Should they be pushed toward independence, or helped with tasks they should be able to handle?

There are a number of different substances that are utilized to treat disabling anxiety or depression, often combined with psychotherapy to maximize success. These include benzodiazipines (for example, Valium, Ativan, Xanax), tricyclics (for example, Elavil, Tofranil, Siniquan), SSRIs (selective serotonin reuptake inhibitors; for example, Prozac, Zoloft, Paxil), atypical antidepressants (for example, Serzone, Effexor, Remeron) and others. Older people usually require smaller doses of these medications for treatment and can suffer adverse effects, such as drowsiness, impaired coordination, or cognition at higher levels. Relaxation techniques such as biofeedback, meditation, and exercise, along with behavior modification, may also have a role to play.

Though we all want to maintain autonomy throughout our lives, we must also be realistic as age takes its toll on us. If infirmity imposes limitations that would seem reasonable to an unbiased observer, we should be willing to acquiesce. We can debate these restrictions with family, friends, and physicians, but if they are in agreement, and we believe they have our best interests at heart, we should go along with their recommendations. There are times, however, when the issue of autonomy may be so important, that an elderly person may be willing to risk injury to remain in control, and his or her family and physicians may have to give in. This was brought home to me by an incident involving my mother several years ago.

My mother, who was then 89 years old, was brought into the hospital with a broken and dislocated hip. As recovery progressed, she was sent to a rehabilitation unit and began walking. Some mild problems with balance were noted and her doctors felt that she should permanently relinquish her slippers (scuffs with low heels and no backs) because they made her too unstable. She refused, saying she had worn these slippers all of her life and they were fine for her. After arguing to no avail, my sister and I took them away against her wishes, telling her she would have to wear flat slippers. But as soon as she left the hospital, she went and bought another pair of her old slippers, which she now wears around her apartment. She wanted to be in control and would not let anyone else dictate to her what she could or could not wear. So far, she has not fallen while using these slippers.

It may also be possible to have a degree of independence even with significant physical impairments, if one is willing to develop and accept a "shared dependency" with people other than a spouse. By that I mean a group of older people who work together to help each other out when necessary. It is preferable to establish this support network even before any disability occurs, one of individuals who live close to one another and who are concerned about one another and perhaps have common interests. Couples, widows, widowers, and singles could all be included. Perhaps one person has poor vision and needs to be taken shopping as he or she cannot drive. Another person might have severe arthritis and needs to be assisted with household chores. Someone else needs help with bookkeeping. These are just examples of how the network could function and allow people to live semi-independently with certain disabilities. In many communities, these types of arrangements are already utilized informally, usually by siblings or groups of old friends who live near one another.

FRANKNESS ABOUT SHORTCOMINGS

Being candid about disabilities and acknowledging problems that have resulted from illness or aging are also important if dignity is to be maintained, although these issues are rarely discussed in public. Rather than being embarrassed and trying to hide flaws, one should make an effort to speak about them openly, when and where it is appropriate, understanding that these matters are beyond one's control and they do not mean that someone is lazy, unintelligent, or offensive in any way. Most often, impediments are obvious to casual observers anyway and one looks foolish when attempting to conceal them or deny their existence.

As examples, an individual with Parkinson's disease or other types of tremor may hold on to one hand with the other to prevent it from shaking, or keep it hidden behind his or her back, rather than admitting the illness. Once that has been done, there is no need to feel ashamed and the shaking may actually be reduced because of less anxiety. Another example might be a person who has had a mild stroke and has been left with slightly slurred speech. He or she is very self-conscious about it and does not converse much in social situations, hoping that other people will not be aware of this condition. It may be even worse if there is drooling in addition to the slurred speech. The affected person may become withdrawn and isolated with an impact on the quality of his or her life that is disproportionate to the physical problem. Another example might be someone with visual impairment who cannot drive at night but will not reveal it because of embarrassment. Or someone who is afraid to go out alone because of dizzy spells, but will not tell anyone about them. Or a man who has chest pain with physical activity but will not acknowledge it to his golfing buddies.

It may also be hard for seniors to concede any minor problems with memory and the slowed reaction time that are accompaniments of aging. Too often, people feel they will be disregarded if they are cognitively compromised in any way and will be shunned by others if they are suspected of having Alzheimer's disease. So they may try to cover up their deficiencies involving memory without realizing they are not unique, and that many other older individuals have similar impairments. If they do not remember a face, a name, or a situation, they should say so, without an extensive apology. (Perhaps they can also joke about it and say they are having a "senior moment".) By telling family or friends that their memory is not as good as it once was and that they cannot remember something, they will no longer have to feel ashamed and try to conceal it. This will eliminate some of the stress from social interactions and result in better communication and improved relationships.

Increased fatigue and daytime sleepiness is another area that causes embarrassment for some of the elderly and limits their activities. If medical treatment does not help, it should be discussed with those individuals with whom they have frequent social contact. Certain strategies may also be useful in prevention, such as a nap prior to any engagement, avoidance of alcoholic beverages, and changing the schedule of medications.

Dealing with bodily functions that have gone awry is extremely traumatic for many seniors who frequently choose to ignore these subjects. To preserve dignity, however, it should be explained to those who are close to the involved person. Urinary and/or bowel incontinence is a particularly difficult issue for the elderly to confront and causes a great deal of embarrassment, perhaps because it is often associated with senility. However, with an increasing number of advertisements on television and in the print media in recent years for adult diapers and medical help for incontinence, it is something that more and more people are aware of. If the problems with incontinence can be managed with diapers, medication, or other aids, then there may be no reason for it to be discussed publically. Urinary frequency (having to urinate very often) is also a common occurrence in older people. Eructation (belching), flatus (passing gas), drooling, use of dentures, unpleasant breath, and various tics and twitching can all be seen among the elderly as well. Unfortunately, some seniors are so upset with these various conditions that they become reclusive rather than trying to find ways to deal with them.

When our bodies act in ways we cannot regulate to produce undesirable effects that are frowned upon in polite society, there is no need for us to be ashamed. Though it may be hard for us to accept this rebellion and our inability to keep normal physiology in check, that is the way it is and denial will not change things. Being candid and willing to speak about personal matters is not something easily done by everyone, especially those who are modest and essentially private people, unaccustomed to discussing bodily functions. It is worthwhile trying, however, for once a problem is acknowledged to others, it is less stressful since we do not have to work at keeping it under wraps.

APPEARANCE

As we get older, it is necessary to pay special attention to our appearance. Once we are retired and do not have to go into work regularly, or do not have children around the house, it is easy to fall into a pattern of sloppiness and ignore our personal demeanor. We may think people's impression of us is no longer important and not particularly care about how we look. However, appearances do matter and we lose our dignity if we are slovenly or repellent in our dress or hygiene. And if we seem unconcerned about ourselves, others may be unconcerned about us as well. Some of us may also allow our apartments or homes to fall into disrepair and not paint them or attend to our lawns and gardens. The interiors may become cluttered and dusty, with objects askew and infrequent cleaning. This may cause neighbors to become antagonistic toward us and people may perceive the condition of our homes as reflective of our state of mind.

An effort should be made to be neat and clean whenever going out in public, being certain that one's clothes are not stained or torn. This does not require buying new and expensive outfits, but merely taking care of what one already has. Men should be clean-shaven, or their beards should be neatly trimmed. Hair should be in place and not permitted to run wild. Diligence with personal hygiene is also extremely important, even if it is difficult and time-consuming. If necessary, assistance should be sought from medical personnel and family. Homes should be maintained to the best of a person's ability, taking into consideration any physical or financial constraints. This will make the neighbors happy and make one seem more in control of his or her environment. Keeping up the home also increases its value, so they will be worth more to one's children or whomever the heirs may be.

COGNITIVE VITALITY

Maximizing cognitive abilities as we grow older is essential to successful aging and maintaining dignity. I have mentioned certain behavior patterns in this chapter that can contribute to cognitive vitality, such as remaining relevant and independent, and I will emphasize the importance of goals and objectives in the next chapter. As I have discussed previously, deterioration of intellect is not inevitable with aging, with the aging brain having considerable plasticity and with learning still possible. Intellectual stimulation as we grow older enhances cognitive function and protects against dementia, and cognitive training programs can be helpful.[16] "Studies suggest that lifelong learning, mental and physical exercise, continuing social engagement, stress reduction and proper nutrition may be important factors in promoting cognitive vitality in aging. Manageable medical co-morbidities such as diabetes, hypertension and hyperlipidemia also contribute to cognitive decline in older persons."[17] Smoking and excess alcohol can play a role as well. All of these factors are under our control to at least some degree, indicating that we can influence the changes that occur in our brains and it is up to us to make the right choices. The key is to be active, both physically and intellectually—the best treatment for aging.[18]

CONCLUSION

I have touched on health issues, exercise, nutrition, and other areas to give readers an idea of some important ways older people can augment their feelings of self-worth, confidence, and dignity by maintaining their physical and cognitive abilities. For those who would like to delve more deeply into these topics, see the "For Further Reference" chapter at the end of this volume.

8

IT'S NEVER TOO LATE

Additional Strategies in the Quest for Dignity and Vitality

———————— • ————————

Even such is Time, which takes in trust
Our youth, our joys, and all we have,
And pays us but with age and dust.

—SIR WALTER RALEIGH
EPITAPH

————————

Age is a great equalizer. Whether we are rich, powerful, or famous, brilliant or average in intellect, middle-class strivers or impoverished welfare recipients, we all face the same problems as we grow older. Wealth offers no protection from Alzheimer's disease. Power is no shield against heart attacks. And our cells undergo the same changes, whether we are from Watts or Beverly Hills, Scarsdale or the South Bronx. Because of the universality of the aging process, one would like to imagine there might be a "brotherhood of the aged," allowing all older people to understand one another's pain and commiserate on the deterioration they suffer in common. One might also imagine there would be an absence of competition and that one-upsmanship would cease, with status and income less important than they had been in earlier years. But of course, it is not like that. The barriers that existed previously do not crumble as the years advance. People remain in the same isolated social pockets, with the same viewpoints until the time they die.

Still, a brotherhood of the aged is an ideal we should all consider and there are certain measures we should take to avoid inflicting indignities on our fellow travelers on the dwindling road of life. Those who are fortunate should not be ostentatious and flaunt their affluence in front of those who have difficulty making ends meet. Live well if you can and enjoy the benefits of wealth, but do not brag about what you have achieved or the material goods you have accumulated. Do not denigrate anyone whose life you perceive as a failure, or those who are not as successful as you are. And be compassionate to the needy and the impoverished. It is important for us to remember that happiness is not predicated on material success, and that love and fulfillment do not require money. Many people who are not rich, famous, or powerful have found a contentment in life that others would envy and that is the bottom line.

GOALS AND OBJECTIVES

When we are young, with careers ahead of us and children to raise, we all have visions of the future, with certain long-term goals and aspirations we wish to achieve. Performing well at a job, reaching a particular position, creating something important, and attaining financial independence are among the ends we set for ourselves. Overwhelmingly, these goals revolve around our jobs and our families. In addition to our distant objectives, we have daily and short-term goals, which may or may not be related to our major aims, but give our lives some coherence and structure. What happens when we retire and our careers are over, or our children grow up and move out of our homes? Should we just sit around eating, sleeping, and watching television, waiting to die?

Though goals and objectives may differ from those of our youth, it is just as important to have them as we grow older, perhaps even more so. We do not want to get by on memories alone, existing in the past. We need to have reasons to arise every morning and look forward to each day; to plan for the future though our time may be short. We need to have some purpose in our lives, even if through a very personal vision. Since job, career, and family are gone, it is important to find new outlets for our energies and not allow them to dissipate without direction. We need to find new ways to be productive and get the most out of the time allotted to us. And if we are lucky, we can inject a new fervor and excitement into our lives.

With the contentious world of business and the desire to make money now behind most older people, it is important to establish new values that are not tied as much to financial rewards and acquiring things. More attention needs to be paid to spiritual accomplishments: nurturing relationships, helping other people, becoming active in charities, developing intellectually, and unleashing creative talents. And for those who are believers, greater participation in religion is another option that may give one's life purpose.

Very often, objectives in later life evolve from interests we had before, perhaps having lacked enough time to cultivate them fully. Thus, fulfillment may be found in a business venture dabbled in previously, but to which we had been unable to devote much attention before retirement. Or a hobby of collecting coins may be totally absorbing. Or improving a golf game may consume one's time. Or working to raise money for a particular charity may become a fixation. Or spending a day or two teaching inner city children to read may provide gratification. Or studying the Bible more intensively may provide answers. Of course, goals do not have to come from past interests but can develop from exposure to new ideas, new realizations, and new opportunities. And they can come at different times during our later years, leading to one goal at a certain point and another goal at another time. There is no reason goals cannot be changed several times over the years, as one's needs and values evolve.

It is also unnecessary to focus on one objective at a time—a single driving motivational force. One can have goals in different areas that provide excitement to varying degrees, but in combination make one's life satisfying. Just as financial planners advise diversified portfolios in terms of investments to assure safety and success, diversified interests in life with numerous friends are more likely to make one happy (assuming good health).

In pursuing goals and objectives, we need to find things we can be passionate about. This can include a devotion to particular people, such as a mate, children, grandchildren, or friends. Or participation in special causes: political, cultural, social, religious, educational, or health related. Or games—golf, tennis, bridge, Scrabble, chess, and the like—can impel one to get out of bed in the morning. Or one can develop obsessions with objects of various sorts and become a collector. Or find enjoyment in activities such as traveling, dancing, taking a college course, gardening, managing finances, a new occupation, hunting, fishing, or boating. Or unleash your creative side and paint, sculpt, write, knit, quilt, do woodworking.

Relationships

Whether young or old, relationships with other people are essential in terms of emotional well-being and overall happiness. However, they alone are not enough to sustain a person, if one does not have our his or her own personna. It is wonderful to have a spouse to love and a strong marriage, but spouses die and then one has to carry on alone. Or a spouse can become disabled and his or her partner must take on the role of caregiver. That is why it is critical for each partner in a marriage to do things apart from his or her spouse, for each to have his or her own goals and interests, and be able to run his or her own life apart from the other.

Many older individuals, overwhelmingly women, want to live their lives through their children. They want to be involved with every aspect of their offsprings' existence, assisting with their grandchildren, as was done in previous generations with the extended family. These days however, there is not the same need for physical help in raising children. Modern appliances make doing the laundry much easier and prepared meals are readily available. And there is usually convenient day care that can be utilized if both parents are working. Of course, there are still many tasks in which grandmothers can be helpful and it is nice for children to have the love and warmth grandmothers can provide.

However, it is not healthy for either the adult children or their parents for the latter to interject themselves into their offsprings' daily routine. Both need to let go and be independent of each other, maintaining separate identities and separate lives. At the same time, there is no reason why grandparents cannot help out periodically with their grandchildren, such as baby-sitting, furnishing backup care, and playing a small role in raising them. They can even offer opinions on important decisions relating to the grandchildren, but only when asked to do so by the parents and without trying to dominate or direct the process of child rearing. And certainly they can follow the progress of their grandchildren from afar, be enthusiastic and proud of their accomplishments, loving them and deriving pleasure from them. It is important also to remember that children can move away from their parents, or become estranged from them for various reasons. Neither children nor grandchildren should be the central focus of older peoples' lives, causing them to neglect their own interests.

In addition, too close a relationship between children and parents can at times have a constraining effect on older individuals. Some children see their parents as members of a different generation and out of touch with today's world. They may not allow their parents the freedom to be themselves, telling them they seem foolish or silly for doing things they enjoy, or even mocking them for trying to act young. In these situations, it may be difficult for the parents to know when the criticism is warranted and when it comes from the children's own insecurity. However, in a proper relationship between parents and children, neither can be blamed for interfering in the other's lives.

Currently, friends provide most of us with a support apparatus. Thus, preserving and nurturing these relationships should be a goal for older people. When a spouse dies, or someone is afflicted by a major illness or injury, friends are often the ones depended on for solace, sometimes as much or even more than families. With children and grandchildren scattered around the country or even the world, and the extended family a faded photograph from the past, only friends may be available. Shared confidences, shared ideas and shared interests all contribute to building a solid friendship, but a commitment to spend time together is also necessary to foster a relationship. This may entail going out to lunch or dinner, shopping, seeing a movie, attending church, and so forth. Without any blood ties, friendships last because people want them to and they are willing to extend themselves to strengthen the bonds.

Even if desired, making new friends when one is older can be very difficult. Many people do not open themselves up to new relationships because they are insecure, fixed in their ways, or perhaps depressed. This is unfortunate, since as people grow older, previous companions die and leave a void that cannot be easily filled. And when it is necessary to move to new surroundings, such as a smaller apartment or an assisted living residence, there is often the hope that new friends will be made to make life more enjoyable; people with whom to talk and accompany one through both the good times and the bad. Even greater barriers to friendship arise if a person is disabled and lacks mobility, or has an impairment of hearing or vision, but friends remain important to everyone.

> What though youth gave love and roses,
> Age still leaves us friends and wine.
>
> —Thomas Moore
> Spring and Autumn

Causes

Involvement in a cause may develop because of an affinity for a particular organization or a particular issue. Individuals may aid a cause by giving their time and energy, donating money, or both. Sometimes they have special talents that can be utilized, administratively or creatively, or they may simply function as foot soldiers for an organization. Volunteerism is in itself a goal for many seniors, with the belief that it keeps their minds and bodies active, even as they are performing good works and helping others. It is also an opportunity for them to get out of the house, meet and interact with other people. There are numerous examples of people who retired and subsequently started or became involved in organizations of volunteers who gave something back to their communities in health-related, educational, or environmental projects, or other socially beneficial programs.[1]

POLITICS. Older people tend to vote in greater percentages than the population at large and because of this are courted by political parties and individual candidates on both a national and a local level. For example, in 1998, 28 percent of those voting in the elections for the House of Representatives were sixty-five and older.[2] People in this age range were more than twice as likely to vote as those from age eighteen to twenty-four in recent elections. In some states on election day, they may comprise one-third or more of the vote and are often moved by matters that affect them directly, such as Social Security, Medicare, taxes, or various local problems.

Depending on their orientation, older people may actively serve either political party, sometimes working for a candidate, sometimes championing an issue. They may also support third parties, independent candidates, nonpartisan groups (League of Women Voters, Concord Coalition), or advocacy groups for senior citizens (Gray Panthers, AARP). Some may also work for ballot initiatives or referenda on a local or statewide basis, or constitutional amendments nationally.

The *New York Times* in April 1999 carried a feature article about an eighty-nine-year-old woman who was walking from Pasadena, California, to Washington, D.C. (over 2,500 miles) to protest the failure of Congress to pass campaign finance reform, stopping at various points along the way to proselytize about this problem.[3] This shows that anyone can make a political statement and engender support for an issue in which he or she believes.

SOCIAL. Social causes run the gamut from the expected charities such as the Red Cross or the United Way to child advocacy, gun control, pro-choice, antiabortion, women's rights, elimination of drunken driving, family values, control of violence on television, and so forth, along with a multiplicity of environmental concerns. There are usually national organizations espousing differing stances on all of these subjects, with regional and local chapters that are always seeking members. On some issues, the positions taken may also encompass religious convictions, and not infrequently, supporters of these causes will cross the line into political activism to try to advance their views.

Participation in fraternal organizations, such as the Masons, the Shriners, and the Eagles, combine socialization with social causes. These groups meet regularly for camaraderie, but also sponsor events that raise money for charities. The American Legion and the Veterans of Foreign Wars might also be considered in this category, though their orientation is more political, supporting veterans' rights and a conservative agenda.

Seniors are also involved in trying to improve education, either directly or indirectly. They may solicit funds for schools or educational organizations, or act as teacher's aides in the classroom, augmenting instruction. As aides, they can provide individual guidance for some children with problems, enabling them to learn. This is a wonderful opportunity for older people to have contact with the young, absorbing the stimulation and energy the children generate, while performing a useful task that is immensely satisfying. Those who are active in this area are usually fervent about it, saying they get as much out of it as the children do. One can also function as a mentor to a child on a one-to-one basis, assisting a boy or girl with poor self-esteem, perhaps from a broken home and lacking good role models. Some extremely affluent individuals have carried this even further, acting as mentors to entire classes of students in inner city schools, promising to help them obtain a college education with financial aid. Another area that can be gratifying is working as a literacy volunteer with adults who have never learned to read.

Many health-related organizations focusing on distinct disease entities with chapters around the country have seniors involved in their operations, trying to raise money, helping to educate people about the illnesses, and providing support to patients and afflicted family members. Among the organizations that fit this description are the American Cancer Society, the American Heart Association, the National Stroke Association, the Alzheimer's Association and the Parkinson's Disease Foundation. Though the above disorders are certainly more prevalent among the elderly, older people also work on problems that do not ordinarily affect them, like AIDS, multiple sclerosis, and juvenile diabetes. They also volunteer at hospitals and have a considerable impact on patient care, being involved in administrative chores, transporting patients around the facilities, and boosting morale by distributing flowers, newspapers, and so on, in an educational capacity and providing emotional comfort.

Some seniors also enlist for assignments in third world countries, either with the Peace Corps or private charitable organizations. They may go individually or as couples if married, and stay for months to years. Their function depends on their skills and can include teaching various subjects, working in hospitals or clinics, helping farmers, and/or working on building projects.

For the most part, people who have been involved in these ventures feel they have been wonderful experiences, for what they have seen as well as for what they have done.

CULTURAL. Promoting favorite cultural causes is also important for some older people, with both national and local organizations benefiting from their work. Support may be generated for museums, the opera, symphony orchestras, chamber groups, theatrical organizations, and the like. In addition, seniors are active in local library associations and historical societies, with some providing backing to the Daughters of the American Revolution and similar groups that act in both the cultural and the social spheres. Again, they perform administrative chores, sponsor fund-raising events, and act as volunteers for different tasks. Some cultural institutions are dependent on their seniors' efforts and money for their survival and try to recruit older people to join their organizations.

RELIGION. For many of the elderly, involvement in religious worship and the traditions of their religion is essential. This may merely entail church attendance on Sundays or certain other times, providing financial support, and adhering to church doctrine in their daily lives. Or following the precepts of Judaism, Islam, Buddhism, or whatever religion they believe in. However, other individuals choose to play a greater role. They may proselytize, handle administrative or organizational functions for their local churches, work on affairs to raise money (bake sales, dances), or even teach the Bible or Sunday school. With more free time available, some also join study groups or formal classes to learn scriptures and various other aspects of their religions.

The central role that religion plays in the lives of many older individuals cannot be overemphasized, with their faith serving to sustain them in a world that some see as threatening and where they no longer feel in control. Whether that faith was followed when they were younger, as they see their peers dying and are approaching death themselves, they search for meaning in their lives. Belief in God and their religion can provide that meaning for them, bringing them peace and contentment in their later years.

In addition to the feelings of contentment and well-being gained by religious adherents, a recent report has demonstrated an added benefit of longer survival by those who attend religious services.[4] Previous studies had suggested that religious observance resulted in a reduced incidence of anxiety, depression, and substance abuse; fewer suicides; lower blood pressure; and fewer strokes. Greater social support for members of religious congregations was also noted. Though subjects who attended religious services frequently were healthier at baseline, their survival was still greater than the general population, even when this was taken into consideration.[5]

GAMES. An obsession with various games also motivates numerous older people, with an objective of improved performance, or merely frequent play with the enjoyment it provides. Some find the competition exciting, but the social aspect of these games is usually as significant as the game itself, if not more so. An element of physical aptitude and fitness may be necessary for tennis, and minimally with golf or bowling, but most of the games are more sedentary. They include card games like bridge, pinochle, hearts, gin, and poker, and board games like chess, checkers, mah-jong, and Scrabble. Bocce and dominoes also have their adherents. People may take these games quite seriously, with devotees utilizing golf, tennis, or bridge lessons, either individually or in groups, to enhance their play. A number of games like chess, bridge, pinochle, and Scrabble are quite complex and cognitively stimulating, and their adherents believe it helps to keep them sharp. Crossword puzzles are similarly challenging for many individuals.

Some seniors, mainly men, are involved passively (though often passionately) in sports, watching football, baseball, and basketball on television, or going to the ballparks to see their favorite teams. As fans, they also follow reports on their teams in the newspapers, magazines, and on television, and can argue the pros and cons of personnel moves and strategies that their teams employ.

Over the past few decades, gambling has become a major form of entertainment for many older people, some of whom have become addicted and impoverished because of its allure.[6] "In a national survey, Harrah's Casino found that 27 percent of Americans over the age of 55 visited a casino at least once last year. In Illinois, a recent survey found that 40 percent of gamblers who visit that state's 12 riverboat casinos are over the age of 55; 30 percent are retired."[7] For most seniors, gambling is a way to provide a little excitement, socialize and pass the time. Initiation often starts innocuously with bingo at a church or community center. This may lead to attendance at a professional gaming establishment, where the payoffs are higher, but with a greater risk of losing money. The slot machines are particularly popular among the elderly, who will also play roulette, blackjack, craps, or any of the other games. In the Midwest, excursions on the gambling riverboats attract many older people, with the proliferation of casinos on Indian reservations also a big draw. Those with more money and greater interest may travel to the gambling meccas of Las Vegas, Nevada, and Atlantic City, New Jersey. Though gambling can ensnare individuals of any age group, the elderly, on fixed incomes, can least afford to lose large sums of money.

Collecting

Those with a passion for "things" or objects of any sort may become collectors, their goal being to acquire examples of the items they covet. They may simply be interested in quantity, or try to obtain objects with specific qualities they deem desirable. Collecting is a wonderful avocation for all ages, but may be especially appropriate and satisfying for older people who have more time. Any type of object is fair game for the collector, from "garbage" to fine art. Prices can range from pennies (or even nothing) to millions of dollars for any individual item. And people do not have to be wealthy to be collectors. All they need is the interest in something and the time to pursue it. If they educate themselves about the objects they wish to collect and develop a good eye for determining quality, their collections can grow significantly in value over the years.

A middle-class couple of modest means who purchased contemporary art in New York City from the 1960s to the 1990s, amassed a collection that was eventually worth tens of millions of dollars. They had paid a small fraction of that, buying paintings they believed to be of special merit by artists who were then unknown. The collection occupied every available niche in their small apartment and was finally donated to a major museum to be maintained in their name. With a discerning eye, they were able to choose outstanding works before the artists became famous. They learned about their subject by reading, going to galleries and museums, and speaking to artists and gallery owners, becoming well versed in the art and the artists during this period.

For most people however, collecting involves mundane objects that require minimal expenditure to accumulate, depending on how greatly they are in demand by others. Some collections have little or no monetary value, but may still provide great pleasure to the collector and thus are valuable because of that. Examples of this may be different types of rocks, seashells, leaves, pressed flowers, buttons, spools, bottle caps, and matchbook covers. Other collections necessitate small outlays of money when started, but subsequently can be worth large sums if other people become interested and a market develops for resale. In this category could be included baseball cards, posters, and colored bottles. There is almost a childlike quality about some collectors, with a certain innocence in the way they confer value on objects.

People collect virtually everything imaginable, whether of natural origin or man-made. Collectors clubs, newsletters, Internet websites about collecting various things, and books about these objects soon become available, covering every area. Items embraced are as diverse as marbles, various kinds of dolls and their paraphernalia, birdhouses, Walt Disney memorabilia, typewriter ribbons, bakerlite jewelry, Occupied Japan pottery, vintage clothing, Coca-Cola memorabilia, postcards, Depression glass, cookie jars, Victoriana, art deco items, art nouveau pieces, and books on every subject or by every author. The list can go on and on.

A major aspect of collecting is the "quest." For those who are bitten by the bug, the search for objects can generate an intense high and finding something special or rare can induce euphoria. While the quest is something that can be pursued in one's local geographical region, it can also provide extra enjoyment when traveling, or may even be the impetus for traveling. It is not necessarily money but time one must be willing to spend to discover the objects of one's desire. Collecting can potentially furnish a goal for every individual that is unique to that person. It also promotes social interaction, as one buys, sells, trades, and discusses one's collections with other people with the same or similar passions.

For older people, collecting may also be a subconscious reaction to all the losses they have been suffering. In stark contrast to losing friends, physical prowess, identity, and so on, they are acquiring new objects, indicating they still have some power and control. But whatever psychological needs collecting may meet, people are seduced because it is fun.

Creative Pursuits

Creative impulses and nascent talents that may have been suppressed by the exigencies and demands of youth may be able to blossom forth during a more leisurely time when we are older. There are almost limitless ways to be creative and the form of self-expression chosen might depend on past experiences, interests, and knowledge acquired. Sometimes the presence of a mentor already working in a particular field may provide one with guidance and inspiration. Whatever we do, it is important to keep in mind that attempts at creativity do not require recognition from others. And this should also not be perceived as work, with a product resulting that can be marketed. While we can try to sell what we have created if desired, this should not be the primary goal and there should be no illusions about the possibility of making money from one's art. Grandma Moses was a one in a million phenomenon.

It is also true that not everyone can be creative and one should not be discouraged if one is not so inclined. Besides the necessity for at least a modicum of talent in the area of choice, discipline is required to generate any sort of art. If one discovers that this is not meant for them, simply find another interest.

In many urban and suburban areas there are classes or individual instruction available if one wants to work in a specific medium, but needs to learn how to get started or how to improve one's skills. Whether one partakes of these opportunities is contingent on how intensively one wants to learn and how much one wants to spend. Adult education courses in community colleges and high schools are one resource that can be utilized, and some large senior centers also offer classes in different art forms. Art supply stores may sponsor classes as well, or be able to find instructors if one wishes to take private lessons.

Painting is probably the most popular type of artistic expression among seniors, with work done in watercolors on special paper or in oils or acrylics on canvas or canvas boards. Sculpture is a more difficult form to master and also more expensive, depending on the medium. Working in pottery entails using a potter's wheel with its idiosyncrasies, a kiln and knowing how to apply various glazes and paints. Other creative pursuits include woodworking and carpentry, knitting, crocheting, needlepoint and quilting, gardening, and cooking and baking.

Writing allows great flexibility, since it can be done in whatever time is available and without the need to purchase expensive equipment; however, a computer and word-processing software will certainly make life easier. One can choose to write fiction or nonfiction, poetry or prose, short stories or novels. Music also attracts many older people and they participate according to their talents and level of interest. Some start instrumental or singing lessons after retirement, others become members of local orchestras, opera companies, chamber groups, or chorals, with periodic concerts and performances. There are even those who become involved with country-western or jazz groups, barbershop quartets, or as pop music singers. The theater also furnishes a forum for creativity, the venue generally being local community groups, with every age range included. Some senior centers also have their own theater companies just for their members.

Activities

There are numerous other activities that older people enjoy and find stimulating. Working is one of these, a significant calling for a large and growing proportion of seniors that will be discussed separately. Several of the activities mentioned here could be placed under other headings, as there is an overlap in some of these areas.

TRAVEL. Traveling to different regions is an important objective for many older individuals, how and where they go encompassing a wide spectrum. Affluence is not a necessary prerequisite since people can travel inexpensively if they desire (though wealth obviously does play some role). However, a certain percentage of seniors do not like to travel at all, either because of illnesses or unexplained fears. Others are only interested in visiting their families, and seeing their children and grandchildren. It has been said that travel broadens an individual, and, in the past, a person was not considered educated unless he or she had been to a number of foreign countries. But with television and the movies, we are able to get some feeling for other parts of the world without having gone there. Still, we cannot truly savor another country unless we have been physically present and immersed in its culture. Obviously, certain destinations and itineraries have to be avoided if travelers are not in good health, and other responsibilities (for example, caring for a spouse who is ill) may also be limiting factors. Since 9/11 and the war in Iraq, the possibility of encountering terrorism in various countries has also been a consideration in making travel plans. And many individuals are fearful of flying.

Recreational vehicles seem to have a special allure for some seniors, who are on the road much of the year, covering the depth and breadth of the United States and Canada. This allows them to live in a "home" of their own, while moving about and sightseeing. An entire movement has developed around RV (recreational vehicle) living, with organizations, newsletters, and Web sites.[8] It is estimated that there are hundreds of thousands of elderly and retired people who have chosen this lifestyle.

As another alternative, many older individuals journey to elder hostels in the United States and abroad, where they can stay inexpensively and are given lectures or classes on topics of interest. Twenty years ago, Elderhostel offered a few courses at New England colleges and had 240 participants.[9] It has grown so dramatically that there are now 10,000 courses in its catalogues, with more than 300,000 people a year attending in both traditional and more esoteric sites. This is indicative of the desire that seniors have for learning and new experiences.

Special tours to different parts of the world that target older people are also increasingly common, providing opportunities to visit new places at reduced prices. Mature travelers (those over fifty-five according to the Travel Industry Association) have a penchant for high adventure as well, including safaris, rafting trips, treks, sea kayaking, hot air balloon travel and horseback riding.[10] "A study for the A.A.R.P. found that travelers 50 and older spent more than $30 billion on vacation travel in 1994. Since then, by all accounts, their numbers, expenditures and travel options have increased sharply."[11] Many airlines, railroad companies and bus companies also give senior discounts, lowering the cost of any journey.

Some older people who love to travel have the grit and determination to carry on no matter what their circumstances might be. In September 2003, my wife and I were on a guided tour of Italy that required considerable walking and physical exertion. Our group included an eighty-eight-year-old man who was hard of hearing and had minor problems with vision, but was otherwise in fairly good shape. In the Sardinian port city of Algheiro, he did not see a curb bathed in shadow and fell forward on to his face, breaking his fall with his out-stretched hands. He received a deep gash in one hand and abrasions on his nose and chin. Downplaying his physical injuries, he later said that the major damage was to his pride. After having his wounds cleaned and bandaged, then resting that afternoon, he rejoined the tour the following day, with long hours of sightseeing and lectures, eager to discover new vistas and artistic treasures.

OUTDOOR ACTIVITIES. Hunting, fishing, boating, and sailing are other recreational pursuits that invoke passion in their proponents, overwhelmingly men, though the chance to engage in these diversions depends on geograph-ical location. Boating, sailing, and fishing can be done on the ocean or on in-land waters. One can engage in sailing competitively or merely for relaxation, and either locally or over great distances. And what you do in terms of power-boating depends on the craft at your disposal. Long boat trips along coastal waters around the United States, heading up to Canada and Alaska, or down to the Carribean are all possible with the proper boat and expertise. Similarly, fishing can run the gamut from sitting on a pier to fly casting to deep sea ad-ventures. Fishing can reduce stress, is not physically taxing, and does not have to be a budget buster. Hunting is of course limited to rural areas and usually focuses on deer, geese, or ducks. However, trekking through the woods and handling a gun are not tasks that every older person is capable of doing.

DANCING. As mentioned previously, many older people enjoy dancing. Though it is easier to go dancing if you already have a partner, it can be an opportunity to meet new people of the opposite sex under nonthreatening circumstances if you are single, widowed, or divorced. Dancing lessons may also be available in your community, through senior centers, YMCAs, the school systems, or privately. Some communities and some churches also schedule regular dances aimed at seniors. In addition to these, one can go dancing at nightclubs or at special affairs, or enter dance competitions, which are becoming quite popular.

STUDYING. Returning to school, either in pursuit of a degree or merely to gain knowledge of certain subjects, is also becoming an important pastime for seniors, with individuals who are determined to graduate from high school or college or even obtain a graduate degree. These can be acquired for a person's own feelings of self-esteem, or can be used in preparation for teaching or possibly another career. Most people, however, take nonmatriculated courses because they are interested in a particular area of study and want to learn more about it. "According to the National Center for Education Statistics, 1 in 3 Americans over 50—23 million—were engaged in some sort of adult education in 1998, more than double the 11 million (18 percent) who were involved in 1990–91."[12] There are many venues for senior education, both formal and informal, affiliated with educational institutions or freestanding. One is the Plato Society—the Perpetual Learning and Teaching Organization that was founded at the University of California–Los Angeles in 1980. These groups have expanded dramatically since that time, as more older people want to learn. Some universities have even set up residential communities for seniors near their campuses, so these seniors can attend courses and participate in the intellectual life of these institutions.[13]

Conclusion

Aside from improving quality of life, social and productive activities in older people have been shown to enhance survival independent of physical fitness.[14] This was demonstrated in a large study with a thirteen-year follow-up, controlled for multiple risk factors. The way in which these activities conferred survival benefits was unclear, though all-cause mortality appeared to be reduced. (Social activities included church attendance; visits to the movies, restaurants, and sporting events; day or overnight trips; playing cards, games, and bingo; and participation in social groups. Productive activities comprised gardening, preparing meals, shopping, unpaid community work, paid community work, and other paid employment.) "This study contributes to a growing body of research in gerontology that recognizes the importance of social engagement and productive activity as essential features of successful aging."[15]

Another study suggested that in addition to longevity, the risk of dementia is reduced in older individuals who are involved in certain leisure activities (after adjustment for baseline cognitive status).[16] The activities included six cognitive pursuits: reading newspapers or books, writing for pleasure, doing crossword puzzles, playing board games, participating in organized group discussions, and playing musical instruments. Participation in eleven physical activities was also measured: tennis, golf, swimming, bicycling, dancing, group exercises, team games, walking for exercise, housework, baby-sitting, and climbing more than two flights of stairs. Reading, playing board games, and playing musical instruments were found to be associated with a lower risk of dementia. Among the physical activities, only dancing had a reduced occurrence of dementia. The mechanism behind the lower risks was unclear and whether participating in these leisure activities truly protects against dementia remains unproven.[17]

PETS

The care of a pet, or pets, and the companionship they offer, provides a reason for living and solace in difficult times for many elderly people. Dogs and/or cats are the common recipients of their affection, but unusual animals and birds may also be kept by some seniors. If individuals or couples do have pets in their homes, they usually limit them to one or two, but occasionally, excessive numbers can create a nuisance. No matter how many pets someone has, if he or she becomes more feeble or cognitively impaired with aging, it may be necessary for another person to assist them in giving the animals adequate care. But whatever the physical or financial burden that pets may entail, there is no denying the great emotional benefits they bestow.

EMPLOYMENT

For some older people, retirement is not a desirable state and they want to continue working until they are prevented from doing so by death or disability. This goal may be due to a lack of financial resources or a paucity of other interests, but there are also individuals who have been working all their lives and love their jobs, with the structure and routine that is imposed on them. Indeed, there are many individuals who are now working productively into their nineties or even beyond.[18] They may derive great pleasure and a sense of accomplishment from what they do, and have nothing outside of work that is equivalent. In addition, their sense of identity and feelings of worth may be tied to their jobs and they are unwilling to surrender these. If pressed, they may cut down on the hours they work, but will not give up their jobs completely, unless forced to do so. Of course, with the decline in the stock market at the beginning of this decade and its effect on many pension funds, retirement may not be an option for many people and they are happy to have any job. "According to a survey by AARP, more than one out of four people ages 50 through 70 who suffered stock-market losses over the past two years have postponed retirement, returned to work, or started looking for work."[19] But even before the sharp drop off in pension funds, many Americans had chosen to retire later.[20]

The ability to work through our sixties, seventies, or even older is contingent on our health, the type of job we have, and the situation in the labor market. Commonly, in corporate America, forced layoffs and early retirement have targeted older workers in the name of cost savings despite the fact they are more reliable, take less time off, and are involved less with drugs and alcohol. In addition, they have greater skills in dealing with people. A person in his or her fifties or sixties who has been laid off and needs to, or wants to work may find himself or herself seeking a new job with a new company, often having to start all over at a lower wage, or even taking a menial job. It may be necessary for the worker to accept this situation, not just for the money, but for the benefits he or she can obtain.

With the population growing older, the retirement age is being pushed back (and will probably be pushed back further) to preserve Social Security. It is already scheduled to rise slowly from sixty-five to sixty-seven, and many economists feel it should go to seventy to relieve the financial pressures on the Social Security system.[21] As Dr. Robert Butler, the editor of *Geriatrics*, has stated, "It does not seem reasonable and economically sustainable to have 65 million skilled and educated Baby Boomers sitting idle. When older persons remain active in the work force [*sic*] they contribute to a productive economy and make financial contributions to, rather than requiring payments from, Social Security trust funds."[22] American businesses must find ways to keep seniors working. Corporations, unions, and employees will all have to move together and make adjustments to reduce the pain this coming transition will undoubtably bring.

A recent survey has shown that the idea of retirement as merely a time of leisure for older Americans is already changing.[23] People want to be more engaged and more productive than past generations and do not want their retirement to be similar to that of their parents. Sixty-five percent of those surveyed felt that retirement is "a time to begin a new chapter in life by being active and involved, starting new activities, and setting new goals." Only 28 percent thought of retirement as "a time to take it easy, take care of yourself, enjoy leisure activities, and take a much deserved rest from work and daily responsibilities." The survey found that "40 percent are working for pay in retirement, or plan to after they retire, while an equal percentage do volunteer work or plan to." Of course, fulfillment of these aspirations may depend on the availability of meaningful jobs, either for pay, or in the voluntary sector.

FINANCIAL MANAGEMENT

Since the majority of people currently do not have paying jobs after age sixty-five, their income depends on their pension funds, 401Ks, savings, and Social Security. Managing their money well is essential if they are to make the most of their assets and ensure their long-term financial security. This is particularly true after the financial meltdown that occurred in the stock markets from 2000 to 2002. Unfortunately, many older people are not knowledgeable about investments and not aware of the differences in returns and risks of various financial instruments, often making poor choices. They may listen to friends or family members about where to place their money, or even strangers who sound persuasive. And because they are financially naive and too trusting, the elderly also at times fall victim to scam artists and con men. It is important for all of us to remember that if an investment seems too good to be true, it usually is and we should stay away from it. There is no easy way of making money and anything with a high rate of return always involves a high level of risk. Also, we should not make snap decisions or be pressured into any arrangements without adequate time for consideration and consultation. Before we hand anyone money or sign up for any "deals," it should be given plenty of thought and discussed with other people in whom we have confidence and who are experienced in economic matters.

To increase sophistication and general knowledge about finances, it may be worthwhile taking classes that deal with money management and investments. Courses on these topics may be found at community colleges, libraries, high school adult education sections, or senior centers. Seminars and lectures may also be advertised in the local newspapers or on the radio or television, either free or requiring a small fee. However, one has to be wary of these, as often the lecturer is trying to drum up business for his or her own firm, selling stocks, annuities, insurance, or other types of investments, or is seeking clients as a financial planner. Always look for any possible conflicts of interest before accepting that what you are being told is valid.

Many books have also been written on the subject of financial planning and investing, some of which are quite good and some of which are worthless, or even dangerous. Here, too, one must watch to be certain the author is not pushing a specific agenda, but is providing useful information about different options. Your local library or the AARP might be able to recommend the best books for you, as might a reputable financial planner, or your accountant. In addition, some of the financial magazines, such as

Fortune, Money, Your Money, Smart Money, Worth, and *Barron's* (which are also suggested reading), should be able to assist you in choosing the most salient books.

If you have significant assets, you can consider the use of a financial planner to aid you in managing your money. However, these are pros and cons to this approach. The biggest pro is that you are enlisting a person who is purportedly objective and erudite, and should be able to help you maximize your returns and protect your assets. The con is that these individuals are not always what they are advertised to be and may be pushing a specific type of investment that is inappropriate for you. If you are going to use a financial planner, find one who is certified and also endorsed by your accountant, or someone else whose judgment you trust. You also want a planner who will work for a set fee rather than on a commission basis, eliminating conflicts of interest in directing you to particular financial instruments. In addition, you need a person with whom you can communicate well and who will be available to answer any questions that might arise.

Very often in a marriage, one partner, usually the man, assumes the role of handling financial matters and making the decisions regarding investments and allocation of assets. This usually continues as the couple ages. However, this pattern can be disastrous if the person in charge of finances dies or becomes cognitively impaired and the second partner is suddenly faced with financial decisions about which he or she may be totally ignorant. It is important in a marriage for both partners to deal with monetary issues together and for both to understand the economic ramifications of their choices. Also, if an older person has cognitive problems and is widowed or single, it may be necessary for the children, other close relatives, or the person's attorney to step in early to manage his or her money, to be certain it is not squandered on foolish schemes or given away to strangers.

In the past, the population over age sixty-five was the most impoverished segment of our society, with many simply concerned about survival and the necessities of life. Since the advent of Social Security and Medicare, this is no longer true, with the government's safety net allowing older citizens some degree of security. Though these programs provide significant support for the elderly, many have found they do not meet their total needs. That is why pension plans and savings, along with astute financial management are so important in our later years. Because older people are generally risk averse, many do not receive an adequate return on their money. This will change only if they make a concerted effort to become more knowledgeable financially and invest whatever capital they have appropriately.

PREPARATION

One of the most significant strategies for coping with aging to maintain dignity and vitality is early preparation—doing things when you are younger that will improve your life when you are older. This is true not only in terms of financial arrangements, but also in matters of lifestyle and mental set. One should start considering the evolution of one's life early on, asking the questions, Where am I going? and What do I want to do with my life? It is helpful to have a general schema devised in terms of how long you want to work and at what job, how much money you will need when you retire and how you intend to accumulate it, and what you want to do after retirement or when the children are gone.

Certainly, by your forties these issues should be on your mind and you should try to be realistic about your employment situation and financial potential. If you are married, your planning should be done together with your spouse, with contingencies discussed for each of your deaths. It is much easier analyzing needs and the possible paths your lives might take after a partner's death, when both of you are healthy and the planning can be done in an orderly, logical, nonpressured manner. (Concern about how a spouse will do when you are gone is a practical sign of love and not merely morbid rumination.) And living within your means, budgeting, and saving should be a continuing goal throughout your life, putting something aside annually to prepare for the future. Even if the amount saved is small when you are young, it is a good pattern to establish and maintain until more money is available. Also, the earlier you start, the more money will accumulate, particularly in IRAs (individual retirement accounts) and tax-sheltered programs.

Physical fitness and taking proper care of your body when you are young is another area that will impact greatly on you when you are older. Though one can initiate an exercise program at any time, the younger you do it, the more substantial the benefits will be. Exercise should be a lifetime activity that continues as you age. The longer you wait to start, the harder it may be for you to achieve a desired level of functioning. However, for those who have been remiss, it is worthwhile beginning at any age, for you can always be better than you are. In addition to exercise, physical fitness entails watching your diet and avoiding excessive amounts of fatty foods, not smoking cigarettes or abusing drugs or alcohol, all of which will come back to haunt you as you grow older.

As essential to your happiness in later years as your physical and financial status is the development of interests that will sustain and motivate you. I have mentioned the various goals and objectives that people need when they are older to make life exciting and pleasurable. These passions, outside of work and families, should be started when you are young, then developed over the years, accelerating when your children leave home and as the time of retirement nears. If there is nothing that energizes you, you should actively seek out an interest, exploring various options, studying them carefully, and possibly making a trial run here and there if something is in the least enticing. Then, when you retire, the seeds that have been planted will be ready to blossom and you can expand on your early work. Preparation in this area is critical. You cannot just suddenly retire at some age and begin a new life from scratch without an inkling of what you are going to do. That path inevitably leads to boredom, restlessness, and depression.

Even without regard to the future, you should try to be intellectually and socially engaged all of your life. You should know what is going on in your community, the nation, and the rest of the world, and participate. You should be aware of social changes, current events, political matters, and cultural developments. It is also important that you keep up with any technological advances, so that you do not feel out of touch and isolated by the Internet, the computer revolution, and whatever else may follow. And acquiring a store of information should be a lifelong process. Though living this way will be preparation for when you are older, it is merely the right way to live at any time. In other words, the tenets for maintaining dignity and vitality as you age are the same as for living well when you are younger.

DEALING WITH GRIEF

Grief is intense sadness and despair as a reaction to losing someone we love, which interferes with our ability to function normally. We express grief through a process called "mourning." There cannot be grief without love, or emotional involvement. Invariably, it signals that a change has occurred, or is going to occur, in the life of the person who is grieving, in terms of an important relationship. (Individuals may also grieve because of the loss of a pet, or of something else of significance to them, such as a house burning down or a favorite piece of jewelry that was stolen. It may also occur with loss of a job or loss of status.) Grief may be exaggerated by someone who is depressed, but grief itself can lead to depression. Though everyone's grief is different, as is the loss to which they are responding, there are certain behavior patterns that are fairly predictable. The way we deal with grief and the increasing losses we sustain as we grow older can affect every aspect of our lives.

The most common cause of grief is the death of a loved one. Profound grief may also be seen in conjunction with a disabling illness or injury in someone dear to us, where that individual is impaired to the degree that he or she will never again be the person he or she was and in a way is lost to us. Grieving occurs as well when we ourselves are disabled and cannot do the things we did in the past. We may also be wrapped in a cloak of grief upon learning that we have a terminal illness and are going to die, mourning our own anticipated death.

The loss of someone we love results in grief because that person, who was such an important part of our life, is no longer there for us physically and emotionally, producing a great void within us. There was an interdependency that no longer exists, forcing us to reshape our lives. Though the predominant feelings are those of overwhelming sadness, often there is guilt as well associated with the loss, with the belief we had not loved the other person enough, or had been remiss in doing or not doing certain things, or simply that we had survived while the loved one had died. Restlessness, difficulty sleeping, physical pains, and various other health problems frequently accompany grieving. There may also be feelings of anger that this person has been taken from us, directed toward the loved one, society, God, fate, or ourselves. Usually, aside from the sadness, we are not conscious of the different feelings that are encompassed by grieving, which makes it more difficult to come to terms with them. With the disability of a loved one, however, anger may be closer to the surface, as we are forced to confront this person regularly, who is no longer the same individual we loved. The anger may be more intense if we have to take care of this person on a continuing basis, interfering with the way we lead our lives even more than his or her death.

The most often seen and usually the most painful grief occurs with the death of a spouse. Since women on average live longer than men, they are generally the ones who survive and have to deal with this. "Almost half the 20 million American women age 65 and over are widows; fewer than 10 percent of them are thought to remarry."[24] The adjustment to the death of a spouse can take as long as two to four years, though many survivors suffer longer term problems, including depression, alcohol and prescription drug abuse, and greater susceptibility to diseases.[25]

Our own loss of function or disability induces anger as well as sadness at the realization of the limitations that have been imposed on us. This may occur as part of the aging process, as we break down in various ways or develop the illnesses associated with aging and can no longer do the things that were previously automatic. If there are enough other areas in our lives that are pleasurable, we eventually accept the losses and carry on with living, though we may still grieve to some degree. Sometimes, where the function lost was critical to our sense of self, normal grieving may evolve into depression, even to the point of wanting to end life, particularly if we cannot care for ourselves adequately and feel we are a burden to others.

Knowing we have a terminal illness and are going to die also produces grief, which is rooted in a number of concerns. There is disappointment and sadness over leaving those whom we love, the things that were never done in the past, and the future that will not be shared. Perhaps as well, there is an element of guilt about not being able to meet our responsibilities because of death. In addition, there is worry about being an encumbrance physically, emotionally, or financially to our loved ones while we are dying. We may also be very angry about our impending death, wondering why it had to happen to us at this time. The knowledge we are going to die may also make us fearful, as we are unaware of what lies ahead and do not know whether there will be pain and suffering.

I have mentioned some of the emotional components of grief, but there are others as well that may appear at different stages of mourning. Initially, when learning of the death of a loved one, we react with shock and disbelief, followed by a period of denial. Then we tend to become apathetic and depressed, perhaps withdrawing from social contact. During this time, there is an unwillingness to do anything or make decisions and we seem almost in suspended animation, going through the motions of living. After this there is usually a gradual acceptance and a reentry into the world with a resumption of activities. These are not necessarily sharply delineated stages with a smooth transition, but often overlap. And many people may skip a stage or remain fixed in a particular plane from which they cannot escape. The duration of the entire process varies greatly, usually in the realm of months to years. This may be determined by the individual's coping mechanisms and resiliency, his or her dependency on the deceased, age, and the support apparatus available as well as numerous other factors. Even after recovery, when a person is functioning again, some residua of grief often lingers. Sometimes we fail to grieve by immersing ourselves in activities or throwing ourselves into new relationships to avoid experiencing the loss.

Grief commonly elicits sympathy from family, friends, and acquaintances of the bereaved. However, if it is too intense or overly histrionic, or persists for an inordinate period of time, it begins to grate on people's nerves, and compassion may turn to disinterest, or even disgust, or even worse, pity. Our inability to handle grief may thus destroy our fragile wall of dignity. What should we do to constrain our grieving and keep it within acceptable boundaries?

We must understand that though our grief is unique to us, as is our loss, other people also lose loved ones and suffer as we have suffered. We must mourn appropriately, then carry on with our lives, remembering our loved ones.

As Ernest Hemingway expressed so beautifully toward the end of *For Whom the Bell Tolls*, the people we love live on after death within us and we owe it to them to go on living as productively as we can. Robert Jordan, who has been wounded in battle and is going to die, says to his love Maria, who does not want to leave him, "Listen. We will not go to Madrid now, but I go always with thee wherever thou goest. Understand? . . . I go with thee. As long as there is one of us there is both of us."[26]

We are responsible for the memories of our loved ones and should celebrate their lives rather than focusing on their deaths. We must fight the tendency to withdraw and isolate ourselves, and return to living after the necessary period of mourning. We cannot keep feeling sorry for ourselves.

Most of the evolution from a state of grief to acceptance and normalcy occurs because of adjustments and changes within ourselves that are part of the restorative process. Though we have to do the heavy lifting ourselves, help is available from many sources to ease the burden and we should use them as necessary. Family and friends are the first line of support and we should not hesitate to call on them in whatever role we require of them. They can provide us with both physical and emotional comfort, and appropriate sympathy. In most circumstances, they have also shared our loss, having known our loved one who has died. This permits shared memories and reminiscences as well, which are often helpful in a time of grief. They may also be able to assist us with simple tasks, like shopping and preparing food and so on, that we might neglect while we are mourning.

Religion can also offer us solace and, if we have faith, we should turn to God and his ministers to provide answers for us and help relieve our pain. For many, the power of faith and of prayer is a spiritual balm that can heal all wounds. This may be even more important as we age. Whether previously observant or not, death and illness are two crises that commonly direct us toward religion with the hope that belief in God and acceptance of His precepts will bring us peace. This assistance in the transition between life and death seems to be a universal attribute of all religions.

Help can also be obtained through various support groups, some which have been formed to respond to particular illnesses, such as breast cancer, prostate cancer, Alzheimer's disease, Parkinson's disease. Many hospitals, communities, and churches also have bereavement groups for relatives of those who have died, to guide them through the process of mourning for as long as it takes. There are bereavement counselors available as well in some communities to assist people. Family physicians may also be a valuable resource to help those who are grief-stricken understand what has happened and alleviate fear and anxiety through brief psychotherapy. Medications on a short-term basis to reduce anxiety and allow sleep may be beneficial. The use of psychiatrists and psychologists should probably be limited to those people who have excessive difficulty in managing their grief, or where it has gone on too long and interferes with their lives.

Since everyone goes through the process of mourning in his or her own way, those watching the person trying to escape the pain should not be judgmental, thinking it should have been done differently. I provide two examples of how individuals dealt with a loved one's death:

P.R. was a 90-year-old man in good physical shape and mentally sharp. After living in the New York metropolitan area all of their lives, he and his wife had moved down to an inexpensive condominium community in Florida when he had retired from an administrative job in the city, managing to get by on a small pension and Social Security. For nearly ten years, he ministered to his wife with breast cancer as she went through surgical procedures, courses of radiation, and chemotherapy. Deeply in love, he was greatly supportive of his wife during her illness, having been married to her sixty-four years when she finally died. Several hours after returning from her funeral, one of his neighbors, a woman in her eighties who had been a close friend of his wife, came over to his apartment with chicken soup and freshly baked pastries. She stayed for a while to commiserate with him and the following day brought him dinner. They were married three months later and lived together, apparently happily, for four years before he died of a massive stroke.

R.K. is an 82-year-old woman who is a breast cancer survivor with cervical spine arthritis and a neuropathy. Her pain is controlled for the most part with small amounts of medication and she leads an active life, playing golf and bridge and traveling a lot, with elegant apartments in Connecticut and Florida. Married to a banker for over fifty years, she cared for him during a five-year decline and eventually death from diabetes, congestive heart failure, and prostate cancer. A year after her husband's death, she met a charming man of her age at a golf range, who started a conversation, then asked her out to dinner. Within three months, she moved into his apartment. Now, after three years, they are still living together, sharing each other's lives. Because of financial arrangements, they do not want to get married.

There are some people who might find these relationships shameful, saying that not enough time had elapsed for proper mourning between the deaths of the longtime spouses and the new connections that were made. But we all want love and companionship and when the opportunity knocks in the sunset years of our lives, perhaps it should be grasped. We do not have much time left and it may not happen again. It does not negate feelings for the loved ones that have died. In addition, sometimes the period of mourning starts to occur before the death of a spouse, when the illness is long and drawn out, and the death is expected.

DEALING WITH LONELINESS

Loneliness can, of course, occur at any age, but is more characteristic of the elderly than the young. There are a number of reasons for this. After retirement, there is no longer daily contact with other people on the job and, thus, there is a lessening of the social intercourse that was a part of our lives. Children have moved out of the house and as one ages further, spouses as well as more friends and peers die off. Physical handicaps and disabilities may develop, making it more difficult to get out of the house, which interferes even more with socialization. Some may also have to take care of impaired spouses, which limits freedom and the ability to get around.

It is essential that older people not allow themselves to be defeated by loneliness, which can lead to depression and a surrender of the will to live. Friendship is the best weapon in this battle and one should do all he or she can not only to maintain old relationships but also to initiate new ones, which is not an easy task as one grows older. Physical isolation must also be battled and older people must force themselves to get out of their houses and become involved in the communities around them. Joining groups of people who have similar interests, whether discussion groups at the library or working for particular causes, and sharing activities with other individuals, such as playing bridge or golf or exercising in an aerobics class, are very important for an older person's well-being. Religious services are other opportunities to be with people, and offers various other roles. Though each person has to find his or her own way out of loneliness, it is important to remember that "prevention is the best cure." By not permitting oneself to fall into the chasm of loneliness, it will not be necessary to worry about climbing out.

Over the past ten years, the Internet has become a new tool for older people to deal with isolation. For example, in our nursing homes, the plague of loneliness infects much of the population. But some geriatric experts have found that the use of the Internet and e-mail can revitalize nursing home residents, improving their morale and manifestations of depression.[27] It has been shown that a large number of these people can be taught how to use a computer and communicate by e-mail. If the institutionalized elderly can do it, certainly those on the outside can also do it, utilizing e-mail and chat rooms to alleviate loneliness and enrich their lives. It is also important that older people using the Internet be aware of possible scams and misuse of information, keeping personal data out of the hands of unscrupulous schemers.

COUNTERACTING SOCIETY'S AGEIST BIAS

Older people have considerable power both economically and politically, but have not yet learned how to wield their power effectively to reduce society's ageist bias. This must be accomplished if the indignities that society imposes on individuals simply because they are old is to end.

A major portion of the nation's wealth is controlled by people over sixty-five, in their pension plans, other retirement vehicles, and the assets they have accumulated over a lifetime. As stockholders in virtually every large corporation, they should be able to force an end to age discrimination and help older employees obtain better treatment. Given their tremendous buying power, they should also be able to influence the media to start depicting the elderly in a more favorable light, and to develop television programs and movies that are aimed at older audiences. Recently, a number of corporations have begun to realize that a major market exists among older people that has not been served adequately and are starting to address this deficiency.[28] Some companies have become "senior friendly" in an attempt to generate more business in this growing affluent group with a vast amount of discretionary income. Because of the financial stakes, companies can no longer afford to show indifference to seniors.

With the growing number of older people in the United States and the fact that they vote in higher proportions than any other segment of the population, they should be able to assert themselves even more strongly from a political standpoint, so that greater attention will be paid to their agenda. At their direction, legislation should be passed that further bars age discrimination, levels the playing field for senior citizens, increases low-income senior housing, provides better Medicare drug benefits, and protects Social Security and Medicare. As a priority, they should also have the police target criminals who prey on the elderly, particularly the con men and scam artists. Society will not transform itself spontaneously in terms of its ageist bias. Only political and economic pressure can produce the social changes that older people need.

RANDOM THOUGHTS ON AGING

Having discussed the major areas of concern in terms of maintaining one's dignity and vitality, following are some general precepts to keep in mind as we grow older.

- Our attitude and approach to life is important as we age. We can either perceive the glass as three-quarters empty or as one-quarter full and it will affect the way we live. Being depressed not only makes us unhappy, but all of those around us as well.
- We are who we are, both in fact and in other people's perceptions. We must try to be at peace with ourselves and accept what we have done with our lives. Whether successful in our own eyes or not, it is not beneficial to be resentful of the past, including career decisions, choices of mates, and lack of financial security. What has happened cannot be altered.
- While we are all capable of change and learning at any stage of our lives, our personalities have already been forged and our patterns of behavior are fairly fixed. If we are truly unhappy about who we are, we can try to live differently in the time we have remaining, working at something new. Though it is possible for us to bring about change, we should be realistic. We can dream, but it should not run our lives. It is unlikely we are going to become a scratch golfer at age seventy, or write the great American novel.
- Since the past is set and we do not know what the future holds, the only period we can do anything about is the present. We should live well, for our time is short.
- We should deal with the enmities and antagonisms that have colored our lives, and come to terms with the people we dislike. This can be done openly or within ourselves, but we should not let hatred fester, for it will only poison our own systems.
- Be kind to other people, forgiving them their failings and overlooking small mistakes, remembering our own imperfections. At the same time, we should not let others take advantage of us, or we will feel duped and unhappy later on.
- Self-respect entails respect for others. We should treat everyone as we ourselves would wish to be treated.
- Having survived into old age, we should try to give something back to our communities, for that makes our lives more meaningful.

- Though bringing joy to other people is important, we have to live for ourselves as well, since we do not know what will come after death. We should try to find enough pleasures of both mind and body to sustain us while we are still alive.
- It is still important to be productive when we are older. However, productivity can be measured differently—using our time well. This can mean reading a good book, walking five miles, or helping someone.
- Find a peaceful time every day for renewal. Whether it is through meditation, prayer, walking, or any form of conscious solitude, it is necessary to give our lives balance.
- We should not withdraw into ourselves, nor share our lives with a single companion. We should interact with the world around us, with different people of all generations.
- We should maintain a "youthful" outlook as we age. By that I mean, remaining curious about life, with a willingness to explore and try new things.
- Age imposes limitations on us. The older we get, the more limitations we face, though it is different for everyone. At each stage of life, we must do the best we can within our own limitations.
- Burning the candle at both ends is not necessarily bad. Having many interests and activities can make our lives exciting.
- Don't gossip. This is a characteristic often attributed to older people that is demeaning. If our lives are interesting and fulfilling, we do not have to talk about others.

POSITIVE THINKING

It has recently been suggested in several studies that those individuals who are optimistic about life as they age and have a positive attitude live longer.[29] Whether this is cause or effect is uncertain, as is what people can do to develop a positive attitude and make themselves happier. Feeling empowered, or having some degree of control over their lives, as well as being aware and knowledgeable about their environment, did seem to increase peoples' happiness and was correlated with longevity. These people seemed to be more conscientious about the way they conducted their lives, engaging in healthier actions and avoiding riskier behavior (smoking, eating poorly, driving without seat belts, excessive alcohol, drug abuse, and so on).

PIRO

I have examined many factors that must be considered in the attempt to preserve dignity as we age. However, four of these are of primary importance in the struggle and can be represented by the acronym PIRO:

P   stands for continued physical fitness and physical activity as we grow older.

I   symbolizes maximizing our independence whether we are healthy or disabled.

R   signifies remaining relevant in our interactions with other people and understanding the world around us.

O   stands for the objectives and goals we should always have, to provide reasons for us to continue living.

> "Enjoy yourself, it's later than you think.
> Enjoy yourself, while you're still in the pink.
> The years go by, as quickly as a wink.
> Enjoy yourself, enjoy yourself,
> It's later than you think."
>
> —Guy Lombardo
> *Enjoy Yourself*

9

OVER THE HORIZON

Aging in the New Millennium

————•————

Trying to control the future is like
trying to take the master carpenter's place.
When you handle the master carpenter's tools,
chances are that you'll cut your hand.

—LAO-TZU
TAO TE CHING

————

During the early decades of the twenty-first century, advances in scientific knowledge and technology will dramatically change everyone's lives, particularly those of the elderly. While the more affluent will benefit initially from the innovative products that are being developed, they will become available to people in all social and economic groups as their cost diminishes. Even now, many high-tech companies are searching for ways to tap into the expanding senior market, utilizing computer applications, communications systems, and discoveries in biotechnology.[1] In the years ahead, we can expect the living environment of the elderly to be significantly altered, the aging process to be modified, and society itself to undergo a metamorphosis.

CHANGES IN LIVING ENVIRONMENT

While the aggregate of nursing home beds and assisted living residences have been rising over the last quarter century in tandem with the growth of the elderly population, the number of these units will begin to decline in the near future, as older people remain independent longer in their own dwellings. This is partly because seniors will be healthy deeper into old age, while their life expectancy continues to increase. Other important factors supporting their independence will be the transformation of their living environment with so-called smart homes,[2] the use of "robotic companions" and "smart cars," allowing even many of the disabled elderly to live alone rather than being institutionalized, or having a "human" attendant constantly with them.

Smart Homes

As a starter, every home will be equipped with a computer that is programmed to help it run efficiently, requiring limited attention from its occupants. This computer will be networked to all the appliances and machinery in the home, as well as to various sensors installed in appropriate locations. (Presently, the average American home has 40–50 microprocessors in it and this is anticipated to increase to 280 within five years.[3] Most of these are embedded microprocessors that are hidden in various objects, including appliances, toys, automobiles, and so on, monitoring and controlling different functions.) As voice recognition software will be standard in all computers within a few years, it will not be necessary for anyone to have special knowledge or training to interact with his or her electronic assistants. People will be able to direct the computers to alter their home environment or meet other needs simply by telling them what they want done, if the task has not already been preprogrammed. The machines will also communicate with people by "talking" to them, providing information such as when a task has been completed or asking if there are new tasks that need to be performed, based on previous behavior patterns.

These new "occupant-friendly" houses will have motion sensors in each room, causing lights to go on and off as people enter and leave, reducing the danger of falls and injuries. (If someone does fall, the computer will be aware of it and will alert the appropriate responders.) Television cameras will allow monitoring agencies to look into every room if there is a question of a resident being ill or injured. People with cognitive impairment will be verbally reminded to take medication, eat and drink the required amounts, and perform various other tasks. The temperature in each room will be self-regulating according to the presence or absence of people, with perhaps only the bedroom and bathroom being comfortably heated at night, and the temperature in the remainder of the house adjusted as programmed, but able to be overridden by voice command. Oil and gas for heating will be delivered as requested by the computer, without anyone's intervention. Speakerphones will be present throughout the house allowing phone calls to be answered or made by someone simply saying a key word, with the person able to have a conversation while moving about the house or seated with his or her hands free. At the occupant's command, the shower or bath will also go on at the desired temperature and turn off when he or she is finished. When that person is ready for sleep, the bed will also be warmed to the level he or she finds comfortable, by merely giving the directive. Similarly, the stove or microwave oven will be able to make tea or coffee as ordered, or even a complete meal, reading the coded instructions on the food packages to prepare each part properly. The ovens and burners will also switch off automatically, eliminating any concern about fires. Indeed, smoke, heat, and carbon monoxide alarms will be more sophisticated, alerting occupants and firehouses if there are any possibilities of danger. And bills and taxes will paid be by people's banks electronically, after their approval by voice or computer.

In the early part of the twenty-first century, television, radios, and CD players will also be operated by voice command, with movies or other entertainment programming ordered from a central source. High-definition, large-screen televisions will be commonplace with visual quality greatly improved over current equipment. Within one to two decades, however, every home will have an entertainment machine. Through virtual reality, this equipment will allow each individual to become part of the program he or she is watching. This may be effected with a bubblelike screen around the viewer or with that person wearing a headset. Each of us will also be able to conjure up any kind of programming we desire, old or new, from movies to Broadway shows to sporting events to news stories. In addition, through interactive television or high-definition videophones, friends and relatives will always be available to us for conversation and companionship. No one will ever have to dine alone if they do not wish to do so, with a three-dimensional screen in the dining area.

Entry into our homes will no longer require keys. Our thumbprint on a pad outside our doors will suffice, though retinal patterns may also be used to gain entrance and make our homes aware of our presence. Eventually, as voice recognition improves enough to ensure security, our voices may be utilized to open the doors and "start up" our homes. A tiny implanted chip under our skin may also be employed to activate our homes and allow our computers to locate us in any area of our homes, or even outside. This technology might be valuable for keeping track of people with Alzheimer's disease who tend to wander. The global positioning system would always be able to find them when they were missing and away from their homes, no matter where they went. In July 2003, the Intel Corporation announced that they and the Alzheimer's Association were going to join together in a research initiative to try to harness computer technology to the care of Alzheimer's patients.[4]

The Internet

Currently, by using the Internet and various chat rooms, people who are homebound are able to interact socially with others, have discussions, share ideas, and alleviate feelings of isolation. These activities will be enhanced in the future as costs are reduced and voice instructions operate all computers. Faster chips, broadband access, and improved digital technology will be combined to let participants in chat rooms actually chat with each other in real time, while being able to see the individuals to whom they are talking (as will interactive television). Facial expressions and reactions will be clearly visible, as seniors develop new online friends and become members of online communities. People can already play various games with their Internet companions or their computers, travel to different places for virtual reality tours, shop at various Web sites, and so forth. In addition, they will also be able to have books downloaded from Internet bookstores, and if they have problems with vision, their computers will read the books to them. And shopping for everything from clothing to furniture will be done increasingly over the Internet, permitting people to buy whatever they need or desire without stepping out of their homes. (It seems unlikely, however, that the Internet will be able to provide us with online hugs.)

Working at home in the twenty-first century will be further facilitated by new technologies. This will allow many older people to perform various functions without commuting. In a virtual office, they will be able to communicate face to face with their co-workers, with people coming together for conferences on their television or computer screens.

Smart Cars

Even though it will not be as necessary for older people to leave their homes in the years ahead, they will be less reclusive even if disabled because their automobiles will be able to operate without a driver, providing them with more freedom. These so-called smart cars may be available within the next ten years and certainly within the next twenty. Again, they will be activated by voice pattern, thumbprint, or some other personal identifying characteristic rather than a key. Instead of people climbing behind the wheel to drive these vehicles, they will merely tell them where they want to go, sit back, and relax. The car's computer will then transport the occupant to his or her destination, using the global positioning system or other determinants of location to move the car to the required site, where it will be given instructions on which driveway to enter or where to park. Motion sensors, radar, or other sensory detection systems in the automobile will help it maneuver through traffic, avoiding other vehicles, pedestrians, and various hazards. Computers in different cars will also be in radio contact with each other, allowing traffic to move smoothly and avoid accidents. With these improvements, elderly people unable to drive a car because of poor vision or other limitations will be able to visit friends or family, go shopping if they wish, go out to dinner or the movies, or even go on dates without imposing on others. An alternative system that may be in use earlier is that of "smart roads," where highways are embedded with sensors that feed back to a main computer that assumes control of the vehicles on the road after they have given their destinations.

Robotic Companions

Even more significant than occupant-friendly houses and smart cars for the elderly will be their robotic companions (RCs), making their lives easier and safer and permitting them to do things that might not otherwise be possible. These robotic companions will be particularly helpful for disabled and feeble older people, but valuable as well for those who are physically and cognitively intact. The RCs would "live" with seniors in their homes, acting as companions and also assisting them with the tasks of daily living. They would respond to their friend/master's verbal instructions, both with actions and verbal acknowledgments. The RCs would have to be fairly large, possibly human size, in order to perform the required physical work. They would each have their own computer and operating systems, programmed according to the needs of their individual friend/master and able to communicate electronically with the smart home, smart car, and other computer systems. They would also be equipped with various sensors to "see" and "hear" what is going on about them and know what is happening in their environment. Their shape, the number and form of their limbs, and other extensions would depend on what functions they might be required to accomplish, and the addition of new limbs, or removal of old limbs, might be necessary if they were given new tasks. Ideally, the RCs would be endowed with some anthropomorphic qualities that might help older people more readily identify with them. Each one would be named by its friend/master who would summon it when needed.

As programmed or by specific command, the RC would execute all the household chores, relieving its master of those responsibilities and associated stresses. It would clean the house regularly—dusting, vacuuming, and washing, using appropriate cleansers and detergents. Removing the dirty bed linens, towels, and clothes, it would wash and dry all the laundry, fold and stack the pieces, and put them away. It would make the bed with new linens and put out new towels. Though these tasks and their frequency might be programmed in, its master could order the bed to be changed or a new wash to be done if he or she had been incontinent or there had been other problems. (Many older people are mortified by having soiled bedsheets or clothes, but find it too demanding physically to constantly wash and clean everything. Having an RC would eliminate this concern.) Cooking and shopping would also be handled by the RC. It could provide a meal either by following instructions from its master, or it could be programmed by a family member or visiting nurse to prepare and serve particular meals if its master was incapable of giving instructions. Programming could occur from distant locations, so that a visit would not be necessary each time the meal content or schedule was changed. RCs could also be directed to cook meals for special diets, for example, low salt, low fat, diabetic, etc, and gourmet dishes or ethnic foods to suit individual tastes.

For those older people incapable of feeding themselves, the robotic companion could take over that role as well, making certain their charges ingested adequate amounts of food and fluids. Meals could be pureed when needed, or mixed with thickeners, and even if feeding were laborious, the RC would show infinite patience in spooning out nutrients to its friend/master. The RC could also check the food stocks regularly with its scanner and order provisions from a delivery service at the local supermarket when different items in the pantry or refrigerator were running low. When the food was delivered, the RC would put everything away. Being cared for by their robotic companions, elderly people would no longer be afflicted by malnutrition or dehydration.

Substituting for a home health aide, the RC could also render help with other tasks of daily living such as bathing, washing, and general hygiene. If the person were disabled enough, it could perform the job completely, changing underwear or diapers if its friend/master was incontinent. (Again, these tasks could be preprogrammed, if its master could not furnish directions.) The RC could also dress its charge and get him or her up in a wheelchair if it were necessary, placing him or her in front of the television or offering other forms of entertainment. The companion could play cards, checkers, chess, or other games if its friend/master was able and interested. It could also engage in conversation, relate the latest news, or be a general source of information. Perhaps it could even provide words of comfort and support if it were programmed properly, like a friend who was available at all times. If guests came to visit, it could hang up their coats and serve them drinks, snacks, or meals.

In addition to acting as a home health aide, maid, and companion for many older people, the robotic companion could serve as a visiting nurse and physical therapist for those who were housebound. As a visiting nurse, it could supervise and administer medications as programmed to do so by the patient's physician or actual nurse. It could also take blood pressure, pulse, and temperature and measure blood sugars, oxygen levels, and other important parameters. This information could be forwarded to the nurse or physician, who could then adjust medications or change other orders. Its constant attendance and monitoring of the patient would allow for frequent corrections in the patient's regimen, resulting in superior care. In its role as physical therapist, the RC would regularly put its master through range of motion or other appropriate exercises, as well as helping him or her with ambulation. The RC would also serve as a transporter for any disabled person, taking him or her by car for doctor's appointments or any other important meetings outside the home. In all of its functions, the RC would be ready for action twenty-four hours a day, at its friend/master's beck and call, needing no sleep and performing the most menial and repellent tasks without complaining.

Smart bedrooms have already been developed that use microchips to monitor people's temperatures, metabolic rates, cardiograms, and blood sugars,[5] as have smart toilets that measure weight, fat content of stools, and urine sugars. This data can be transmitted to the person's physician who can utilize it in patient management. A robot is also presently available that does vacuuming and cleaning in the home, using onboard sensors to avoid obstacles.[6] It apparently does a reasonable job cleaning, though it has some problems in tight corners. A lawn mowing robot can be currently purchased as well and a snow shoveling robot should be commercially available shortly.

THE AGING PROCESS AND DISEASES OF THE ELDERLY

Though scientific progress will transform the aging process itself in the next ten to twenty years, people who are currently middle-aged or older may not reap much benefit from these modifications. However, their children and grandchildren will. Our generation or the one following may be the last to die prematurely from heart disease, strokes, and cancer, with life expectancies in the Western industrialized countries increased significantly, from 80 to about 120 years or more. And not only will people survive longer, but they will be healthier and more active and able to enjoy their old age to a much greater extent than is true today. Our generation is already living longer than that of our parents, and our children will live longer still. However, we also feel healthier, younger, and more vibrant than our parents' generation as we are aging. We considered our parents old at fifty or sixty and they also thought of themselves as over the hill. At fifty, sixty, or seventy today, many are still raring to go, looking forward to the challenges ahead. (Age categories will also have to be redefined as average life expectancy increases. If people live to 120, middle age might be from 50 to 85, with old age from 85 to 120.)

Preventive maintenance will be the catchword for physicians and other medical personnel in the future. Their goal will be to keep people healthy and avoid illnesses, rather than to treat them once they arise. There will be frequent checkups and diagnostic evaluations of patients, much of which will be totally automated. A person will come to a "health station" (or physician's office) periodically where he or she will have all physiologic parameters measured, including blood pressure, pulse, temperature, EKG, EEG, urine composition, and blood chemistries. Blood will not have to be drawn to be analyzed, but instead will be surveyed by spectrophotometry through the skin. On a routine basis, total body scans will be performed to search for evidence of cancer and other diseases or various structural changes, with more specific testing of organ systems when indicated. Of course, if a person does become sick, rapid diagnosis using the above techniques will aid in treatment, and new therapeutic modalities will be available to maximize patient recovery and restoration of function.

Genetic profiles on everyone will be a standard part of the assessment, used to determine an individual's susceptibility to a host of illnesses. This will be of particular value in assessing the risk of different types of cancers and hereditary diseases. Even today, women with or without certain cancer suppressor genes can be made aware of the possibility that they might develop breast or ovarian cancer. Soon, this will be true for many other cancers as well as other diseases. Another aspect of genetic profiling will be to match pharmaceutical agents with the people receiving them to be sure the most effective drug is being used.

More sophisticated computers and software programs in the future will be the key to improved patient evaluation, both from a preventive standpoint and to treat illnesses. When a patient comes to see a physician, he or she will have vast amounts of data available. In addition to body scans, physiologic determinations and genetic profiles, there will be information on past illnesses, responses to therapy, allergies, and total medical history. Computers will assist in putting everything together to arrive at a differential diagnosis, though the doctor's judgment will be required to decide on the most likely cause, using intuition and past experience as well as factual information. And once the diagnosis is established, the computer will review the medical literature, presenting the physician with all the therapeutic options and their probabilities of success. Then, finally, a computer will be used to monitor the patient during treatment to see whether the option taken is working and the patient is recovering. If the expected progress is not occurring, the physician will be alerted and another pathway can be utilized.

Within several decades, nanotechnology will also play a major role in diagnosing and treating various ailments under computer control. Machines, sensors, and robots too small to be seen by the human eye will be placed in people's bodies to travel through their bloodstreams and lymphatic pathways and around different organs and body cavities to monitor their status and perform certain tasks. These might include destroying cancerous cells, cleaning away atherosclerotic plaques, repairing damaged joints, and delivering drugs to targeted cells.

In the years ahead, the ravages of age, degenerative disorders, and diseases affecting each organ system will be able to be attacked and reversed by various means, including increased replacement of body parts, giving credence to the fantasy of the "bionic man." Research and development by medical technology companies and medical schools is already active in this area and the fruits of their labor will become more available to us.

THE CARDIOVASCULAR SYSTEM

As we enter the twenty-first century, diseases and malfunctions of the cardiovascular system are the most significant causes of death and disability in the industrialized world. A number of different techniques are being used to address these disorders, including cardiac bypass surgery, angioplasty, stenting, thrombolysis, valve replacement, and permanent pacemakers. Currently, lasers and microscopic scalpels as well as expandable balloons can be threaded by catheter into arteries in different areas of the body to open up the vessels. All of these procedures have been continually improved since they were first introduced, decreasing the associated risks and complications.

Veins from a different area of the body, an animal blood vessel, or a teflon graft can also be used to replace an obstructed section of an artery. In time, we can expect new blood vessels that are grown in cell cultures as well as in genetically engineered animals to be used as substitutes for human arteries that are blocked or damaged. Or with special techniques, new arteries may be encouraged to grow within the person who requires them, providing blood flow to tissues that were lacking it. All of these advances, of course, would primarily benefit the elderly, where atherosclerosis causes so many problems. However, in the future, it is also likely that the use of various medications and gene therapy may greatly reduce the ubiquity and severity of atherosclerosis, eliminating blockage of the arteries and rendering many of these procedures unnecessary.

A little over three decades ago, the transplantation of a human heart was viewed as science fiction, until Dr. Christian Barnard performed the first one in South Africa in 1967. Now they are seen as extraordinary surgical feats, but certainly achievable and with a high rate of success, given the improvement in drugs that suppress rejection. Heart transplants are employed only when a person's heart has been irreparably damaged and can no longer function effectively, utilizing someone's heart who has died from a noncardiac cause. However, the utility of this operation has been limited by the small number of hearts available, with many good candidates dying before acceptable organs can be found. In the future, genetically engineered animal hearts (or hearts grown from our own cells) may be used to fill the need, though totally artificial mechanical hearts are also being developed and may ultimately serve as substitutes. Eventually, as the supply of hearts increases, older people who until now have not been considered for heart transplants, may become worthy candidates.

The Brain and Central Nervous System

Since the brain is a network of billions of interconnected neurones, with a multiplicity of pathways linking all the cells, transplanting large sections of the brain that are damaged or not working properly is presently not believed to be feasible. However, there are other ways to approach the problems of central nervous system diseases. Stem cells, which can be harvested from various sources, both fetal and nonfetal, when transplanted into animal brains have been shown to migrate to damaged areas and have replaced some of the dead tissues. The significance of this is immense for people with neurological diseases or injuries, holding out the possibility that their deficits may be able to be improved at some time in the future.[7] These could potentially be used to replace damaged brain in strokes, Parkinson's disease, Alzheimer's disease and head trauma, and could restore severed pathways in spinal cord injuries.

However, stroke, the major cause of brain injury, will be reduced by improved prophylaxis—finding susceptible individuals and cleaning out their blocked arteries before a stroke happens. Or giving medication that prevents clots from forming in these blood vessels. Or lowering cholesterol and other blood lipids so that atherosclerosis does not even begin. It may also be possible to use specific substances immediately after a stroke has occurred to protect the brain tissues and minimize damage. Or thrombolysis will restore blood flow to the brain by dissolving the arterial clot and reversing the effects of the stroke. Then, if none of these avenues are successful, stem cells may be used to repair the areas that have been destroyed.

Alzheimer's disease may be eliminated by compounds that prevent the deposition of abnormal substances (beta amyloid) in the brain and dysfunction of the brain cells. Parkinson's disease may be halted at an early stage by the use of other compounds that work on different cells. And transplants of primitive stem cells to regions of the brain that have degenerated may be used to reconstitute neural pathways that have been lost. But in both diseases, genetic manipulation may ultimately be utilized to prevent the brain cells from being damaged and destroyed.

Cures for multiple sclerosis and ALS (Lou Gehrig's disease) will probably also occur in the next ten to twenty years. Various genetic diseases such as Huntington's chorea and the cerebellar degenerations will be solved through gene manipulation. One of the major causes of disability in the United States, traumatic brain injuries, will be less of a problem as the new techniques are utilized to replace the damaged cells with transplants of primitive neurones that will differentiate into the cells that are needed. Implanted electrical stimulators may also be used to control seizures, tremors, and different types of tics.

Mental Illness

Diseases that affect mood, thought processes, and behavior, including garden-variety anxiety and depression, will also be better managed in the future with new medications, genetic modification, and possibly new behavioral techniques.

Sensory Systems

Techniques that improve hearing and vision will greatly enhance quality of life for many older people in the twenty-first century. Some of the disorders that impair these senses are genetic in origin and may be treatable when the underlying abnormalities are elucidated. Others are caused by different types of injuries, either direct or indirect, that results in damage to the sensory organs. These can often be alleviated by replacement of the damaged part (a new lens after removing a cataract), or augmenting function that still remains (use of a hearing aid). These kinds of approaches should work even better as the design of the substituted elements is further refined. On the horizon, there is also the possibility of replacing useless eyes and ears with small cameras or receivers that connect to computers and the appropriate pathways in the brain to restore lost function. There has already been some experimental work with "artificial eyes" that are able to detect gross black and white forms and movement. Taste and smell, which decline with age, may be able to be corrected as well with certain compounds or new populations of cells in designated locations.

Musculoskeletal System

Many of the problems in this area involve degenerative joint disease and arthritis that cause pain and limit activities. Joint replacement with artificial joints of metal and plastic is already a well-established option for people with these conditions. Usage will only increase as better joints are fabricated and operative techniques evolve. New substances may also be developed that retard wear and tear in the joints and strengthen joint cartilage. Implanting new cartilage from cell cultures into deteriorated joints may be effective as well in restoring mobility to the joints. Utilizing cells directly in the damaged joints to manufacture new cartilage is another mechanism that might prove to be efficacious.

Osteoporosis is presently being treated with various drugs that promote calcium deposition in the bones. Muscle weakness is common as well in older people, leading to the appearance of frailty. In the future, through exercise programs and newer medications, osteoporosis will be reduced and muscle strength dramatically improved. Frailty in the elderly will be replaced by vigor and robustness that will heighten self-esteem and permit activities that were previously abandoned.

Organ Replacement

Various organs besides the heart that can be destroyed by infectious agents or chemicals, such as the liver, the kidneys, the lungs, or the pancreas, will be replaced more easily in the years ahead, allowing people with these problems to survive into and through old age. The substitute organs may come from animals (pigs, sheep, chimps) that are raised for this purpose, with possible genetic engineering to make the donor organs more compatible with the recipient. Growing these organs from the person's own cells in cell culture may also become feasible. Improvements in dialysis and artificial livers may be used as well to increase short- and long-term survival and better quality of life.

Several laboratories have recently been able to culture human stem cells, a primitive cell that is capable of developing into many different types of mature cells. This heightens the possibility that specific tissues and even organs from a particular individual will be able to be produced in the laboratory using his or her own genetic material. These tissues or organs could then be surgically implanted back into this person to substitute for organs that were malfunctioning, with no danger of rejection. Initially, this scenario will occur in people who have vital organs that are seriously damaged by disease or injury. However, as the technique becomes more commonplace and less costly, it will be used to replace organs or tissues that are worn out or less effective because of aging. Thus, a person may ask for a new heart because he or she can't exercise as vigorously as in the past. Or a skin graft may be requested for cosmetic reasons because the skin is wrinkled and pigmented, even though it is still functional. The day will come when our own genetic material in newly grown cells and organs will be used routinely to rejuvenate each of us by replacing old parts.

Cancer

Cancer and the aging process appear to be interrelated problems that are currently being tackled in various scientific laboratories. Many researchers believe that the secret of what makes cells cancerous will also reveal the mechanism of aging. While surgery and chemotherapeutic agents may be successful now in curing specific cancers, they do not allow a universal approach to the disease that unlocking its genetic key may provide. As mentioned earlier, the number of times a cell may divide is programmed into it at its inception. Like a biological clock, the telomere in the genetic material of the cell controls how many additional times that cell may divide, with a finite number of divisions possible from the time the organism itself was conceived. If this mechanism fails, then the cell becomes able to reproduce itself wildly and cancerous growth ensues. When scientists determine how telomeres work, they will probably be able to prevent cancer. In addition, it is likely they will be able to reprogram cells and allow them to divide longer, replacing damaged ones with fresh new cells and rejuvenating the recipient.

OTHER ASPECTS OF THE AGING PROCESS

There are other aspects of aging that need to be addressed as well in relation to improved functioning and quality of life. One of these is the decrement in memory and cognitive abilities that occurs as we grow older and is present in everyone to varying degrees. As we search for answers to Alzheimer's disease and dementia, we may find answers to the less severe impairment of memory and intellectual ability that is commonplace in normal aging. We may discover that particular nutrients, vitamins, or drugs are helpful in arresting or preventing cognitive decline by augmenting chemical transmission between the neurones, or by encouraging new connections (synapses) between these cells, or by growing new neurones. Or perhaps there is a genetic solution to this problem. Or perhaps there is an answer we have not even considered. Increasing amounts of research dollars in both the public and the private sectors will be directed to this area in the years ahead. Only when this problem is solved and our minds are able to perform better as we age, will we be able to fully enjoy the extra time we have been granted.

Another question that needs to be answered is why some ninety-year-old people are able to live on their own and manage quite well, while others of the same age, though not demented or physically ill, need significant assistance in running their daily lives. The reasons for these differences, when not the result of disease, have to be explored. Perhaps depression or mental outlook plays a role. Or perhaps there is a brain center for initiative and self-reliance that is more developed in some people.

In our quest for eternal youth, continued sexuality is part of the formula, as perceived by most individuals and by society. With different therapeutic measures now in use, sexual function in older people has been enhanced significantly and will only improve further with new medications that are being developed. At some point perhaps, in our idealized world, we can imagine men and women one hundred years old, but looking young, making love, and rushing off to play tennis or some other activity, fully enjoying life after retirement.

An AARP publication summarized what we might all expect from medical science in the next ten to one hundred years:

- A scan of your genetic structure (with billions of bits of data about the estimated 80,000 genes in your body) will detect symptoms or susceptibility to particular diseases.
- Nanobots—minuscule robots—will deliver medications to affected cells to prevent or treat disease. Or they will clear clogged arteries or repair damaged tissue.

- You can have your checkup anywhere, anytime. You can have your vital signs tested by machines at the drugstore and send the results to your doctor by the Internet for analysis.
- Hospitals will fade away. A surgeon in Boston will do your hip replacement at your home in Cleveland via virtual reality. The doctor will view the surgical site on a screen and remotely manipulate surgical instruments inserted by a technician.
- Implanted biochips will monitor your vital signs, alerting you or your doctor to an impending crisis.
- Replacing diseased or worn-out body parts will be as routine as replacing auto parts today.[8]

The four ways that survival and quality of life will be bolstered in the future include replacement of organs, genetic manipulation of cells, new drugs that work in various ways on our cells, and lifestyle changes. Though the promise is there of greater longevity and a healthier, more rewarding life for all of us, self-destructive behavior by some individuals may negate the possibilities of new therapies and relegate these people to an early demise or significant disabilities. We each have to take care of our own bodies and cannot expect medical science to undo all the abuse to which we have subjected ourselves. The most obvious types of self-destructive behavior include cigarette smoking, immoderate alcohol intake, and the use of drugs. Repeated dietary indiscretions, overeating, a sedentary lifestyle and a lack of physical exercise also exacts a toll on our bodies. In addition, driving recklessly or at excessive speeds, taking physical risks, or engaging in violence can potentially result in severe injuries or even death that can foreshorten life or make it less pleasurable. But if we act reasonably and show proper respect for our bodies, old age may be long and satisfying.

SOCIAL CHANGES

In the future, with the elderly comprising a larger segment of our population, changes will occur in current social mores and beliefs, and in the workings of society. Two factors guarantee a transformation. The first is the increased political power of older people because of their greater numbers and willingness to participate in the political process. The second is the heightened economic power of the elderly, with an even higher proportion of national wealth in the years ahead controlled by retired older people.

Older people will also learn how to better use their power. This means that politicians will have to pay more attention to the needs of seniors and pass legislation that meets their expectations. American corporations will also be aiming more of their products at seniors and new businesses that cater to older people will come into being. Thus, the smart cars, smart homes, robotic companions, and other innovations that I mentioned earlier are more likely to be developed and produced in quantity, as there will be consumers ready and able to buy them. More mass entertainment will be directed toward seniors as well, with movies and television stressing themes that are of interest to an older audience. Advertising content on television and the radio will target the elderly, with older men and women pitching products instead of young, nubile kids. In Japan, a mall has already been built that particularly targets seniors, with products that invoke nostalgia or cater to older people's needs.[9] Having opened in the fall of 2002, it is extremely successful, and other similar ventures are expected to follow.

Though society's attitudes toward the elderly may well improve in the future, some generational conflict can still be anticipated. There will still be envy of seniors' wealth and influence, and some younger men and women will be confrontational and discourteous, as is true today. Another reason for animosity between the generations is that in the next few decades, smaller numbers of young people will be working to "support" greater numbers of the elderly who are on Social Security. Though the heightened productivity of American workers may make this sustainable for a while, some adjustments will undoubtedly be necessary to ensure that those who need Social Security will get it, without putting undue pressure on those who are still working.

The increase in life expectancy will raise the question of when people should retire and the suitability of mandatory retirement ages in the corporate world, academia, and government. If people live to 120 and are generally in good health, should they be made to retire at age 65? That would mean they would work an average of forty years and be retired for an average of fifty-five years. (If current survival is to age seventy-nine, the numbers are forty and fourteen.) Not only would longer survival put a greater burden on society to assist these retirees, but one could assume that the retirees themselves would be subject to boredom and malaise. However, if we allowed these individuals to keep working and maintain their positions and seniority until age eighty or ninety, younger people would be frustrated by their inability to advance and assume leadership roles. And perhaps innovation would be stifled by having the same employees in place for years.

If they are cognitively and physically sound, older people should be able to work longer than the current retirement ages and setting a mandatory retirement age should depend on changes in life expectancy in the years ahead. (Working longer, older people would also have time to accumulate more wealth by putting money away in tax-free retirement accounts, allowing it to compound. With people employed into their seventies and eighties, the Social Security system would be aided as well, as these workers would be putting more money into the fund, rather than taking it out.) However, it would not be good policy to permit individuals to remain ensconced in specific jobs indefinitely, since that would be unfair to those below them and might lessen worker enthusiasm and productivity. One solution to this problem might be to place limits on the length of time any person could continue in one position regardless of age, perhaps rotating people into different roles. This would ensure upward and lateral mobility for everyone and fresh approaches to management and problem solving.

Older people might also be encouraged to embark on second careers, even though they may have been on a particular track for most of their lives. This might be in a completely divergent area, rather than an allied field. Many individuals might find satisfaction in new careers that were emotionally and socially productive, rather than financially lucrative, especially if they had been well compensated before; for example, teaching or social work instead of investment banking. Or if they had been in low-paying service jobs previously, they could opt for something that was more economically rewarding after returning to school or receiving additional training. Perhaps some people who were financially secure would perform volunteer work or help out nonprofit agencies without remuneration. Or they might work for political parties or special interest groups or fulfill creative impulses. Though, currently, people-oriented rather than technical jobs appear to be the strong suit of the elderly, in the future, enhanced cognitive function should allow older people to handle the most intellectually demanding positions.

There are some researchers in gerontology and cell biology who believe that a human life expectancy of 160 to 180 years is feasible, with a good quality of life for most people. If they are correct, think of what this might portend for the Social Security system or the allocation of time between work and retirement. Yet, we may find there are less available jobs for everyone because of increased productivity fueled by the computer revolution, permitting businesses and government to operate with reduced personnel. Then the priority would have to be employment for younger people to stem any social unrest. Indeed, society may actually have to create make-work jobs to keep people occupied. However, the number of individuals in service jobs can certainly be increased to provide a better level of service, even though it may not be absolutely necessary or help the corporate bottom line. And the elderly could play a role here. With more teachers, we could reduce class sizes to help students learn. More doctors and nurses would be able to spend more time with their patients. More salesclerks would be able to pay more attention to customers. More computer support personnel would cut waiting time and provide greater support. Though hiring all these people and keeping them employed would be costly, society would benefit greatly from this expense.

Continuing Education

Currently, we attend school during childhood and our early adult years, perhaps taking a course here and there afterward. However, it might make sense as we live much longer lives to return to school periodically, not only to improve our skills in our chosen fields, but to learn more about living well, with courses in the humanities and philosophy, literature, and psychology. We would derive so much more out of these subjects in the light of our life experience. It would also give us the opportunity to explore new areas of interest and possibly discover new careers. We might envision a year or two of further university study for those who desired it at ages forty to forty-five, sixty to sixty-five, and eighty to eighty-five, or at any age. While courses could be taken over the Internet, it would be preferable for individuals to return to the classroom, where there would be social interaction with new people and discourse that would be stimulating. Corporations might even encourage their employees to take these study sabbaticals, then return to work fresh and invigorated.

Leisure Time

Regardless of measures taken to increase the number of jobs, people are going to find themselves with huge amounts of additional leisure time in the future that they must find ways to fill. Particularly for those living into their nineties, or even one hundred and beyond, this will be the overwhelming fact of their lives—a challenge that must be met by the individuals themselves, with the help of society. Playing golf or cards every day for fifty or sixty years will not be enough for most older people, who will want to use their minds and bodies in a more productive fashion. Perhaps there will be special schools and training centers set up for the elderly (who would actually be considered middle-aged), with counselors, therapists, and teachers to assist them in finding activities that are rewarding, to make their extra years of life truly satisfying.

10

OBSERVATIONS AND CONCLUSIONS

Ultimately, man should not ask what the meaning of his
life is, but rather he must recognize that it is *he* who is asked.
In a word, each man is questioned by life; and he can only
answer to life by *answering for* his own life; to life he
can only respond by being responsible.

—VIKTOR E. FRANKL
MAN'S SEARCH FOR MEANING

Growing old is a succession of steps on the path of life leading eventually to death. We can influence the route we take in a number of ways and improve the quality of our lives as we age, but must acknowledge the inevitability of death. That said, we should still attempt to protect our minds and bodies as much as possible from the ravages of aging. This does not entail battling to remain young, but merely trying to remain in control of as much of our lives as we can for as long as we can. The situation is quite different from what it was a millennia ago and even a century ago, when life expectancy was shorter and the elderly were isolated survivors among the multitudes of the young. Now, the elderly are a growing minority with their own subculture that crosses race, ethnicity, and gender. Still, their voices are not always heard.

Even though people are living longer and better than in the past, nature and society still conspire to rob us of our dignity and vitality as we age. And the older we get, the more successful these adversaries seem to be in their depredations against us. Our cells and tissues deteriorate, and different diseases take their toll. Our organs may be damaged and stop working normally, and expected bodily functions are no longer reliable. And in addition to these changes, society puts up barriers that make it even more arduous for us to live well, causing us to feel obsolete and subservient. Because of this discrimination, it is more difficult for us to fulfill our potential and enhance our happiness in our later years, having to deal with societal slights and insults as well as our physical dissolution. Yet, in most cases, we manage to resist and carry on with our lives.

At any age, we can still fight to secure our dignity against the consequences of growing older and society's attempts to constrain us. That does not mean we will always be successful, but the struggle itself is essential if we are to preserve our self-esteem. It is also important for us to understand there are aspects of our lives that we can affect and others over which we have no power. The part within our domain must be managed to our advantage and we must take responsibility here for our actions—for our failures as well as our achievements. And that which is beyond our control, must be accepted: illnesses, disabilities, loss of loved ones. True dignity is not complaining over the cards that life has dealt us and being envious of others, but making the most of the hand we have. We cannot go around feeling sorry for ourselves, lamenting our situations and what has occurred in the past, for that accomplishes nothing. We are who we are and that will not change.

We must also recognize that time is precious to all of us, an irreplaceable commodity, and that at any moment in our lives, the only time we have is the present, the future being uncertain. When we are young, decades are in the offing, but when we are old, our years are meager. We must use them well. Working within our limitations, we must try to overcome the afflictions imposed on us by chance, or our own missteps. We must utilize our remaining potential to the fullest extent possible, for our dignity is at least partially determined by what we do with what we have. No matter what our status may be, we must try to maximize both our productivity and our pleasure, to make our lives worth living.

THE AGING PROCESS

Normal aging occurs on both a cellular level and throughout each organism. The changes that take place in the cells are manifest in various tissues and organs of the body, and are visible as diminished functional abilities. The actual mechanism responsible for aging is not yet clear, but we do know that as cells become old, their capacity to divide decreases and that this is programmed in genetically. Their metabolism also slows, reducing the production of proteins, while also affecting carbohydrates, fats, enzyme systems, and

DNA. With cellular performance faltering, the organism as a whole becomes more susceptible to disease, with impairment of the immune system and less reserve. All organs become less efficient and fail more easily with any insults to that specific organ or the body in general.

A diminution in muscle mass and general strength is another expected result of aging, with bones more fragile and liable to break more easily. The lungs are less elastic and oxygen exchange is not accomplished as readily. The heart muscle becomes stiffer and thicker, and the maximal heart rate is reduced. The liver is smaller in size and there is less enzymatic activity. The kidneys also shrink and there is attenuated blood flow and decreased renal function. Hormone production is lowered as well, with the sexual organs particularly affected. Vision and hearing are significantly less acute, along with the other sensory modalities. The brain also atrophies and loses cells, leading to mild degrees of cognitive compromise and problems with balance and coordination.

DISEASES OF OLD AGE

Diseases with a predilection for the elderly compound the normal changes that are part of aging, magnifying any functional decline. Illnesses affecting the brain are the most devastating, causing dementias, speech difficulties, paralysis of extremities, and impairment of gait and balance. Cardiac dysfunction produces chest pain, shortness of breath, fatigue, and fluid retention. Pulmonary compromise is manifested by shortness of breath and oxygen hunger. Hip fractures hinder walking and mobility. Degenerative spine disease can be responsible for back and leg pain, and can also affect ambulation. Multiple complications can develop from diabetes and hypertension. Different types of cancers are also more common in older people, some catastrophic, others curable.

AGING, ILLNESS, AND THE LOSS OF DIGNITY AND VITALITY

Because of the effects of the aging process and diseases on us, we are more likely to have our protective armor of dignity chipped away as we grow older. Our ability to walk and get around may be decreased, with our balance deficient and weakness or pain restricting our movements. We may be chronically short of breath or experience chest pain on exertion. Our vision may deteriorate to the point where we cannot drive and are unable to read. Bladder and bowel control may be difficult and we may soil ourselves at times. Our memories start to fail and our thinking is not as clear as it had been. Anxiety or depression may also limit our activities and we stay in our houses more, interacting less with other people. Suddenly, we discover we can no longer shop for food and other necessities. We may have problems reconciling our checkbooks and managing our financial affairs. Then, a point may be reached when we have lost our autonomy and are no longer in charge of our own lives, with various aspects of our independence surrendered or taken from us. In addition, our peers have died off and we have fewer friends and family available to provide love and support. And our pride, self-confidence, and self-esteem begin to wane.

Unless there is a specific illness or injury that supervenes, our loss of independence is usually a gradual process, where we cede certain functions to others willingly or have them seized despite our opposition. We may find that we are being helped with physical tasks we may or may not be able to handle ourselves. The administration of our lives and the daily decisions begin to be made by someone else. Living in our own homes may become impractical and we may have to move in with one of our children or perhaps to an assisted living residence. Though at the onset the help we are given may be minimal, it continues to increase over time. And eventually, family members can no longer furnish the care we may require. Home health care aides may step into the breach and we may be allowed to remain at home with their assistance—strangers giving us medication and helping with the tasks of daily living. However, even this may not be enough for some of us and we may be sent off to spend our final days in the confines of a nursing home, where any shred of dignity we might have left is torn from us.

SOCIETY AND THE ELDERLY

On top of our physical and cognitive problems, society is not kind to us as we grow older. Younger people tend to overlook older peoples' experience, while society as a whole disregards them and does not pay attention to their needs. If they wish to work and are capable, they may be unable to retain a job or find new employment because of ageist bias. The media either ignores their needs and interests, or depicts them in stereotyped ways. Many reside in age-related ghettos because they are uncomfortable out in the world and there is not enough of an effort made to help them fit in. Because older people are vulnerable, they are also victims of a disproportionate amount of crime, both scams and violent offenses. And they are the butt of ageist jokes that ridicule them because of their limitations and disabilities.

STRATEGIES FOR HOLDING ON TO DIGNITY AND VITALITY

Given all the elements arrayed against the elderly, what can be done to preserve our dignity and vitality as we grow older? As I have shown in this book, there are a number of strategies, both major and minor, that can be employed in this battle, but it is essential to maintain a positive mind-set. If we feel that whatever we do is of no value and will not help us, it is useless to try, for they certainly will not help. But if we believe we can modify our fate, at least to some degree, our struggle can be rewarding. Some of the strategies are as follows:

- The aging process must be accepted. It is normal to grow old with all the attendant difficulties that are part of aging.
- We must try to remain physically fit, as this impacts on many other aspects of our lives. Aerobic conditioning is vitally important and we should attempt at least an hour of vigorous exercise daily, unless there are medical contraindications.
- Proper nutritional rules should be followed and we should eat a well-balanced diet, avoiding excessive calories, fats, cholesterol, and so forth.
- We should not smoke and we should avoid abuse of alcohol and drugs, including prescription medications.
- Regular medical checkups can lead to early diagnosis of a number of conditions, allowing certain cancers to be cured, diabetes and hypertension to be treated, and a percentage of heart attacks and strokes to be prevented.
- Sexuality and intimacy among older people are normal and desirable, and we should not make value judgments about what other people do.
- We must remain intellectually and socially relevant so that we are not marginalized by other segments of society.
- We must do whatever is necessary to remain independent as long as possible and in every way possible, taking into account illnesses or disabilities. This is not to underestimate the problems this may entail for some people.
- If limitations on our activities are unavoidable, a shared dependency with a group of our peers should be sought if this is feasible—where we can help them with some aspects of their lives and they can help us with others.
- We should be candid about our disabilities and shortcomings, rather than trying to hide them from the world at large and looking foolish in our attempts.
- We should avoid constantly complaining about any hardships. It is undignified and people soon become desensitized and less sympathetic.

- It is important that we pay attention to our appearance even if we are retired. Appearances do matter and dignity is lost if one is careless in his or her dress or hygiene.
- Goals and objectives are vital at every stage of life and are necessary for all of us as we grow older. When careers are over and children are out of the house, we need to have reasons to get up every morning and look forward to each day. We need to have things that excite us, our own personal goals that give our lives substance and motivate us to keep going.
- We must be able to deal with grief and loneliness, for as we age, more of our relatives and friends will die. If we allow grief to continuously overwhelm us, our lives will no longer be worth living. And we must find ways to conquer loneliness and make new friends.
- We should not ignore the spiritual aspect of our existence, for that can bring us peace and contentment, and help us in our search for meaning.
- We should prepare for being old when we are young, as that will make the transition easier.

Whatever our goals and objectives are in later life, we should try to derive as much pleasure as we can in the time we have. There will not be other opportunities. Aging well means enjoying life. However, we should also try to give something back to others: those who are close to us, our communities, and the world at large. Being totally self-involved will not bring us happiness. There should be a balance between what we do for ourselves and what we do for others. And relationships are important and should not be neglected. Shared time with our spouses, children, friends, and other loved ones should be held dear.

We should also not try to tidy up our lives in preparation for death. There should always be projects that remain unfinished when we die.

I have mentioned a number of factors that play a role in empowering us as we age while helping us preserve our dignity. Four of these are critical:

- *Physical activity.* We must condition ourselves through regular exercise.
- *Independence.* No matter how difficult it may be, we should try to maximize our independence and self-sufficiency.
- *Relevance.* We must be aware of what is happening in the world around us.
- *Objectives.* As we age, we must have goals and objectives, some of which we are passionate about.

We all have an innate dignity that is shaped through the years by our experience hammering on the template of our genetic composition, becoming strong, but malleable. It provides protection from life's misfortunes, the abuses of society and those of our fellow human beings, allowing us to live according to our own precepts and beliefs, unable to be broken by external forces or internal doubts. We should do everything in our power never to relinquish this.

NOTES

—————————————— • ——————————————

CHAPTER 1

1. Mick Jagger and Keith Richards, "Mother's Little Helper," *Flowers*, 1967.

2. S. Burner et al., "Nation's Health Care Expenditures Projections through 2030," *Health Care Financing Review*, 14, no. 1 (1992): 4.

3. R. Yanick and L. Ries, "Cancer in the Aged—An Epidemiologic Perspective on Treatment Issues," *Cancer* 68 (1991): 2502.

4. Peter Peterson, *Gray Dawn* (New York: Times Books, Random House, 1999), 12.

5. R. Katzman and R. Terry, *The Neurology of Aging* (Philadelphia: F. A. Davis, 1983), 10.

6. Bernice Neugarten, in J. Rowe and R. Kahn, *Successful Aging* (New York: Pantheon Books, 1998), 9.

7. Centers For Disease Control and Prevention in Sheryl Gay Stolberg, "U.S. Life Expectancy Hits New High," *New York Times*, September 12, 1997.

8. J. Rowe and R. Kahn, *Successful Aging*, 10.

9. K. A. Pillemer and D. Finkelbor, "The Prevalence of Elder Abuse: A Random Sample Survey," *Gerontologist* 28 (1988): 51–57.

10. Sir William Osler, *Osler's Principles and Practice of Medicine* (New York: D. Appleton, 1927).

11. Thomas R. Cole, *The Journey of Life* (Cambridge: Cambridge University Press, 1992), xxv.

12. J. Rowe and R. Kahn, *Successful Aging*, 39.

13. Dylan Thomas, "Do Not Go Gentle into That Good Night," in *The New Oxford Book of English Verse* (Oxford: Oxford University Press, 1984), 942.

CHAPTER 2

1. Ralph Waldo Emerson, *Essays: First Series—Prudence* (Boston: Little-Brown, 1968), 607.

2. Michael Fossel, *Reversing Human Aging* (New York: William Morrow, 1996), 10.

3. Leonard Hayflick, *How and Why We Age* (New York: Ballantine Books, 1996), 122.

4. Ibid., 123.

5. Michael Fossel, "Telomerase and the Aging Cell—Implications for Human Health," *JAMA* 279 (1998): 1732–1735; Nicholas Wade, "Cell Rejuvenation May Yield Rush of Medical Advances," *New York Times*, January 20, 1998; and Nicholas Wade, "Cells' Life Stretched in Lab," *New York Times*, January 14, 1998.

6. Nicholas Wade, "How a Gamble on an Obscure Theory of Aging Paid Off," *New York Times*, February 17, 1998.

7. Gina Kolata, "Pushing Limits of the Human Life Span," *New York Times*, March 9, 1999.

8. Mark Williams, *The American Geriatric Society's Complete Guide to Aging and Health* (New York: Harmony Books, 1995), 12.

9. Roger Rosenberg, "Editorial: Time and Memory," *Arch Neurol* 59 (2002): 1699–1700.

10. See, for example, Nicholas Wade, "Scientists Say Aging May Result From Brain's Hormonal Signals," *New York Times,* Science sec. October 10, 2000.

11. Nicholas Wade, "A Pill to Extend Life. Don't Dismiss the Notion Too Quickly," *New York Times*, September 22, 2000.

12. Nicholas Wade, "Study Spurs Hope of Finding Way to Increase Human Life," *New York Times*, August 25, 2003.

13. Brian Vastag, "Cause of Progeria's Premature Aging Found. Medical News and Perspectives," *JAMA* 289 (2003): 2481–2482.

14. Philip Horner, "Editorial: Regeneration in the Adult and Aging Brain," *Arch Neurol* 59 (2002): 1717–1720.

15. R. Katzman and R. Terry, *The Neurology of Aging* (Philadelphia: F. D. Davis, 1983), 15–16.

16. Hayflick, *How and Why We Age*, 165.

17. Ibid., 160.

18. See Gina Kolata, "Chasing Youth, Many Gamble on Hormones," *New York Times*, December 22, 2002.

19. M. Vance, "Can Growth Hormone Prevent Aging?" *N Engl J Med* 348 (2003): 779.

20. Steven Lamberts, "Editorial: The Endocrinology of Aging and the Brain," *Arch Neurol* 59 (2002): 1709–1711; and M. Blackman et al., "Growth Hormone and Sex Steroid Administration in Healthy Aged Women and Men," *JAMA* 288 (2002): 2282–2292.

21. Susan Schiffman, "Taste and Smell Losses in Normal Aging and Disease," *JAMA* 278 (1997): 1357–1362; and C. Murphy et al., "Prevalence of Olfactory Impairment in Older Adults," *JAMA* 288 (2002): 2307–2312.

CHAPTER 3

1. B. Schoenberg, "Epidemiology of Dementia," *Neurology Clinics* (May 1986): 447.

2. Y. Liao et al., "Quality of the Last Year of Life of Older Adults: 1986 vs 1993," *JAMA* 283 (2000): 512–518.

3. M. Aronson et al., "Dementia—Age Dependent Incidence, Prevalence, and Morbidity in the Old-Old," *Arch Int Med* 151 (1991): 989.

4. C. Qiu et al., "The Influence of Education on Clinically Diagnosed Dementia Incidence and Mortality Data from the Kungsholmen Project," *Arch Neurol* 58 (2001): 2034–2039.

5. W. Kukull et al., "Dementia and Alzheimer's Disease Incidence," *Arch Neurol* 59 (2002): 1737–1746

6. H. Karp and S. Mirva, "Dementia in Adults," *Clinical Neurology* (Philadelphia: A. B. Baker, 1986), chap. 32, p. 1.

7. Kukull et al., "Dementia and Alzheimer's Disease Incidence," 1737–1746.

8. B. Winblad et al., "A 1-Year, Randomized, Placebo-Controlled Study on Donepezil in Patients with Mild to Moderate AD," *Neurology* 57 (2001): 489–495, and N. Trinh et al., "Efficacy of Cholinesterase Inhibitors in the Treatment of Neuropsychiatric Symptoms and Functional Impairment of Alzheimer's Disease," *JAMA* 289 (2003): 210–216.

9. Ruth Bonita, "Epidemiology of Stroke," *Lancet* 339 (1992): 342.

10. F. McDowell and J. Cedarbaum, "The Extrapyramidal System and Disorders of Movement," *Clinical Neurology* (Philadelphia: A. B. Baker, 1986), chap. 38, p. 19.

11. M. Mittlemark et al., "Prevalence of Cardiovascular Diseases among Older Adults," *Am J of Epidemiology* 137 (1993): 311.

12. G. Dewhurst et al., "A Population Survey of Cardiovascular Disease in Elderly People: Design, Methods, and Prevalence Results," *Age and Aging* 20 (1991): 353.

13. Economics and Statistics Administration, "Table Number 131, Deaths by Age and Leading Cause: 1993," *Vital Statistics* (Washington, DC: Economics and Statistics Administration, 1996).

14. Gina Kolata, "Vast Advance Is Reported in Preventing Heart Illnesses," *New York Times*, August 6, 1999.

15. R. Ross, "Mechanisms of Disease: Atherosclerosis—An Inflammatory Disease," *N Engl J Med* 340 (1999): 115–126.

16. A. Chobian et al., "The Seventh Report of the Joint National Committee on Prevention, Detection, Evaluation and the Treatment of High Blood Pressure," *JAMA* 289 (2003): 2560, and Thomas Kottke et al., "JNC 7. It's More Than High Blood Pressure," *JAMA* 289 (2003): 2573.

17. Chobian et al. "The Seventh Report," 2560.

18. Mark Williams, *Complete Guide to Aging and Health*, (New York: Random House, 1995), chap. 24, p. 389.

19. E. Laumann et al., "Sexual Dysfunction in the United States," *JAMA* 281 (1999): 537–544.

20. Mark Williams, *The American Geriatric Society's Complete Guide to Aging and Health* (New York: Harmony Books, 1995), 32.

21. D. Fesanich et al., "Walking and Leisure-Time Activity and Risk of Hip Fracture in Post Menopausal Women," *JAMA* 288 (2002): 2300–2306.

22. Geoff Winkley, "Hip Fractures," *EMedicine*, sec. 2 (2002).

23. American Cancer Society, *Cancer Facts and Figures 1993.*

24. Catherine Boring, "Cancer Statistics 1993," *Ca—A Cancer Journal for Clinicians* 43, no. 1 (January–February 1993), 7.

25. R. Yanick and L. Ries, "Cancer in the Aged—An Epidemiologic Perspective on Treatment Issues," *Cancer* 68 (1991): 2502.

26. Ibid.

27. Nadine Brozen, "Decades after Midlife Mark, a Frontier for Mental Health," *New York Times*, March 16, 1998.

28. Brenda Pennix et al., "Depressive Symptoms and Physical Decline in Community-Dwelling Older Persons," *JAMA* 279 (1998): 1720–1726.

29. Mark Williams, *Complete Guide to Aging and Health*, 193–194.

30. Jane Brody, "Hidden Plague of Alcohol Abuse by the Elderly," *New York Times*, April 2, 2002.

31. Christopher Wren, "Many Women 60 and Older Abuse Alcohol and Prescribed Drugs, Study Says," *New York Times*, June 15, 1998.

32. James Lubitz et al., "Health, Life Expectancy, and Health Care Spending among the Elderly," *N Engl J Med* 349 (2003): 1048–1055.

33. James Lubitz et al., "Longevity and Medicare Expenditures," *N Engl J Med* 332 (1995): 999–1003.

34. Vicki Freedman et al., "Recent Trends in Disability and Functioning among Older Adults in the United States," *JAMA* 288 (2002): 3137–3146.

35. James Fries, "Reducing Disability in Older Age," *JAMA* 288 (2002): 3164–3166.

36. Williams, *The American Geriatric Society's Complete Guide to Aging and Health*, 385.

37. June Stevens et al., "The Effect of Age on the Association between Body-Mass Index and Mortality," *N Engl J Med* 338 (1998): 1–7.

38. A. Vita et al., "Aging, Health Risks, and Cumulative Disability," *N Engl J Med* 338 (1998): 1035–1041.

CHAPTER 4

1. Erica Goode, "New Study Finds Middle Age Is Prime of Life," *New York Times*, February 16, 1999.

2. C. Morin et al., "Behavioral and Pharmacological Therapies for Late-Life Insomnia," *JAMA* 281 (1999): 991–999.

3. R. Petersen et al., "Current Concepts in Mild Cognitive Impairment," *Arch Neurol* 58 (2001): 1985–1992; D. Bennett et al., "Natural History of Mild Cognitive Impairment in Older Persons," *Neurology* 59 (2002): 198–205; and M. Elias et al., "The Preclinical Phase of Alzheimer Disease," *Arch Neurol* 57 (2000): 808–813.

4. See, for example, Roger Rosenberg, "Editorial: Time and Money," *Arch Neurol* 59 (2002): 1699–1700.

5. Sara Rimer, "For Aged, Dating Game Is Numbers Game," *New York Times*, December 23, 1998.

CHAPTER 5

1. Sara Rimer, "Families Bear a Bigger Share of Long-Term Care for the Frail Elderly," *New York Times*, national edition, June 8, 1998.

2. Peter Kilborn, "Disabled Spouses Are Increasingly Forced to Go It Alone," *New York Times*, May 31, 1999.

3. Richard Schulz and Scott Beach, "Caregiving as a Risk Factor for Mortality," *JAMA* 282 (1999): 2215–2219; and Janice Kiecolt-Glaser and Ronald Glaser, "Chronic Stress and Morbidity among Older Adults," *JAMA* 282 (1999): 2259–2260.

4. Schulz and Beach, "Caregiving as a Risk Factor for Mortality," 2215.

5. Tamar Lewin, "Report Looks at a Generation and Caring for Young and Old," *New York Times*, July 11, 2001.

6. Sara Rimer, "Study Details Sacrifices in Caring for Elderly Kin," *New York Times*, November 27, 1999.

7. Lewin, "Report Looks at a Generation and Caring for Young and Old."

8. Sara Rimer, "Blacks Carry Burden of Care for the Elderly," *New York Times*, March 15, 1998.

9. Nicholas Kristoff, "Once Prized, Japan's Elderly Feel Abandoned and Fearful," *New York Times*, August 4, 1997.

10. Robert Butler, "Editorial," *Geriatrics* 53 (1998): 8.

11. Sana Siwolop, "The Many Life Styles of Senior Housing," *New York Times*, sec. 11, May 16, 1999; and Sara Rimer, "A Niche for the Elderly, and for the Market," *New York Times*, May 9, 1999.

12. J. C. Conklin, "Nursing Homes Add 'Special Care,'" *Wall Street Journal*, August 7, 2000.

13. "They Didn't Live So Long for This," *New York Times*, April 26, 1999.

14. Hila Richardson, "In Long Term Care," *Health Care Delivery in the United States*, ed. Anthony Kovner (New York: Springer Publishing, 1990), 175–208.

15. A. Scitovsky and A. Capron, "Medical Care at the End of Life: The Interaction of Economics and Ethics—The Nation's Health" (Boston: Jones and Bartlett, 1990), 382–388.

16. Richardson, "In Long Term Care."

17. National Center for Health Statistics, "Americans Less Likely to Use Nursing Home Care Today," *HHS News*, January 23, 1997.

18. Sheryl Stolberg, "Study Finds Pain of Oldest Is Ignored in Nursing Homes," *New York Times*, June 17, 1998.

19. "They Didn't Live So Long for This."

20. Sara Rimer, "An Aging Nation Ill Equipped for Hanging Up the Car Keys," *New York Times*, December 15, 1997.

21. "Safety and Mobility of the Older Driver," *JAMA* 278 (1997): 66–67.

22. Thomas Cole, *The Journey of Life* (New York: Cambridge University Press, 1997), xix.

CHAPTER 6

1. Betty Friedan, *The Fountain of Age* (New York: Simon and Schuster, 1993), 41.

2. Thomas R. Cole, *The Journey of Life* (New York: Cambridge University Press, 1992), 64–65.

3. Ibid., 163–165.

4. David Rosenbaum, "Social Security: The Basics, with a Tally Sheet," *New York Times*, January 29, 1999.

5. John Tagliabue, "In France, Nothing Gets in the Way of Vacation," *New York Times*, August 24, 2003; and Fred Brock, "Victims of the Heat. Victims of Isolation," *New York Times*, business section, September 14, 2003.

6. Julie Flaherty, "A Company Where Retirement Is a Dirty Word," *New York Times*, sec. 3, December 28, 1997.

7. Fred Brock, "Slow to Learn the Lessons of Ageism," *New York Times*, Sunday business section, December 2, 2001.

8. Francis X. Clines, "Glenn Is Ready to Say Goodbye to All That," *New York Times*, June 13, 1998, national edition.

9. R. Butler and A. Luddington, "Aging Research: John Glenn's New Mission," *Geriatrics*, 53 (1998): 42–48.

10. Don Terry, "In This Brand-New City, No Shortage of Elders," *New York Times*, March 4, 1999.

11. Sara Rimer, "New Needs for Retirement Complexes' Oldest," *New York Times*, March 23, 1998.

12. Ibid.

13. Alan Feuer, "High Rise Colony of Workers Evolves for Their Retirement," *New York Times*, August 5, 2002.

14. Ivor Peterson, "As Taxes Rise, Suburbs Work to Keep Elderly," *New York Times*, February 27, 2001.

15. Robert Butler, "Commentary: Living Longer, Contributing Longer," *JAMA* 278 (1997): 1372–1373.

16. Bill Carter, "Faces on TV Get Younger and Comedy Is Not King," *New York Times*, May 24, 1999.

17. Anne Jarrell, "Models, Defiantly Gray, Give Aging a Sexy New Look," *New York Times*, sec. 9, November 28, 1999.

18. Douglas Frantz, "Sweepstakes Pit Gullibility and Fine Print," *New York Times*, July 28, 1998; and Douglas Frantz, "Phone Swindles Steal a Page from Publisher's Playbook," *New York Times*, July 29, 1998.

CHAPTER 7

1. Ruth La Ferla, "Over 60: Fashion's Lost Generation," *New York Times*, Sunday styles, December 3, 2000.

2. K. Mukamal et al., "Roles of Drinking Pattern and Type of Alcohol Consumed in Coronary Heart Disease in Men," *N Engl J Med* 348 (2003): 109–118.

3. Gunnar Eriksson et al., "Changes in Physical Fitness and Changes in Mortality," *Lancet* 352 (1998): 759–762; S. Blair et al., "Physical Fitness and All-Cause Mortality," *JAMA* 262 (1989): 2395–2401; S. Blair et al., "Changes in Physical Fitness and All-Cause Mortality," *JAMA* 273 (1995): 1093–1098; S. Blair et al., "Influences of Cardiorespiratory Fitness and Other Precursors on Cardiovascular Disease and All-Cause Mortality in Men and Women," *JAMA* 276 (1996): 205–210; E. Simonsick et al., "Risk Due to Inactivity in Physically Capable Older Adults," *Am J Public Health* 83 (1993): 1443–1450; Pekka Kannus, "Preventing Osteoporosis, Falls and Fractures among Elderly People," *BMJ* 318 (1999): 205–206; A. Hakim et al., "Effects of Walking on Mortality among Nonsmoking Retired Men," *N Engl J Med* 338 (1998): 94–99; L. Fried et al., "Risk Factors for 5-Year Mortality in Older Adults," *JAMA* 279 (1998): 585–592; L. Sandvik et al., "Physical Fitness as a Predictor of Mortality among Healthy Middle-Aged Norwegian Men," *N Engl J Med* 328 (1993): 533–537; R. Paffenbarger et al., "The Association of Changes in Physical-Activity Level and Other Lifestyle Characteristics with Mortality among Men," *N Engl J Med* 328 (1993): 538–545; W. Kraus et al., "Effects of the Amount and Intensity of Exercise on Plasma Lipoproteins," *N Engl J Med* 347 (2002): 1483–1492.

4. L. Kushi et al., "Physical Activity and Mortality in Postmenopausal Women," *JAMA* 277 (1997): 1287–1292; I. Lee et al., "Exercise Intensity and Longevity in Men," *JAMA* 273 (1995): 1179–1184; Michael Pratt, "Benefits of Lifestyle Activity vs Structured Exercise," *JAMA* 281 (1999): 375–376.

5. Jane Brody, "Panel Urges Hour of Exercise a Day; Sets Diet Guidelines," *New York Times*, September 6, 2002.

6. R. Butler et al., "Physical Fitness: Exercise Prescription for Older Adults," *Geriatrics* 53 (1998): 45–56; Holcomb Noble, "A Secret of Health in Old Age: Muscles," *New York Times*, October 20, 1998; Sara Rimer, "Older, Wiser, Stronger: Grandmas Head for the Weight Room," *New York Times*, June 21, 1998; M. Fiatarone et al., "High-Intensity Strength Training in Nonagenarians," *JAMA* 263 (1990): 3029–3034.

7. R. Butler et al., "Physical Fitness: Exercise Prescription for Older Adults," *Geriatrics* 53 (1998): 45–56.

8. Ibid.

9. I. Lee et al., "Body Weight and Mortality," *JAMA* 270 (1993): 2823–2828; J. Stevens et al., "The Effect of Age on the Association Between Body-Mass Index and Mortality," *N Engl J Med* 338 (1998): 1–7; and A. Vita et al., "Aging, Health Risks, and Cumulative Disability," *N Engl J Med* 338 (1998): 1035–1041.

10. K. Fontaine et al., "Years of Life Lost Due to Obesity," *JAMA* 289 (2003): 187–193; and J. Manson and S. Bassuk, "Obesity in the United States—A Fresh Look at Its High Toll," *JAMA* 289 (2003): 229–230.

11. W. Thompson et al., "Mortality Associated with Influenza and Respiratory Syncytial Virus in the United States," *JAMA* 289 (2003): 179–186.

12. Susan Jacoby, "Great Sex—What's Age Got to Do with It? The AARP/Modern Maturity Survey on Sexual Attitudes and Behavior," *Modern Maturity* (September–October 1999): 41.

13. E. Laumann et al., "Sexual Dysfunction in the United States," *JAMA* 281 (1999): 537–544.

14. Robert Butler, Editorial: "The Viagra Revolution," *Geriatrics* 53 (1998): 8–9.

15. Jane Gross, "Wielding Mouse and Modem, Elderly Remain in the Loop," *New York Times*, June 15, 1998.

16. K. Ball et al., "Effects of Cognitive Training Interventions with Older Adults," *JAMA* 288 (2002): 2271–2281.

17. H. Fillit et al., "Achieving and Maintaining Cognitive Vitality with Aging," *Mayo Clin Proc* 77 (2002): 681–696.

18. Christine Cassel, "Editorial: Use It or Lose It," *JAMA* 288 (2002): 2333–2335.

CHAPTER 8

1. Jane Brody, "Ways to Make Retirement Work for You," *New York Times*, July 24, 2001.

2. Robin Toner, "Shift by Older Voters to G.O.P. Is Democrats' Challenge in 2000," *New York Times*, May 31, 1999.

3. Frank Bruni, "89 and 2000 Miles to Go for Democracy," *New York Times*, April 27, 1999.

4. H. Koenig et al., "Does Religious Attendance Prolong Survival? A Six Year Follow-Up Study of 3968 Older Adults," *Journal of Gerontology*, 54A, no. 7 (1999): M370–M376.

5. Ibid.

6. Brett Pulley, "Glitzy Pastime, Gambling, Entices Elderly," *New York Times*, July 2, 1998.

7. Ibid.

8. Tom Chaffin, "The Song of the Road Leads over the Hill," *New York Times*, January 23, 1999.

9. Sara Rimer, "An Alaska Trek Makes Elders of the Aging," *New York Times*, September 2, 1998.

10. Edwin McDowell, "Travel Industry Finds Adventure Is Now Ageless," *New York Times*, February 20, 1999.

11. Ibid.

12. Jodi Wilgoren, "Golden Years Brings New Emphasis on Learning," *New York Times*, December 26, 1999.

13. Jay Tokasz, "White Hairs Settle in among the Ivy," *New York Times*, March 21, 2001.

14. T. Glass et al., "Population Based Study of Social and Productive Activities as Predictors of Survival among Older Americans," *BMJ* 319 (1999): 478–483.

15. Ibid.

16. J. Verghese et al., "Leisure Activities and the Risk of Dementia in the Elderly," *N Engl J Med* 348 (2003): 2508–2516.

17. J. Coyle, "Use It or Lose It. Do Effortful Mental Activities Protect against Dementia?" *N Engl J Med* 348 (2003): 2489–2490.

18. Douglas Martin, "To Be Old, Gifted, and Employed Is No Longer Rare," *New York Times*, sec. 3, January 14, 2001.

19. J. R. Brandstrader, "Great New Gigs—Retirees Are Jumping Back into the Labor Pool, for Fun and Profit," *Barron's*, March 24, 2003.

20. Mary Williams Walsh, "Reversing Decades-Long Trend, Americans Retiring Later in Life," *New York Times*, February 26, 2001.

21. Richard Stevenson, "Sides Are Squaring Off on Raising Retirement Age," *New York Times*, July 12, 1998.

22. Robert Butler, "Medicare and Beyond," *Columbia College Today* (Fall 1998), 40.

23. Sara Rimer, "Older People Want to Work in Retirement, Survey Finds," *New York Times*, September 2, 1999.

24. John Cutter, "Coming to Terms with Grief after a Longtime Partner Dies," *New York Times*, women's health, June 13, 1999.

25. Ibid.

26. Ernest Hemingway, *For Whom the Bell Tolls* (New York: Charles Scribner, 1968), 463.

27. Associated Press, "E-Mail and the Internet Brighten Nursing Homes," *New York Times*, November 23, 1999.

28. Fred Brock, "Catering to the Elderly Can Pay Off," *New York Times*, business section, February 3, 2002.

29. See, for example, Mary Duenwald, "Power of Positive Thinking Extends, It Seems, to Aging," *New York Times*, November 19, 2002.

CHAPTER 9

1. Dana Canedy, "Gadgets to Go Gentle into Age," *New York Times*, October 17, 1998.

2. Anne Eisenberg, "A 'Smart Home' to Avoid the Nursing Home," *New York Times*, April 5, 2001.

3. Katie Hafner, "Honey, I Programmed the Blanket," *New York Times*, May 17, 1999.

4. John Markhoff, "Intel and Alzheimer's Group Join Forces," *New York Times*, July 25, 2003.

5. John O'Neil, "'Smart Toilet' Keeps Track of Health," *New York Times*, May 18, 1999.

6. Scott Kirsner, "Making Robots, with Dreams of Henry Ford," *New York Times*, December 26, 2002.

7. Sandra Blakelee, "In Early Experiments, Cells Repair Damaged Brains," *New York Times*, science section, November 7, 2000.

8. Susan Crowley, "Hello to Our Future," *AARP Bulletin*, 41, no. 1 (2000): 3.

9. Howard French, "Hot New Marketing Concept: Mall as Memory Lane," *New York Times*, January 7, 2003.

FOR FURTHER REFERENCE

———————————————— • ————————————————

NUTRITION

Total Nutrition from the Mount Sinai School of Medicine. Edited by Victor Herbert, MD, and Geneel J. Subak-Sharpe, MS (New York: St. Martin's Griffin, 1994). Huge book with every bit of information related to eating and nutrition.

Jane Brody's Nutrition Book by Jane Brody (New York: Bantam Books, 1987). Still excellent advice by the health columnist for the *New York Times* on proper eating and nutrition for good health.

Beyond Cholesterol: The Johns Hopkins Complete Guide for Avoiding Heart Disease by Peter Kwiterovich, MD, Director, Lipid Research Unit, Johns Hopkins School of Medicine (Baltimore: Johns Hopkins University Press, 1989). Good advice on proper eating, what it all means, many recipes.

The New Living Heart Diet by Michael DeBakey, Antonio M. Gotto Jr., Lynn Scott, John Foreyt (New York: Fireside Simon and Schuster, 1996). How to eat well and healthy to avoid atherosclerosis and heart disease. Many recipes.

EXERCISE

The Complete Guide to Walking for Health, Weight Loss and Fitness by Mark Fenton (Guilford, Connecticut: Globe Pequot Press, 2001). All aspects of walking, stretching, exercise, nutrition, and so forth.

Running and Walking for Women over 40 by Katherine Switzer (New York: St. Martin's Griffin, 1998). Running and walking programs, beginners and advanced—comprehensive, clothing, shoes, and so forth.

Strong Women Stay Young by Miriam Nelson, PhD, with Sarah Wernick, PhD (New York: Bantam Books, 2000). Weight training and exercise programs to improve balance and strength and reverse bone loss.

MEMORY AND COGNITIVE ABILITY

The Memory Cure by Majid Fotuhi, MD, PhD (New York: McGraw-Hill, 2003). What is memory and how does it work? What happens to the brain with aging? How to protect your brain against memory loss and Alzheimer's disease.

Saving Your Brain: The Revolutionary Plan to Boost Brain Power, Improve Memory, and Protect Yourself against Aging and Alzheimer's by Jeff Victoroff, MD (New York: Bantam Books, 2002). Some good ideas on improving cognitive functioning.

36 Hour Day by Nancy Mace and Peter Rabins, MD (New York: Mass Market Paperback, 2001). Excellent guide for caregivers of people with Alzheimer's disease, dementia, and memory loss.

COSMETIC SURGERY

Change Your Looks, Change Your Life by Michelle Copeland, DMD, MD, with Alexandra Postman (New York: Harper Resources, 2003). Describes various cosmetic surgery procedures and what they entail.

Turn Back the Clock without Losing Time by Rhoda Narins, MD, and Paul Jarrod Frank, MD (New York: Three Rivers Press, 2002). Guide to various cosmetic procedures, both surgical and nonsurgical.

SEXUALITY

Sex over 40 by Saul Rosenthal, MD (New York: Tarcher/Putnam Press, 2000). All aspects of sexuality with aging, various problems, solutions, how to deal with different physical disorders.

GENERAL HEALTH

American Medical Association Complete Guide to Women's Health, edited by Ramona Slupik, MD (New York: Random House, 1996). All aspects of health from puberty to past sixty. Nurtrition, fitness, preventive health care, stress management, sexuality. Every organ system covered.

Power to the Patient by Isidor Rosenfeld, MD (New York: Warner Books, 2002). Symptoms and treatment of various diseases, simplified. Questions to ask.

INDEX

•